Power and Culture

POWER
AND CULTURE

The Japanese-American War, 1941–1945

Akira Iriye

HARVARD UNIVERSITY PRESS
Cambridge, Massachusetts
and London, England

Library of Congress Cataloging in Publication Data

Iriye, Akira.
  Power and culture.

  Bibliography: p.
  Includes index.
  1. World War, 1939–1945—United States.   2. World
War, 1939–1945—Japan.   3. United States—Civilization
—1918–1945.   4. Japan—Civilization—1865–1945.
5. United States—Relations (general) with Japan.
6. Japan—Relations (general) with the United States.
I. Title.
D769.1.I74   940.53'52   80–23536
ISBN 0–674–69580–1 (cloth)
ISBN 0–674–69582–8 (paper)

To
John King Fairbank

PREFACE

THIS BOOK IS an inquiry into the meaning of the war in Asia and the Pacific, 1941–1945, from the perspectives of the two major combatants, Japan and the United States. This binational framework distinguishes the study both from general histories of the war, in which the battles and policies of all belligerents are described, and from works that examine it in the context of a single country. I am fully aware that the emphasis on Japan and the United States necessarily distorts aspects of the war, but my principal aim has been not to write a narrative of the Asian war but to treat it as a catalytic event in terms of which the nature of recent international relations may be explored.

My operative assumption is that the actors in world affairs can be viewed as powers and as cultures, that international relations are interpower *and* intercultural relations. Power defines a nation's armed forces, its strategies, war-making potentials, including willingness to use force, and a political system that makes and imposes decisions on society, as well as less tangible factors such as the perception of global balances and of other countries' intentions. A nation is also a culture in the sense that its boundaries are defined not simply geographically but also by a consciousness of common tradition; the sharing of religious, artistic, and literary roots; and informal mechanisms such as customs, ways of life, and a myriad of symbols that impart specific meanings to those belonging to the entity. The study of international relations must therefore entail three categories of inquiry: power-level interactions, cultural interchanges, and the relationship between these two sets of relations.

This is a formidable task, and historians have only begun to unravel the complex issues of methodology and analysis inherent in it. In this book I suggest tentative interpretations of one aspect of the phenomenon by examining the meanings the Japanese and Americans gave to the war. They fought fiercely against each other for physical survival; each side mobilized its total resources to destroy the other, and in the end the side that had greater military strength, better strategy, and a more efficient system of production won. At the same time both nations were concerned with more than physical survival and were keenly interested in defining what they were struggling to preserve. They developed visions of what their domestic societies and the entire world would be like when the fighting ended. They sought to articulate their war aims and peace objectives in ways that made sense to themselves, to each other, and presumably to other people.

By tracing the story of the war objectives stated by Japanese and Americans, it is possible to examine the symbolic aspect of the war, and to arrive at certain tentative conclusions about its cultural significance. The contrast between the military and the symbolic aspects of the struggle should enable one to use the Japanese-American war as a case study for understanding the multi-faceted nature of modern international relations. Interestingly, as the book demonstrates, the Japanese and Americans developed a number of similar, and at times parallel, assumptions, so that in the end they both opted for a "conservative" solution—for restoring the kind of international order in which they had once been more compatible. The book explores the question of what kind of international environment was considered most conducive to compatibility among different power and cultural systems. I hope that this approach will stimulate fresh debate about the place of the Second World War in recent history.

THE STUDY OF THE Second World War has been aided tremendously by the opening of the archives in the United States, Britain, Japan, and other countries. Although I have used some of them, I could never hope to exhaust all the available documents. Fortunately, a large number of important monographs on various aspects of the war has been published, some of which are indicated in the bibliography. I am indebted to the pioneering scholars in all countries for their findings and contributions. In concentrating on Japan and the United States, I have freely relied on works by the two countries' distinguished lists of historians. I am particularly grateful to those who have personally and liberally shared their insights with me: Professors C. Hosoya, Y. Nagai, K. Usui, K. Kurihara, S. Asada, I. Hata, N. Hagihara, N. Homma, M. Kōsaka, D. Borg, J. W. Morley, R. Dingman, R. Dallek, J. B. Crowley, W. R. Louis, W. LaFeber, and E. R. May, as well as several colleagues and students at the University of Chicago. The entire manuscript has benefited immeasurably from the careful reading of W. I. Cohen and W. H.

Heinrichs. Professor C. G. Thorne has given me access to an enormous amount of data he has uncovered in the European and Asian archives and has made many valuable suggestions.

During the Second World War, I was in Japan. My father spent most of the period in China, and my future father-in-law in France. I have learned much from their varied perspectives, as I have from my wife, who has divided her life among Europe, Japan, and the United States. But my greatest personal and intellectual debt for this work is to Professor John K. Fairbank, who has embodied for me the finest combination of scholarly integrity, compassion, and loyalty to the idea that one writes history not simply for particular clients but for readers everywhere, transcending national and ideological boundaries. My dedication is a modest way of expressing my gratitude to a great scholar and friend who has inspired me for over twenty-five years.

This study was started during 1974–1975, when I was awarded a generous grant by the John Simon Guggenheim Foundation. Subsequently my research and writing have been aided by funds from the Henry Luce Foundation and from the University of Chicago's Social Sciences Division and the Center for Far Eastern Studies. To Anne Ch'ien, Marnie Veghte, Anthony Cheung, and Sue Iriye I am indebted for cheerful and efficient help as research assistants, editors, and typists.

Chicago   A.I.
July 1980

CONTENTS

1 The End of Uncertainty 1

2 Abortive New Order 36

3 Redefining War Aims 96

4 Japanese-American Rapprochement 149

5 The Making of Postwar Asia 214

6 Conclusion 261

Notes 271

Bibliography 287

Index 297

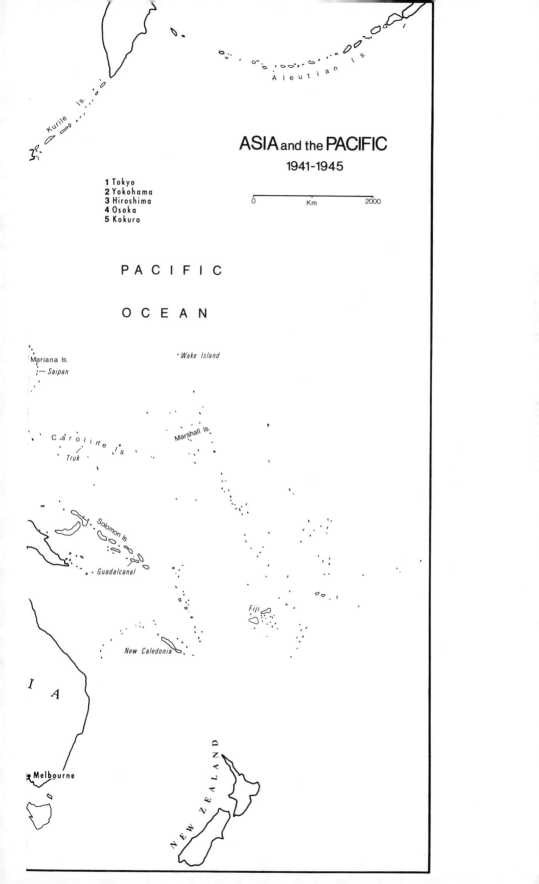

ASIA and the PACIFIC
1941-1945

1 Tokyo
2 Yokohama
3 Hiroshima
4 Osaka
5 Kokura

0   Km   2000

PACIFIC

OCEAN

Aleutian Is.

Kurile Is.

· Wake Island

Mariana Is.
— Saipan

Caroline Is
Truk ·

Marshall Is.

Solomon Is

· Guadalcanal

Fiji

New Caledonia

I   A

· Melbourne

NEW ZEALAND

THE END OF
UNCERTAINTY

1

THE ERUPTION OF war in the Pacific on December 7 (December 8 in Asia), 1941, was preceded by several years of "cold war" between the United States and Japan. As in the more famous Cold War after 1945, the relationship between the two countries had frequently been expressed in terms of fundamental conflict, impending doom, and total confrontation between opposite political and cultural systems. But much as the United States and the Soviet Union later avoided direct armed hostilities, Washington and Tokyo had managed to preserve a relationship that left room for negotiation. More important, despite mutual denunciations and war scares, the two peoples had not severed all ties; on the contrary, belligerent rhetoric concealed an undercurrent of shared interests and outlooks that both sides viewed as largely compatible. However, the very persistence of these outlooks created a sense of uncertainty, because they were at odds with the rapidly deteriorating governmental relations across the Pacific.

War came fundamentally because Japan's military leaders and their civilian supporters decided to close the gap and put an end to the "cold war." They wanted to bring unity to their national experience, so that war would define all political as well as cultural activities. In so doing, they were determined to part, once and for all, from an earlier definition of national life that had underlain Japan's external affairs since the Meiji Restoration. They had been characterized by an effort to integrate the country into the world economy and to achieve rapid industrial development, conditions

[1]

considered essential for collective survival. In order to achieve these
goals Japan had adopted a gold standard, regained tariff autonomy,
pushed its export trade, encouraged emigration and colonization,
and otherwise tried to act like a member of the community of
advanced industrial nations. The task had not always been easy,
and there had been occasional friction with other powers, but at
least until the 1930s there had been a unified perception by the
country's leaders; as a modern industrial state, Japan should cope
with its external problems through the framework of multilateral
agreements with the other advanced nations, according to the
formula of "international cooperation."[1]

In the 1920s the country avidly accepted the framework of
international cooperation embodied in the League of Nations and
the Washington Conference treaties and led by the United States
and Great Britain. The Japanese eagerly turned to Anglo-American
ways, adopting the tenets of Woodrow Wilson's "new diplomacy"
as guides to their own international behavior. The Japanese economy
was fully integrated into the world capitalist system, and the country enjoyed world-power status as the only non-Western member
of the Council of the League of Nations. Japan's problems in Asia
and elsewhere were legion; in China civil war endangered the safety
and interests of foreigners, and in Asia anti-colonial movements
were developing, in part inspired by the Bolshevik Revolution and
supervised by Comintern operatives. Still, Japan coped with these
problems as one of the advanced, colonial, and "treaty" powers
through continuing consultation with the United States and Great
Britain. Although neither Japan nor the Anglo-American powers
were above negotiating separate advantageous deals, the framework
of cooperation through economic interdependence with the other
industrial nations provided the stable point of reference for Japanese
diplomacy.

The world economic crisis that began in 1929 ushered in a
period of confusion and uncertainty in international affairs, in
long-range perceptions as much as in day-to-day relations among
nations. Japan was one of the first countries to decide that the
familiar economic order of unrestricted international trade and
monetary transactions was being replaced by far more particularistic
arrangements and by the division of the globe into autarkic units.
In diplomacy as well, the Japanese saw a trend away from inter-

nationalism and toward regionalism, with a few nations establishing control over wider areas. There would still be "cooperation," but in the form of efforts to maintain equilibrium among these autarkic powers, as exemplified by the "cooperation" between Britain and Nazi Germany during the mid-thirties.

Compared with the situation before 1929, the new pattern was more conducive to uncertainty because there were fewer fixed points of reference; the League of Nations, the Washington Conference treaties, and, most important, the world monetary order based on the gold standard and stable rates of exchange—all were losing their effectiveness as devices for defining international relations. The nations of the world were more determined than ever to effect economic growth, maintain domestic order, and promote national welfare, but they were more willing to use force and to act unilaterally to carry out these objectives without regard for international cooperation. Global interdependence, cooperation, and peace were no longer the prevailing rhetoric; more particularistic conceptions—new order, have-not nations, lebensraum—emerged to provide ideological underpinnings for foreign policies. The assumption that domestic economic development required a peaceful external environment and vice versa, which had sustained the international system of the 1920s, gave way to uncertainty about the relationship between domestic and external affairs and that between power and nonmilitary aspects of foreign relations.

Japanese policy during the 1930s was intended to overcome this uncertainty, but the attempt was only partially successful. At one level there were programs for economic development and for population resettlement in Manchuria and north China under Japanese control. The plan was that "pioneers" from the Japanese mainland would settle in Manchuria and transform the economy to better serve the interests of the expanding empire, especially through increased agricultural output. A twenty-year plan worked out in 1937 called for eventually establishing one million households, totaling five million Japanese, in the area.[2] About half a million Japanese actually migrated to Manchuria during 1931–1945, including some 250,000 farmers who left their villages in Japan to engage in agriculture and dairy industry in the state of Manchukuo. Even teenagers were recruited, 50,000 of them scattering in the frontier regions.[3] The recent arrivals, along with the South Manchuria Railway and the "new zaibatsu" (industrial-financial concerns), hoped that industrialization would go hand in hand with agricultural development, that Manchuria would provide space for Japan's surplus population and also produce enough raw materials, foodstuffs, and manufactured goods to enable Japan to be more self-sufficient.

After 1935 northern China was considered an extension of this scheme. The South Manchuria Railway sent study missions to survey the area's potential resources and needs, and the Boxer Protocol Army (the so-called Tientsin Army) began to exploit the region's mineral resources. The government in Tokyo formally sanctioned these moves, and in 1936, the cabinet drew up a plan for the economic development of north China under the supervision of Japan and Manchukuo. After the outbreak of the Sino-Japanese War in 1937, north China became an important source of supply for the Japanese expeditionary forces, so the newly created Planning Board undertook a special study of economic opportunities there. One result of this planning was the establishment of the North China Development Company in 1938. Capitalized at 350 million yen, of which the government provided half, the semipublic corporation was to engage in transportation, communication, electronics, iron mining, and other enterprises.[4]

In the meantime Japan promoted intraregional trade with Manchukuo and China—the "yen bloc." Exports to Manchukuo and China increased from 25 percent of Japan's total exports in 1936 to over 40 percent in the first half of 1938, and imports from these countries rose from 14 percent to over 22 percent of the total.[5] The concept of a new East Asian order, enunciated in November 1938, was meant to be far more than an empty slogan, it was actually an ex post facto rationalization of Japan's policy of close supervision of economic affairs in Manchuria and north China, calculated to meet the nation's needs as much as possible within the area.

At another level the pan-Asianist doctrine gained influence within and outside the Japanese government. Publicists expounded on the doctrine of Asian solidarity, cooperation, and resistance to Western imperialism (including Soviet communism). Some were traditional right-wing nationalists who felt they had to justify the aggression in China in the name of a holy war against Western influences. But scores of others who were not simplistic chauvinists were genuinely convinced that the nation needed a new ideology under which it could unite in prosecuting the war. They believed that Asian unity was the antithesis of nationalism, individualism, liberalism, materialism, selfishness, imperialism, and all the other traits that characterized the bankrupt Western tradition. Instead, the pan-Asianists stressed themes such as regional cooperation, harmony, selflessness, and the subordination of the individual to the community.

The intensity of this propaganda campaign is, paradoxically, evidence of the tenacity of Western influence in Japanese thinking; author after author found it necessary to stress the supreme importance of liberating one's mind from unconsciously following familiar Western patterns of thought. As Uda Hisashi wrote in his influential 1939 treatise on cultural policy toward China, the Japanese had for too long looked down on things Oriental and dismissed Chinese culture as anachronistic. Outside of the army, few had known much about China or the rest of Asia. Now, however, Japan should "totally put an end to the long period of dependence on and copying after the West." The war in China must be sustained through a new cultural ideology for the new age, beginning with the recognition that Western-oriented scholarly and cultural activities had not served the nation. The country's cultural and intellectual leaders must overcome their past infatuation with Western liberalism and individualism and return to "Japan's innate intelligence." Only then would they be able to grasp the significance of the war in China.[6] The Sino-Japanese War was seen in part as an inner war to cleanse the Japanese mind of Western influences and modes of thought, not just as an action to bring the recalcitrant Chinese to their senses. Once they recognized their past mistakes, the Japanese could proceed to rebuild the world order on the basis of pan-Asianism.

During the late 1930s Japanese propaganda laid tremendous stress on rebuilding, regenerating, reawakening, and rebirth, indicating their self-consciousness about ending Western-dominated patterns and restoring Asia to its past greatness. The East, Japanese writers pointed out with monotonous regularity, had had a tradition of cooperation, harmony, mutual respect, integration, and communal unity, quite in contrast to the West's egoism, constant rivalry, friction, and imperialism. Japan was attempting to recall that proud tradition. As the legal scholar Takigawa Seijirō noted, the new

Asian order would be based upon the negation of Western concepts and the foundation of Asian cultural precepts. Japan, as the depository of traditional Asian virtues, was in a position to take the lead in this task. China, as Japan's closest neighbor, was destined to be its first partner in reconstructing the region's affairs.[7] All of Asia, however, was one, as writers repeatedly asserted, quoting Okakura Tenshin, the turn-of-the-century pan-Asianist. All agreed that economic development was necessary for Asian liberation from Western domination, and cultural unity should ensure that this would not lead to excessive nationalism and imperialism as had been the case in Europe and America.

Despite this rhetoric and the military exploits in China that it sought to rationalize, Japan's external affairs lacked consistency and coherence through most of the decade. Although they talked of a pan-Asianist new order, the Japanese were never successful in making systematic plans to implement their vision. Because Manchukuo and north China were able to supply only a portion of Japan's essential needs, the country continued to depend on sources outside the yen bloc for commodities like cotton, wool, petroleum, rubber, and wheat. The bulk of these commodities came from the United States and from India, Southeast Asia, and Oceania, areas that were tied to sterling and other European currency systems, which maintained protective tariff walls against Japanese imports. Thus Japan almost always suffered a trade deficit with the European countries and their colonies. The United States continued to be Japan's most important trade partner, in spite of the confusion of world depression and the enmity generated by Japanese aggression in Manchuria and China. During the first half of 1938, the United States supplied goods worth 460,000,000 yen, of Japan's total imports of 1,-394,000,000 yen, primarily cotton, petroleum, iron, and machine goods. These were essential for the prosecution of the Sino-Japanese War, and no rhetoric of pan-Asianism could enable Japan to do without them.

The Japanese were well aware that their dependence on extra-Asian markets and sources of supply made them vulnerable to foreign economic pressures. As Saitō Yoshie, a former Foreign Ministry official and confidant of Matsuoka Yōsuke, stated in 1938, sustained boycotts by a Western power would damage the national economy severely and ruin its plans for rapid development. Saitō asserted that fully integrating the economies of Japan and China was the only feasible way for Japan to lessen its dependence on other countries.[8] But the very fact that Saitō had to argue his case in a 400-page volume, printed for confidential circulation within the government, indicates the absence of a blueprint for a pan-Asian economic system.

In fact, lack of adequate knowledge about Asia, let alone a systematic plan of action for the region, was so acutely felt within the government that in September 1938 the Planning Board established a Tōa Kenkyūjo (East Asian Institute) to study ecological, economic, and ethnographic conditions in China, Southeast Asia, and the southwestern Pacific. These surveys were far from completed when the war against the Anglo-American powers began. Within the Foreign Ministry, in the meantime, a planning committee was organized to analyze the effect of world economic trends on Japan's Asian policy. A product of the committee's research was a 500-page volume, which was made available for limited circulation in April 1939. Again the standard clichés were reiterated: the world economic order was being reorganized on the basis of regional blocs, which were stifling Japan's expansive energies everywhere except in Asia. It was incumbent upon the nation to build a new order of economic self-sufficiency in Asia through the cooperation of China and Manchukuo. Japan must expand commercial activities in these countries and promote their industrialization, enabling them to raise their standards of living and contribute to economic growth. Then if there should be war, Japan would be in a much stronger position.[9]

Even this apparently clear-cut assertion contained seeds of uncertainty, however. Japan's bloc policy was justified as a defensive response to the development of regional blocs elsewhere. The implication was that while Japan would go along with present global trends, it would not hesitate to return to the pre-1929 system of more liberal transactions among capitalist countries, if that system were reestablished. Moreover, the East Asian bloc was not truly self-sufficient; Japan, the study noted, still had to obtain oil, rubber, nickel, tin, copper, and other materials from Europe, America, and their colonies in Southeast Asia. Therefore Japan could not be as free of dealings with these countries as pan-Asian policy might dictate. Even as late as 1939, in other words, Japanese foreign policy was not consistently pan-Asianist. An undercurrent of Western-oriented sentiment arose from time to time, as if to warn the nation that a completely autonomous pan-Asianist order was not likely to be realized. Officials recognized the nation's economic dependence on non-Asian countries and knew that dogmatically anti-Western diplomacy could bring about Japan's isolation and not much else.

If anything, the need for some degree of understanding with the Western powers, in particular the United States, seemed to increase as the war in China bogged down. For one thing the military were becoming anxious about their state of preparedness toward the Soviet Union, and the battle of Nomonhan (May 1939) seemed to prove the superiority of Soviet air power and mechanized ground forces. To cope with the crisis, Japan would have to terminate hostilities in China through political means, but that might require the good offices of Britain and the United States. The government in Tokyo was particularly solicitous of America's goodwill and was chagrined when the U. S. State Department announced in July that it was going to abrogate the commercial treaty between the two countries. Instead of driving the Japanese to reduce their dependence on America, however, this announcement made them all the more determined to placate the United States. The growing importance of the American issue belied all the official rhetoric about a new order in East Asia and pointed up the ambiguity and uncertainty underlying Japanese policy.[10]

If little was being implemented in the economic and political realm to implement pan-Asian regionalism, even less was being done about cultural unity. In the late 1930s the only tangible movement to unite Japan and China culturally was the Hsin-min Hui (the People's Renovation Society) in north China. The society was founded under Japanese auspices in December 1937 to bring together occupied China's prominent educators, journalists, and students under the banner of "hsin-min chui-i" or "the principle for the renovation of people," a concept adopted from the Chinese classic Ta Hsüeh (Great learning). From the Japanese point of view, the purpose of this movement was to provide an intellectual and ideological underpinning for the actions of the army of occupation, giving them historic and cultural meaning by stressing the ideal of Asian rejuvenation. From its headquarters in Peiping, the Hsin-min Hui issued newsletters, trained Chinese personnel to establish local branches, opened schools and agricultural experimentation stations, operated radio stations, and otherwise tried to reach out to the Chinese people as an alternative both to the Kuomintang and to the Communist party.

The movement was marred from the start, however, by its close identification with Japanese military policy in China. Several of the Japanese leaders of the society had worked in positions of influence in Manchukuo, and they collaborated with Chinese politicians like Miao Pin and Wang K'o-min, who had parted company with Chiang Kai-shek and chosen the path of reconciliation with the Japanese as the only way to restore peace and advance their own personal interests. These Chinese leaders parroted Japanese slogans about Asian renaissance, economic development without the excesses of Western capitalism, and harmony of all countries. Since most of these ideas could be found in the Chinese classics, the Chinese persuaded themselves that they, rather than the Japanese, were the ideological leaders of the new movement. In any event, the Hsin-min Hui was dedicated to awakening the Chinese people to the dangers of the Kuomintang and the Communists, both of whom looked to the West, whether capitalist or socialist, for inspiration and support. These parties, according to the society's propaganda, were really betraying China by tying its destiny to the interests and ambitions of outsiders. Japan, on the other hand, was the true savior of China, politically, economically, and culturally.[11]

Because the Hsin-min Hui was financially and ideologically tied to the Japanese army of occupation, it did not become an effective movement for cultural pan-Asianism. The Japanese intellectuals and publicists who were active in the movement were mostly right-wing ideologues like Takigawa Seijirō and Fujisawa Chikao. Those who had arrived at pan-Asianism through exposure to the modern Western critique of capitalism and imperialism—men like Miki Kiyoshi, Rōyama Masamichi, Hirano Yoshitarō, and Ozaki Hotsumi —were never enthusiastic about the Hsin-min Hui and groped for other ways to promote their utopian schemes. Several of them gathered around Prince Konoe Fumimaro, hoping that he would provide the focus for a nationwide movement for Asian cultural awakening. Viewing the Chinese provisional regime in north China as a mere puppet of the Japanese army, they also looked to Wang Ching-wei and other prominent Kuomintang officials who might be persuaded to stop resisting Japan and work to save Asia from

Western interference. Even here, however, the alleged union of Japan and China, politically, economically, and culturally, was not necessarily presented as a particularistic proposition. In fact Miki, Rōyama, and others took pains to show that their conception of the new Asian order was not founded merely on the region's geographical and ethnic identity but on some universal principles. The idea, Miki wrote, was to create a more "open Asia." According to Rōyama, it must aim at industrial development, popular welfare, and the advancement of science and technology—a construction hardly distinguishable from a liberal Western order.[12]

Other Japanese who were more centrist were equally concerned with the need for a national movement in close contact with official policy. One such group, Kokusaku Kenkyūkai (the Society for the Study of National Policy), representing middle-ranking bureaucrats, lawyers, businessmen, and academics, held frequent meetings to discuss current affairs, but their discussions tended to be reactive to events and failed to generate an extensive Asian cultural movement. The group included liberal economists and businessmen as well as nationalistic bureaucrats, but it never succeeded in devising a comprehensive scheme for solving national problems. This seems to have been characteristic of the age. Although the Japanese felt compelled to react to world events in some coherent fashion and were beginning to embrace various shades of anti-Western, pan-Asianist ideas, they had no systematic approach to the problems of national defense, development, and identity.[13]

Uncertainty and inconsistency continued to characterize Japanese policy and thinking after 1939, when they were influenced more than ever by events beyond their control. Despite all their talk of a new order in East Asia, they found that developments in Europe were the most important factor in determining Japanese relations with the United States and China. If the government in Tokyo had established a firm framework for carrying out a pan-Asianist policy, it would not have been so shocked by the Nazi-Soviet nonaggression pact or by the outbreak of the Second World War. Prime Minister Hiranuma Kiichirō's self-deprecating remark that trends in international affairs were truly "beyond comprehension" aptly reflected the confusion and ambiguity in Japanese policy. From then on the Japanese began thinking of ways to take advantage of European events to bring about their ideal of an

Asian empire. The inherent instability of that ideal was nowhere more graphically revealed than in the Japanese infatuation with Germany, which grew into an article of faith, so that soon the government and military were convinced that only a German alliance could bring about the new order. Few bothered to ask how a pan-Asianist scheme established through the help of a European power could be free of Western influence. At first even fewer realized that Japan's destiny would be even more closely tied to the policies and strategies of Germany's actual and potential adversaries, above all, the United States.

The twelve-month period between the outbreak of the European war and the signing of the German-Japanese-Italian alliance revealed such a logic of events with stark reality. The Japanese army, frustrated by its inconclusive campaigns in China and shocked by the superiority of Soviet forces at Nomonhan, began to use its perception of "fundamental changes in the international situation" as a guide to strategy. Some top army officials became captivated by this vision and believed the country should take advantage of the European civil war to solve its Asian problems. By encouraging German and Italian victories over Britain and France and keeping the European powers divided, Japan could reduce their interference in China. Also, if Russia and America were compelled to divert their attention to the European conflict, they would be that much less willing to antagonize Japan and might even be prepared to persuade the Chinese to end their resistance to Japan. At the same time it would be easier to extend Japanese influence to areas south of China to obtain much-needed raw materials from the European colonies.

Presumably these developments might have enabled the Japanese to push ahead with their project for an Asian empire, but the reality was far different. Instead of reducing the influence of outside powers, Japan in effect ended up asking for their interference, which came about through two decisions. First, the high-level decision to approach Germany for an alliance was made on the assumption that Adolf Hitler would successfully crush his European enemies, whose colonies in Asia would then be easy prey for Japanese exploitation. Just before he became foreign minister, Matsuoka Yōsuke, who more than any other civilian official was responsible for concluding the Axis alliance, wrote that both the settlement of the war in China and the establishment of a new order in East

Asia depended on events elsewhere. The destiny of Japan and Asia was intimately bound up with that of the whole world.[14] More specifically, he urged that Japan take advantage of Germany's certain triumph in Europe to "construct a new order in East Asia," as he wrote in a memorandum to Konoe Fumimaro when Konoe organized a new cabinet in July 1940. This goal had been reiterated time and again after 1938, but little had been accomplished; now Matsuoka proposed to achieve the objective through an alliance with Germany and Italy.[15] Obviously, an Axis alliance was an expedient tactic, based on a temporary faith in German success. Thus Japan's allegedly firm long-range policy depended on the vicissitudes of a war far away from Asia.

Second, even as they hoped for German victories in Europe, the Japanese wanted to redefine their relations with the Soviet Union and the United States, the two Western powers not yet involved in the war. Matsuoka hoped that these powers, not wishing to be involved in armed hostilities in two separate regions of the world, would want a period of stability and peace in Asia. In his grand design, Japan would establish supremacy in Asia on the basis of an understanding with Russia and the United States. However, such a design necessitated negotiating with these countries, which would enhance their roles in calculations of Japanese strategy. This was borne out by events subsequent to the conclusion of the Axis pact in September 1940. Both the army and the government in Tokyo needed at least a temporary peace with the Soviet Union, so Foreign Minister Matsuoka hastened to Moscow. The result of his trip was that Japanese policy in China and Asia was tied to fluctuations in Japanese-Russian relations, making the country paradoxically more dependent on Soviet behavior than when the army had considered Russia a hypothetical enemy.

The United States also began to loom large as a determinant of Japan's destiny, as Japan sought to reformulate their relationship to accommodate changing world conditions. Konoe, Matsuoka, and other civilian leaders believed that peace in the Pacific could be preserved if the United States pledged not to interfere with Japan's building of a new Asian order. But "noninterference" did not mean inaction or nonintercourse. Japanese officials took it for granted that the two countries would continue to trade and maintain diplomatic relations. Moreover, America might play a role in the settlement of the Chinese war, an idea the army was particularly attracted to in the winter of 1940–41. The army felt that only the Chinese Nationalists' blind faith in American support was keeping them recalcitrant; if the United States interceded to halt the conflict, the Chinese would give up their hopeless cause and begin to cooperate with Japan. These fanciful ideas provided the background for negotiations in Washington between the State Department and the Japanese embassy, beginning in the spring of 1941. The paradox was that Japan was courting American involvement in Asian affairs even while it was bent upon constructing a pan-Asian order.[16] But the Japanese did not perceive this as a paradox—another indication that their policy was more opportunistic than dogmatic and more ambiguous than systematic. The German alliance, far from ending the uncertainty, further confounded the situation. The sense of aimlessness was numbing.

By the spring of 1941, Japanese dissatisfaction was pervasive. Despite Matsuoka's bold strategy, Japan's position had not visibly improved. It was still dependent on the United States for petroleum, and the navy's reserve of fuel oil would last only two years. The neutrality treaty with the Soviet Union, signed on April 13, temporarily assured a status quo in the north, but that was meaningless without an assertive operation in the south to establish a self-sufficient Asian empire. Yet both the army and the navy hesitated to take that step, basically because there was no comprehensive strategic plan for it.[17] Japanese policy was not consistent toward either Germany or the United States. Tokyo politely but persistently refused Berlin's pleas for bold action in Southeast Asia, including an attack on Singapore, to demolish one corner of the British empire. At the same time, the Japanese embassy in Washington tried to convince American officials that the Axis alliance did not really infringe on United States interests or prerogatives in Asia. Still, Japan was determined to settle the Chinese war to its satisfaction and obtain more mineral resources in Southeast Asia, so it would be less dependent on the United States. With all these themes being pursued simultaneously, some concerned officials began calling for a more sharply defined national policy and a more comprehensive strategy to carry it out.

For Ambassador Ōshima Hiroshi in Berlin, the drift and indecision at home were utterly disconcerting. He believed that Japan either had to honor the Axis pact consistently and wholeheartedly, which might mean war with Britain and, probably, the United States, or it had to seek rapprochement with the United States and revert to pre-Axis alliance diplomacy. Ōshima urged the Tokyo government to give up all efforts at reconciliation with the United States. Such efforts would only weaken Germany's resolve to defeat Britain completely, because Germany would not be able to count on Japan to tie the United States down in the Pacific. A German rapprochement with Britain and even with America would mean the failure of Tokyo's policy of keeping the West divided, and Japan would be faced with a united and hostile coalition of Western powers. To prevent this possibility, Japan must do its utmost to assist Germany. "Please have complete confidence in [Germany's] capacity to carry through the war to total victory," Ōshima telegraphed Foreign Minister Matsuoka.[18]

The army was also coming around to this view. Its hope of persuading the United States to play a mediatory role in China had been frustrated by the apparently inconclusive talks in Washington, and sentiment for ending these negotiations was becoming stronger, abetted by the growing conviction among navy staff officers that conflict with the United States was sooner or later inevitable and that negotiations were worthless. That view resulted not from a thorough review of Japanese strategy, but primarily from their unhappiness with the indecisiveness of the civilian government. The navy believed that its position relative to that of the U.S. navy would further decline with time. Either Japan should reach a basic agreement with the United States or it should plan seriously for war. With the first possibility apparently fading, the logical alternative was war in the near future.[19]

Despite such pressures, the Tokyo government continued to court American goodwill, at the same time assuring the Germans that there was no departure from the spirit of the Axis pact. This indecisiveness reflected Japan's continued reliance on external events as a guide to policy as well as its inability to achieve anything through its own initiative. It was symbolic that even the commercial talks at Batavia to secure fixed quantities of East Indies goods ended in failure. Japan was not willing to use force in Southeast Asia, but neither was it ready to dismantle the edifice of Axis diplomacy.

JAPANESE FOREIGN relations before mid-1941 consisted of an unsuccessful attempt to establish a new framework of Asian politics on the ruins of the old order. There persisted a serious gap between the avowal of an anti-Western, pan-Asian system and the reality of continued dependence on Western economic resources, diplomacy, and military vicissitudes. This weakness fortified the American policy of opposition to the Axis alliance and to Japan's moves in China and elsewhere in Asia. From Washington's point of view, Japan was not the enemy that Germany was likely to become—especially if the two powers could be separated. The best way to do this, and to frustrate Japanese ambitions, was to ignore Japan's pretensions as the definer of a new order in Asia and try to compel it to mend its ways and resume its earlier role as a responsible member of the international community.

The United States arrived at this stance, however, only after going through years of frustration in its external affairs. Although not a member of the League of Nations, the United States had in fact been the key to postwar international relations. Its capital, technology, and commodities sustained the world economic system throughout the 1920s, and other capitalist economies looked to America as the financial, business, and political center of the world.

The United States took the lead in ending armament competition, alliances, and ententes as mechanisms for peace and stability. Instead, it continued the Wilsonian policy of encouraging international cooperation among the industrial powers and with the underdeveloped regions. Central to this policy was the concept of "development," which went back to the nineteenth century. "Commercial and industrial development," as many officials, publicists, and intellectuals noted after the 1890s, was being promoted not only among Western countries but also in the rest of the world. And in the words of Benjamin Kidd, the English anthropologist, the Americans "will be the leading representatives of definite principles in the development of the world."[20] These principles were defined by men like Elihu Root and William Howard Taft variously as interdependence, international fraternization, self-control, and peaceful expansion. America should use its resources for internal economic development and also to link the regions of the world closer together through its goods, ships, merchants, and businessmen. This, Taft once remarked, would "bring peoples and governments closer together and so form bonds of peace and mutual dependency."[21]

Wilsonian foreign policy, the basic statement of United States policy until the 1930s, was built upon these concepts and further systematized them. Woodrow Wilson not only accepted the tenets of international economic development, he sought to establish a political framework for it throughout the world. To achieve this end, he believed the advanced industrial countries must refrain from making selfish, particularistic arrangements and from dominating the undeveloped countries, which for their part would need to avoid unstable domestic conditions and irresponsible foreign transactions. They must aspire to "development of ordered self-government," Wilson said.[22] If all the peoples of the world joined in this peaceful, orderly transformation of the globe, they would share equally in the fruits of economic development. Wars, alliances, and armaments would be unnecessary.

Wilsonianism did not disappear immediately after the onset of the depression, but it was severely challenged by the unilateral acts of Japan and other countries and by the rising sentiment of nationalism and unilateralism in America. There was a reaction against Wilsonian internationalism as the United States, like virtually all other countries, became preoccupied with solving the severe economic crisis through price stabilization, devaluation, exchange control, and other measures, which were taken with little regard for their impact upon the international monetary system or world trade. Collective international action fell into disrepute in an environment of economic nationalism and of suspiciousness toward businessmen and bankers that emerged during the depression. The Wilsonian faith in friendly and peaceful relations among nations through economic interaction gave way to indifference to world problems. As Charles A. Beard expressed the prevailing view, national security was derived from attaining "minimum dependence upon governments and conditions beyond [the nation's] control" and developing "its own resources to the utmost."[23]

This nationalistic view was a sharp break from the past, but the administration of Franklin D. Roosevelt accepted it with equanimity, having come to power on the ruins of the Hoover administration's heroic but vain attempt to solve the Manchurian crisis through international cooperation. That experience left American officials shaken, frustrated, and pessimistic about further attempts to preserve the postwar system of international relations. As Japan disregarded the principles underlying that system and as other countries undermined its economic foundation, Wilsonian internationalism became a hollow shell and no longer provided a point of reference for the conduct of American diplomacy.

For a while after 1933 United States foreign policy lost its sense of direction, although it was not altogether inactive. It enunciated a good-neighbor policy in the Western Hemisphere, recognized the Soviet Union, endorsed the League of Nations' embargo of goods to Italy when that country invaded Ethiopia, and enacted neutrality legislation. These steps, however, did not amount to a coherent policy; they were mostly reactive, not creative, responses to changing conditions outside the country. In the mid-thirties the United States sought to stabilize its relations with other nations primarily by recognizing the new realities, including Japan's control over Manchuria and Germany's revisionist thrusts, which aimed at more acceptable boundaries in Central Europe. America was willing to live with these developments simply because it saw no other alternatives. Thus for a while the United States was prepared to maintain some form of stable relations with Japan, refraining from overt support of China or from any action that might give the impression of penalizing or isolating Japan.

Despite the depression and the abandonment of internationalist diplomacy, however, American officials did not give up the idea of economic growth through industrialization. Equally important, economic nationalism did not imply stopping all activities overseas. If anything, the need for oil, rubber, tin, and other raw materials was increasing because of the worldwide trend toward autarky, with each power trying to limit shipments of materials to others outside its own trade bloc. The government in Washington encouraged private firms to continue investing in oil fields and rubber plantations in Southeast Asia and Latin America. In China, despite difficulties caused by the Japanese invasion, American capital investments amounted to $40 million in 1941. In that context, Japanese action in Manchuria and north China was seen as having a negative effect on China's economic development by discouraging the infusion of foreign capital and technology. But because Japan's Asian policy was never consistent, the Americans hoped that in time, Japan would go back to playing its traditional role as a promoter of development through cooperation with Western nations.

When this did not happen, and when the Japanese government in late 1938 enunciated the doctrine of a new order in East Asia, the United States was compelled to clarify its stand and reenter the international arena. Having survived four years in office, President Roosevelt and his aides were finally persuaded that they would have to reformulate the country's foreign policy instead of making ad hoc responses to events. At first, this took the form of trying to restore the framework of international cooperation. For instance, in June 1937 Roosevelt invited Prime Minister Neville Chamberlain to Washington to discuss British-American cooperation, which had all but disappeared after 1933. Shortly afterward Under Secretary of State Sumner Welles proposed an international conference to lay down some basic principles for the guidance of all nations. One such principle, Welles suggested, might be "equal access to raw materials" throughout the world—harking back to the Wilsonian tradition.[24] In October 1937 Roosevelt called for quarantining lawless nations to prevent the disease from spreading to the rest of the world. The idea of an international conference was revived in January 1938, and during the remainder of the year Roosevelt repeatedly appealed to Hitler and to Benito Mussolini to solve international disputes peacefully, more evidence that the American government again considered itself a factor in world affairs and that it wanted to reestablish some system of international cooperation. The Munich settlement of October 1938 fit into that framework, and Sumner Welles characteristically welcomed it, saying, "a new world order based upon justice and upon law" had been established.[25]

This emerging internationalism, which was sometimes called "appeasement," was an effort to stabilize international politics through an understanding by all the major powers—Germany and Japan as well as Britain and the United States—looking to the reopening of the globe to economic activities. In such a scheme the major military powers, which were beginning to come out of the global economic crisis, would have to cooperate with one another and with lesser nations to reduce armament, promote economic interdependence, and settle outstanding disputes peacefully. It was a Wilsonian agenda. That the State Department under Cordell Hull and Welles was the major supporter of this agenda was not surprising, for they continued to formulate their policy statements in the language of international cooperation and interdependence. More notable was President Roosevelt's strong, if transient, interest in such a scheme during 1937–1939. He was sufficiently impressed with an internationalist solution that even after Germany annexed the rest of Czechoslovakia in March 1939, he talked of convening an international conference to obtain the powers' nonaggression pledges and to work out a formula for solving economic problems. Undoubtedly he believed that the American people would oppose any overt act that increased the chances of a war in which the United States might become involved. Also he apparently felt that they would prefer the administration to take some internationalist initiative to prevent war rather than to persist in complete inaction. As late as the beginning of 1940, Roosevelt consented to Under Secretary Welles's peace mission to Europe which, reminiscent of Colonel E. M. House's trip in the early summer of 1914, was designed to assert American interest in internationalism.

Just as the realization of Japan's new order in Asia hinged on events elsewhere, the implementation of American Wilsonianism depended upon events over which the United States had little direct control. Roosevelt's internationalist diplomacy was given a jolt in August 1939, when Nazi Germany and Stalinist Russia signed a nonaggression pact, precipitating the Germany occupation of Poland and the British-French declaration of war on Germany, thus bringing the world another European war. Although the State Department, much like Wilson and House in 1914, saw America's role as that of objective mediator, the reaction of President Roosevelt and most of his aides was more decidedly one-sided and forcefully interventionist. They did not give up their commitment to internationalist principles, but their overriding concern was to maintain the balance of power in Europe which depended on the survival of Great Britain. If the United States did not support Britain, they reasoned, Europe might become united under Germany and confront the Western Hemisphere. Starting with the repeal of the arms embargo in November 1939, official United States policy became more and more interventionist, hoping to ensure British survival without actually getting involved in the war.

This was clearly a power-political approach to foreign affairs, not an internationalist strategy. Although the Roosevelt administration couched its policy in idealistic language to appeal to public opinion, and although the State Department preserved a strain of internationalism, considerations of armament, balance of power, and strategic planning became the major factors in policy. Very often power considerations overshadowed ideological factors as in the decision to maintain official ties with the Vichy regime of conquered France. Likewise, at first the United States did not dispute Britain's particularistic economic policy of according preferential treatment to the members of the Commonwealth. President Roosevelt refrained from condemning the Soviet Union's invasions of Poland, the Baltic states, and Finland. A main objective of American diplomacy during 1939–1941 was to persuade General Francisco Franco's fascist regime to remain neutral instead of joining Germany.

Toward Japan the United States continued what may be termed a neo-Wilsonian approach, hoping it would in time give up its Asian policy and join the other powers in restoring a more open world. Certainly some of the internationalist principles the United States presented during 1938–1939, such as equal access to raw materials, were meant to appeal to Japan no less than to Germany. At the same time, the Roosevelt administration continued to view Japan as vulnerable to economic pressures and to external influence. In July 1939 the United States announced that it would abrogate its treaty of commerce with Japan after January 1940, which was rather out of character with the administration's generally cautious diplomacy at that time. But the announcement can also be taken as an expression of optimism that the United States could compel Japan to renounce regionalism and return to a framework of international cooperation.

This optimism persisted after the outbreak of the European war. The basic need was to prevent Japan from assisting Germany, but officials in Washington continued to believe that Japan was an inferior nation, vulnerable to outside pressures because of its lack of vital resources. They thought it would be relatively easy to restrain Japan through selective economic sanctions and to persuade the Japanese not to commit themselves to the Axis side. When

Tokyo, in September 1940, went ahead with the Axis pact, Washington's reaction was predictable. The United States tried to nullify the effect of the German-Japanese alliance by exhorting China, Indochina (under the Vichy French regime), and the Dutch East Indies not to succumb to Japanese imperialism; by preventing Japan from accumulating large oil reserves; by working out joint strategy with British, Chinese, and Dutch authorities in Southeast Asia; and by telling the Japanese that the German alliance was the major obstacle to understanding in the Pacific. At the same time, the Japanese were told that if they renounced the pact, amicable and cooperative relations would be restored. The Japanese, it was pointed out, would gain far more from such an arrangement than they would from the German pact.

This was a delicate policy. The United States did not wish to drive Japan totally to the German side without being prepared for a two-ocean war. American strategic planning in the winter of 1940–41 was based on the premise that the country could conceivably become involved in a war in Europe and the Atlantic. Diplomatic talks and economic sanctions in the meantime were expected to keep Japan powerless to move, but the United States did not think it necessary to offer Japan specific inducements to stay out of the European war. At bottom was the fact that American relations with Japan were considered much less significant than relations with Germany, whose menace was clearly recognized as formidable. It did not seem that Japan would dare challenge the United States to a war that would be tantamount to national suicide.

Clearly, in the spring of 1941 the United States was not in a position to ingratiate itself with Japan, as had been envisioned by officials in Tokyo. Far from aiding Japan to consolidate its gains in China, America reminded Japan of its obligation to restore China's territorial integrity. Instead of ending uncertainty in the Pacific, the United States played upon that sentiment by persisting in inconclusive talks and stepping up aid to China.

China was becoming important to American strategy because of the European situation. It was obviously desirable to keep Japan mired on the Asian continent to weaken it as an ally of Germany. This necessitated actively supporting China, which had not been done in the past. Before the Sino-Japanese War, most State Department officials had not regarded the Chinese Republic as a principal factor in Asian politics. It had been important more as a test-case of postwar internationalism; the Western powers had been concerned not so much with China as with preserving a cooperative framework for settling international disputes.[26]

Even after 1937, the initial American reaction to the Asian war was to try to settle it through third-party mediation or multinational talks like the Brussels Conference. But the mounting crisis in Europe compelled redefinition of America's Asian policy. China's continuing struggle with Japan could be used to frustrate German ambitions in Europe. Far from being a purely Asian matter, Japan's proclamation of a pan-Asianist new order had implications for the rest of the world. If Japan were allowed to carry out its regionalist scheme while Germany was doing the same in Central Europe, the relative position of Great Britain and hence of the United States would diminish, especially if the European and Asian blocs should combine. If Japan succeeded in controlling the Chinese economy, and China's several hundred millions joined Japan's advanced technology, the whole continent of Asia could become hostile to the West. It was thus imperative to encourage Chinese opposition to the Japanese scheme. More specifically, the United States condemned Chinese collaborators like Wang Ching-wei who appeared ready to accept the Japanese definition of Asian order. If Chiang Kai-shek developed into another Wang, China would become an even greater menace to peace and stability than Japan. The United States must therefore do everything possible to assist the Nationalists politically and economically, especially with capital and technology to aid war-torn China's industrial and agricultural development.

Thus China was becoming the key to America's Asian policy. It should be recalled, however, that at this time aid to China was in no way as important as the European conflict; Asia was still subsidiary to Europe. Whereas America was determined to defend Britain until the menace of Nazi Germany was removed, it had no intention of destroying Japan or of building China up as the major power in East Asia. Some officials in Washington, such as Stanley K. Hornbeck of the State Department and Henry Morgenthau, treasury secretary, urged stern measures to check Japan. They wanted to use economic sanctions and even military force to reduce Japanese power in Asia, but most of Roosevelt's advisers did not agree. They believed in using economic and political pressures to keep the situation uncertain, to keep the Japanese guessing and worried about American policy.

THIS STATE OF uncertainty, a product of Washington's policy of calculated risk, was as frustrating to the Chinese as to the Japanese. To be sure, only a few Chinese officials and publicists openly sided with the Japanese army of occupation and its propaganda about the new cultural order. For most Chinese, pan-Asianism was a thin disguise for Japanese ambitions, and the Japanese themselves were uncertain what it meant. However, waging an all-out war of resistance against the Japanese was not such a clear-cut alternative as it appears in retrospect. Instead of engaging in open confrontation, the Chinese troops, guerrillas, and popular organizations would disrupt law and order in occupied areas and mobilize public opinion against defeatism. Most groups agreed that the best strategy was not to devastate the country through fighting but to wear the Japanese out, at the same time maintaining a high level of production and strengthening unoccupied regions. To obtain essential foodstuffs, raw materials, and foreign exchange, Chinese officials often connived at commercial dealings with the occupied areas. They also resorted to strange diplomatic maneuvers, with emissaries going back and forth between their headquarters and Japanese posts to engage in peace talks. Most of these talks were merely devices by both sides to gain time, but occasionally the Chinese used negotiation instead of fighting to tie the Japanese forces down. Some efforts at peacemaking were genuine, as when Wang Ching-wei and his aides left Chungking to deal directly with the Japanese government. The fate of these collaborators, mistreated by the Japanese and denounced by their compatriots, was a cruel one, but the significance of their effort lay in the symbolism of collaboration; since the war was inconclusive, the Chinese would try to reduce Japanese pressures in every possible way, even negotiation for something less than naked imperialism.[27]

The Chinese were not sure that the war could be prosecuted through conventional means or even that it was a conventional war. To be sure, the presence of the Japanese was humiliating, and the arrogance of the occupation forces and the civilian administrators in coastal cities convinced the Chinese that ultimately they would have to drive out the invaders. But the Japanese military objectives were not always clear. Each new cabinet in Tokyo called for "settling" the "China incident." The Japanese seldom mentioned complete victory, and their officers in China seemed willing to leave much to Chinese administrators. Over the years personal ties and friendships had developed between Chinese and Japanese, and these were not completely broken even after 1937. The Chinese belief in nationalism did not mean that they were necessarily against associating with the invaders.

Chiang Kai-shek himself made frequent nostalgic references in his speeches to his experiences as a young cadet at a Japanese military academy and recalled the discipline, dedication, and frugality of Japanese soldiers. Although he denounced the Japanese invasion and rejected any compromise short of restoration of Kuomintang rule in occupied China, he often pictured the two countries as basically compatible. He had no fondness for Western-style democracy or private enterprise; his vision was of a China combining the traditional virtues of a great culture and the amenities of modern industrialization and bureaucracy. China had to be developed economically, but not necessarily on the Western model. Chiang's insistence on traditionalism and his recognition of the need for industrialization did not put him automatically on the side of the Western countries against Japan.[28]

The Communists rejected Chiang's vision as reactionary, but their outlook was no more Western. Mao Tse-tung pictured China as a "new democracy" that would identify itself with worldwide victims of imperialism. China would lead the less advanced countries in the struggle against colonial oppression, an idea that was congenial to the Nationalists as well. The main difference between the Nationalists and the Communists was in their attitudes toward the Soviet Union. The Communist leaders closely followed the Comintern interpretation of world affairs, and in early 1941 they were still defending the Soviet policy of accommodation with Nazi Germany and neutrality with Japan. The Nationalists were more critical of Russia precisely on these counts and were particularly bitter about Moscow's apparent willingness to mollify Japan at the expense of China. The Soviet Union's selfishness, they thought, was one more reason why the Chinese should not rely too heavily on Russian goodwill or assistance, because it might result in the substitution of Soviet for Japanese domination.

The Chinese leaders found it extremely difficult to make long-range plans, because the Western powers were preoccupied with the European situation, and their willingness to assist China fluctuated with the circumstances of the British war with Germany. There was always the possibility that they would choose to concentrate on the Atlantic Ocean, avoiding armed involvement in Asia. The negotiations between the Japanese and the Americans in Washington were no less disconcerting to the Chinese than to the Germans. The Chinese suspected that if the United States had to choose between war against Japan to protect China or some understanding at the expense of Chinese interests, it would opt for the latter. Then the Chinese would be back where they were earlier in the decade, at the mercy of external powers for their salvation and development. The situation would in fact revert to the conditions of the 1920s.

IN THE SPRING OF 1941, the future of the Asia-Pacific region depended almost entirely upon events outside the area. Japan's quest for Asian autonomy, never entirely consistent, had made its fate less predictable than earlier. The United States now had a definite policy in Europe, but its Asian strategy hinged on the course of the war between Britain and Germany. The Chinese were divided between submission to Japan and hope for Western assistance. In this situation, it is not surprising that Asia's next chapter opened with another major shift in the European war: Hitler's attack on the Soviet Union, launched on June 22.

The Japanese for once saw distinct alternatives: to join Germany in invading the Far Eastern territories of the Soviet Union or to honor the neutrality treaty with Russia. A further question then was whether to take advantage of the German-Russian war by attacking the European colonies in Southeast Asia, thereby bringing the ideal of Asian empire a step closer to fulfillment. Some officials argued for the first course of action, saying that a Japanese assault on the Soviet Union in conjunction with the German offensive in the west would quickly put an end to the Bolshevik regime and remove a menace to Japanese interests in Manchuria and the rest of Northeast Asia. This evidence of German-Japanese cooperation would strengthen the Axis pact, which would weaken the position of the Anglo-American powers and make them respect Japan's position in Asia. As Ambassador Ōshima cabled from Berlin on June

22, "the outbreak of war between Germany and Russia gives us a perfect opportunity to remove, once and for all, the menace in the north and to settle the China incident." If Japan adopted a wait-and-see policy, Ōshima warned, it would lose Germany's trust and damage its own prestige.[29]

Minister Tsutsui Kiyoshi in Bucharest telegraphed Tokyo to express his confidence that Germany would destroy the Bolshevik regime in Russia "at least by the beginning of October." The Soviet Union would disintegrate, and a new government would come into existence in what was left of European Russia. If Japan did not join in attacking the Soviet Union, Germany would owe nothing to Japan and would decide Russia's future with no thought for Japan's desires. To prevent such a disaster, Japan should assault and acquire the Siberian provinces to remove their threat to Japanese interests in Northeast Asia. Of course, such action would violate the neutrality treaty, but Tsutsui believed that the Bolsheviks had already contravened the agreement by supporting anti-Japanese forces in China. Japan was not opposed to Russia and its people but was only determined to overthrow the Bolshevik government, he continued. Once that objective was achieved, the new Russian government would cooperate with Germany, Italy, China, Manchukuo, and Japan in a common struggle against the Anglo-Saxon countries.[30]

Foreign Minister Matsuoka agreed and pressed his cabinet colleagues to sanction yet another shift in Japanese policy. Like Ōshima and Tsutsui, he thought that successful military attacks on Russia would release Japan's armed forces for a move south after the Russian war to capture the rich colonial areas. By that time both Germany and Japan would be so strengthened that American intervention would be unlikely. "We should first go north and then turn south," was the foreign minister's recommendation.[31]

The military leaders in Tokyo, having abandoned hope of American mediation to settle the war in China, agreed that the German invasion of the Soviet Union finally gave Japan an opportunity to act resolutely and end the indecision and tentativeness that had characterized its relations with other countries. But the military did not agree to "go north" first, in part because they needed time to prepare for war against Russia. Twelve divisions of the Kwantung Army, totaling about 350,000 men, were stationed in Manchuria at that time, compared to the Soviet Far Eastern army, which reportedly numbered 700,000. An additional 500,000 Japanese soldiers would have to be mobilized. Realistically, preparations would not be completed until around August 10, and war could not be started for another month thereafter. The military authorities in Tokyo were willing to make such preparations, and at the crucial July 2 meeting of the cabinet ministers and military leaders in the presence of the emperor, it was decided to "solve the northern problem by force" if developments in Europe favored such action. However, the meeting also endorsed penetrating Southeast Asia by force "in order to consolidate the base of our national existence and self-defense." The army would occupy southern Indochina first, at the same time preparing for the anti-Russian offensive. The reasoning was that this would involve comparatively little risk. General Sugiyama Gen, army chief of staff, confidently expressed his view that occupation of southern Indochina would irritate the Anglo-American countries but would not provoke them to war. The navy believed such action would prevent Britain and the United States from taking advantage of a possible Japanese-Russian war. After October, moreover, the rainy season would make it difficult to build airfields in Indochina. Thus, despite Matsuoka's pleas to concentrate on the northern strategy first, Japanese troops began their invasion of southern Indochina on July 28.[32]

If Japan had postponed the southern advance until the beginning of September, when the offensive against Russia was to have started, the subsequent history of the Second World War might have been drastically different. By early August, officers of the Japanese General Staff were losing confidence in a quick German victory over Russia.[33] If Japan had then decided not to cooperate with Germany, the Axis alliance might have been seriously damaged, which in turn might have been conducive to reopening serious negotiations between Japan and the United States, as Prime Minister Konoe wanted. He reasoned that the German attack on Russia without consulting Japan was in effect a violation of the spirit of the Axis alliance and that therefore Japan had a right to repudiate the intent, if not the letter, of the alliance and seek an understanding with the United States. Konoe argued that the German alliance had lost its usefulness and that Japan should seek accommodation with the only power that was in a position to determine the future of the Asian conflict. He wanted to ask the United States to stop its hostile policy in China, help Japan come to a settlement there, and supply Japan with raw materials it would otherwise have to obtain in Southeast Asia.[34] However, the military, while not opposing resumption of the talks in Washington, were convinced that chances for American mediation were slim.[35]

Thus the events of June and July again revealed Japan's tendency to adopt policies in response to external developments. These responses were varied, including preparedness against Russia, occupation of southern Indochina, and resumption of talks with the United States; there still was no coherence in Japanese strategy.

It was in this context that the United States facilitated Japan's search for a coherent policy by speedy retaliation against the occupation of Indochina. On July 24 the U.S. government decided to freeze Japanese assets and on August 1 all export licenses for shipping petroleum to Japan were revoked. The Dutch authorities in the East Indies followed suit and refused to issue export permits without proof of exchange licenses—thus virtually stopping the shipment of oil because payment had to be made in dollars, which were blocked in the United States. After August 5 oil was no longer reaching Japanese shores from either the United States or the Dutch East Indies. Japan could produce about 400,000 kiloliters of oil a year, but the navy easily consumed that much in a month. The reserve, estimated at 9,400,000 kiloliters, would be exhausted in two years unless the nation obtained fresh supplies of oil by some means.[36]

The oil embargo had a tremendous psychological impact upon the Japanese. The ambivalence and ambiguities in their perception of world events disappeared, replaced by a sense of clear-cut alternatives. Hitherto they had not confronted the stark choice between war and peace as an immediate prospect and had lived in a climate of uncertainty from day to day. Now, with the United States resorting to decisive measures, that phase passed. Any wishful thinking that America would tolerate the invasion of southern Indochina was dissipated; either Japan would stay in Southeast Asia at the risk of war with the Anglo-American countries or it would retreat to conciliate them. The military judged that it was too late for conciliation; Japan would now have to consider the likelihood of war, with the United States as its major adversary.[37]

The sense of inevitable crisis was shared by officials in Washington. As Secretary of State Cordell Hull told Secretary of War Henry L. Stimson in July, the United States had "reached the end of possible appeasement with Japan and there is nothing further that can be done with that country except by a firm policy." From this time on it was assumed that there would be war in the Pacific unless the Japanese made drastic changes in their policy.[38] The only question was the timing.

A series of decisions made simultaneously with the oil embargo and the freezing of Japanese assets indicated a dramatic stiffening in Washington's attitude. A Far Eastern command was organized under General Douglas MacArthur, using the Philippines as a strategic base in case of war with Japan. Fighter planes and heavy bombers were to be placed there, a move designed to turn the archipelago into a bastion of U.S. air power and a deterrent to further Japanese aggression. Talks were held with British, Dutch, and Chinese authorities to exchange information and coordinate their defenses in the Pacific. Lend-lease assistance to China started, and the American volunteer air corps, the Flying Tigers, under Claire Chennault obtained aircraft from the United States and Britain to train Chinese pilots and even engage in military action against the Japanese air force. The United States was clearly determined to prevent Japanese domination of Asia.

Although this policy was dictated by power considerations, it is important to note that these steps were coupled with an assertion of certain internationalist principles, indicating Washington's perception that Japan's new Asian order was threatening to become more than mere rhetoric and therefore must be opposed by alternative ideas of international order.

The nature of that order was outlined in August at the Atlantic Conference of President Roosevelt and Prime Minister Winston S. Churchill. The enunciation of the Atlantic Charter complemented the evolving Anglo-American strategy against Axis aggression by defining certain principles for international peace. In the first of the charter's eight points, the United States and Great Britain asserted that they sought no "aggrandizement, territorial or other." Second, they "desire no territorial changes that do not accord with the freely expressed wishes of the peoples concerned." The third point, a compromise between the American doctrine of self-determination and the British regard for empire, expressed the desire "to see sovereign rights and self-government restored to those who had been forcibly deprived of them." Those peoples who had not been independent presumably would not have their "sovereign rights" restored. Fourth, in an obvious allusion to the Axis propaganda about the rights of "have-not" nations, the charter supported the principle that all nations, victor or vanquished, should have access "on equal terms, to the trade and to the raw materials of the world which are needed for their economic prosperity." The next four points further spelled out the ideal world that the Anglo-American allies hoped to bring about after the war, a world in which there would be "the fullest collaboration between all nations in the economic field," where all peoples would "live out their lives in freedom from fear and want," enabling "all men to traverse the high seas and oceans without hindrance," and in which "all nations of the world" would seek to lighten the "crushing burden of armaments."[39]

These principles approximated Wilsonian internationalism, indicating that Wilsonianism was again providing ideological underpinnings for American foreign policy. The older concepts of peace and stability through economic development, prosperity, and interdependence had survived the turmoil of the 1930s and would define the world order after the Axis menace had been removed. Thus the Atlantic Charter was an ideological complement to the concern with balance of power, which had guided Roosevelt's foreign policy since the late 1930s. Great tension remained between the internationalist language of the charter and the more power-oriented strategy, but for the first time since Roosevelt came to power the United States had a sense of direction in its external affairs: essentially a return to Wilsonianism and to the pre-1929 system of international relations in which extensive economic exchanges had been the norm as well as the presumed path to world peace. Some of the problems inherent in that decade would have to be confronted and overcome, such as excessive protectionism and immigration restriction, but it was assumed that internationalism was as viable for the 1940s as it had been for the 1920s.

The Atlantic declaration was a challenge to the Japanese to return to that system and promote their own well-being in cooperation with the United States or else to face the latter's wrath awaiting their path of aggression. Because Washington had already taken decisive steps to curb Japanese expansion, the charter in effect defined for the leaders in Tokyo a world order that would be theirs if they mended their ways. The Americans felt that the Japanese had gone astray, but they could still rescue themselves from their own folly. All they had to do to regain American understanding was to remember the 1920s and reject the militaristic course they had chosen in the subsequent decade.

American faith in Wilsonianism grew stronger after August, even as war seemed more and more imminent, and this feeling provided the setting for White House and State Department talks with Japanese envoys in Washington. Hesitation and uncertainty were replaced by conviction. The famous "Hull note" of November 26 expressed the same doctrine. Presented to Ambassador Nomura Kichisaburō, it enumerated ten points, including the conclusion of a multilateral nonaggression pact among Japan, the United States, Britain, the Netherlands, China, the Soviet Union, and Thailand; Japanese withdrawal of all forces from China and Indochina; negotiations for a new trade agreement "based upon reciprocal most-favored-nation treatment and reduction of trade barriers"; and the stabilization of the dollar-yen ratio. As Secretary Hull noted then and afterward, he was not demanding that the Japanese give up their right to exist as a vigorous and viable nation; he was inviting them to go back to the peaceful and interdependent world of the 1920s, where there had been ample room for Japanese interests and self-respect. The Asia pictured by the Hull note represented his image of what the region would have turned into but for the world depression, Japan's militaristic moves, and the various nations' particularistic trade and monetary policies.

The United States was clearly forcing the Japanese to make a choice, whether to continue the process begun in 1931, even at the expense of war with America, or to return to the framework of the 1920s on the basis of accommodation with the Anglo-American nations. As Ambassador Ōshima said in his September 4 message to Foreign Minister Toyoda Teijirō, "There are only two possible attitudes we can take: either to preserve the spirit of the Tripartite Pact and cooperate with Germany and Italy to construct a new world order, or to abandon the alliance, submit to the Anglo-American camp, and seek friendly relations with England and America." For Ōshima it was only a matter of time before Germany estab-

lished hegemony over Europe, the Middle East, and Africa. It would
be supreme folly for Japan to cut its ties with Germany and seek
good relations with the United States. Even if that resulted in settlement of the China war, it would only "cause Japan to be despised
and isolated abroad, bring about a loss of hope and the atrophy of
the national spirit at home." Rapprochement with the United States
was essentially a backward step, to recapture the atmosphere of the
1920s, which was no longer workable.[40] It would be much better for
Japan to identify its fate with Germany's.

Ambassador Ishii Itarō at Rio de Janeiro disagreed. On September 2 he cabled his superiors in Tokyo, urging them "to perform
a major operation, even if that means turning to other countries for
assistance." He believed that Japan's destiny was bound up with
that of the Anglo-Saxon countries and that the United States, especially, and Great Britain would retain an influence in Asian affairs no
matter what the outcome of the European conflict. What Japan
needed most was a stable and peaceful Asia, even if that meant sharing the continent with these other powers. War with them would
devastate Asia, would seriously damage Japan, and would not solve
the long-lasting conflict between China and Japan. It was regrettable
but essential to settle the Chinese war by negotiating with Britain
and the United States. Ishii was aware of the almost insurmount-
able problems this course of action would create in Japanese domestic politics, but he saw no alternative to "removing all obstacles
in the way of solving the war and establishing peace in Asia."[41]

At the fateful meeting in the presence of the emperor on September 6, Tokyo's leaders tried to see if a middle position was possible. They decided, on the one hand, to continue the talks in Washington to induce the United States to resume normal trade and desist from augmenting its forces in the Pacific. However, if there was
no satisfactory settlement by the beginning of October, Japan was
to be ready for war at the end of the month.[42] Although the Japanese leaders decisively favored Ōshima's resolute stand vis-à-vis the
United States, they wanted to make one final attempt to avoid war
through negotiation. They clearly did not accept Ishii's recommendation for cooperation with the Anglo-American powers. Given the
strengthening of the American position in the Pacific and the stiffening of Washington's attitude, the September 6 decisions could only
mean war.

As the October deadline came and went without war, and the indecisive talks in Washington continued, Ambassador Ōshima and those who shared his views grew impatient. In Tokyo, Konoe was succeeded as premier by General Tōjō Hideki. Tōjō shared the fatalistic view of Japanese-American relations and believed that war in the Pacific was inevitable, but he was under pressure from the emperor and the court to try again to preserve peace. His was a thankless task, since nothing essential had changed in the two countries' relations, and Wilsonian cooperation was no more appealing in October than it had been earlier. To the exponents of pro-Axis strategy, the 1920s symbolized a discredited pattern of old-fashioned internationalism that had benefited only the United States. As Ōshima cabled to Tokyo on October 29, further delay in going to war would strengthen Japan's potential antagonist. Since the success of Japan's Axis diplomacy hinged on decisive action to take advantage of the relative weakness of the Anglo-American powers, last-minute negotiations with the United States made no sense; they would give the Americans more time and sow seeds of mistrust in the minds of the Germans. A new order in Asia was possible only if Japan seized the historic opportunity presented by the collapse of the British empire. "This is our last chance to consult with Germany so that we can coordinate action in east and west in order to secure southern regions rich in important resources . . . We shall be leaving cause for regret for a thousand years if, instead of having a definite idea about the course of the [European] war, we are to adopt an opportunistic attitude."[43]

Some resisted such thinking to the very end. Kamimura Shin'ichi, chargé d'affaires in London, sent a strongly worded telegram to the Foreign Ministry on November 21, urging restraint in view of the growing ties between Britain and the United States, a formidable combination in the event of a break in relations with them. Noting the increases in United States aid to Britain and the consequent growth in British confidence of victory in Europe, Kamimura wrote that British leaders might even desire to crush Japan's strength in Asia, which would be good for British interests after the war. It would be folly to provoke both countries to war at this time. "It is an extremely dangerous situation that we have to start war when our resources have been used up in the Manchurian and China incidents." The best strategy was to be patient and try to reconstruct the nation's strength so it could grow in the future. Japan must accept temporary humiliation and concessions and be ready to resolve the China incident through negotiations with the United States.[44]

Kamimura was waging a losing battle. Adopting his recommendations would necessitate a complete reorientation of Japan's military strategy, foreign policy, and, above all, domestic politics. It would mean going back to the premilitaristic stage of party politics, civilian supremacy, and business culture. The leadership in Japan in the fall of 1941, especially the cabinet of General Tōjō, was not prepared to do this. They believed the only choice was to go forward in search of a pan-Asianist solution. Attacks upon American and British possessions in Asia and the Pacific at dawn of December 7 (8 in Asia), 1941, would be the first step in that direction.

THE JAPANESE-AMERICAN war, then, involved more than just a clash between aggression and resistance or between militarism and peace. Such simple dichotomizing, while undoubtedly accurate at one level of generalization, conceals a far more interesting development: the degree to which the conflict revolved around the question whether a return to the past was possible and desirable. American officials believed the 1920s still provided the basic framework for comprehending international relations. That framework assumed that an international order of stability and peace could be built on economic interdependence among the industrial nations and their cooperation to develop other regions of the globe. The Japanese disagreed and instead opted for a pan-Asianist regional order. This did not mean, however, that they were rejecting all vestiges of Western civilization. They were, after all, as concerned with economic development and prosperity as other peoples, and the new Asian order was by no means defined as a preindustrial one. As commentator after commentator noted on the eve of Pearl Harbor, Japanese policy was aimed at the development and ultimate industrialization of Asian countries. They had in fact already been partially Westernized, one of them noted, and Japan's task was not to de-Westernize them but to "Asianize the Europeanization of Asia."[45] Such a proposition was placed in opposition to what the

Japanese regarded as American and European imperialistic domination of the region. The Americans, on their part, believed that the Japanese scheme was intended to put an end to all Western interests and influence in the East. Both sides exaggerated their differences, but the subsequent years showed that the legacy of Japanese-American interdependence was stronger than the tenuous edifice of pan-Asianism.

ABORTIVE
NEW ORDER

2

NOTHING BETTER illustrates how uncertain American-Japanese relations had been before Pearl Harbor than the sentiment, expressed on both sides of the Pacific immediately afterward, that for the first time in years everything was falling into place. The Japanese rejoiced that their pan-Asianist vision was at last becoming reality; as the novelist Tokuda Shūsei wrote, that vision had been difficult to justify so long as Japan's sole enemy was China; the nation had in fact been engaging in fratricide instead of rallying other Asians to establish a new order.[1] Now, however, the meaning of Japan's struggle was clear; its real enemies in China had been the Anglo-American powers that had sought to enslave the Asian masses. By giving those powers a decisive blow, the Japanese were taking a first strong step to rid Asia of their pernicious presence. Japan's policy after the Manchurian incident was clear for the first time, wrote Nagayo Yoshio.[2] Everything that had happened since 1931 had to do with building the new order in East Asia. The Japanese people, who had been looking at Asia through the eyes of Americans and Englishmen, had now resolutely shaken off this influence to build "a new moral and cultural order."

In the United States, too, there was a widespread feeling that the Pearl Harbor attack revealed the irreconcilable differences between the two countries. Americans believed that the Japanese had long schemed such an outrage even while America was trying to negotiate with them in good faith. The negotiations had been in vain, because the two countries stood for diametrically opposite principles and because the Japanese had never taken the talks seriously. In fact, the two countries had been fated to collide. It was not just that conflicting interests had led to armed hostilities; this was a war between "lawless forces" and the cause of "establishing a just peace," as Roosevelt said on the day after Pearl Harbor.[3] The surprise attack on Hawaii revealed to Americans that Japan was a lawless nation, not fit for the ordinary diplomacy of law-abiding nations. As a State Department memorandum noted, "Loyalty to the Emperor is the most sacred duty of the Japanese subject . . . War and military virtues are glorified . . . Democratic institutions are incompatible with the Japanese philosophy." Given that perception of Japan, it was easy for Americans to persuade themselves that there was a fundamental contradiction between "the ideals expressed in the Atlantic Charter," which the United States espoused, and "Japan's national philosophy."[4] In other words, Japan's sneak attack was not surprising at all; it was but one manifestation of the two countries' irreconcilable philosophies and ways of life.

This type of fatalism helped ensure national unity in both countries. For the first time the Japanese felt united behind a national purpose; debate and bargaining among diverse groups would give way to universal sacrifice and devotion to ideal. All would have a stake in successfully waging war and purging Asia of Anglo-American influences. Now that the United States was involved in an Asian war, the Americans, on their part, could stop arguing about the wisdom of intervening in the European war. They would organize for victory and subordinate their particularistic interests to the larger goal of survival of their way of life. Thus both the Japanese and the Americans came to see their well-being and national purpose as bound up with events in greater Asia. In order to live as they wished to live and preserve their cultural identity, both Japanese and Americans were impelled to pay attention to external events and to become conscious of each other, symbolically as well as physically. They had no choice but to fight.

But the nature of that confrontation was far from clear. Although official propaganda and press commentaries on both sides of the Pacific stressed the theme of fundamental conflict, it was difficult to relate it to specific situations in Asia and the Pacific. Japanese and Americans, when they began thinking about the problem and drawing up plans for the future of the region, found the task even more onerous than the actual fighting between their combat forces.

Wartime Japanese and American designs in China provide a good example. China was a symbol of the struggle between the two; Japan was attempting to incorporate it into its Asian order, while Americans were trying to bring China closer to cooperation with the Western democracies. Which direction the Chinese would take, whether it would become an appendage of the Japanese war effort or a model of liberal-capitalist transformation were obviously significant questions. Both Japan and the United States needed China in a symbolic sense. However, neither of the belligerents could control the political and social orientations of six hundred million Chinese, so they would have to work through their leaders in Chungking, Nanking, Yenan, and elsewhere. How should the Japanese and Americans organize to work with these leaders? Who should be sent to China? What if the Chinese refused to cooperate? Ironically, these questions harrassed Japanese and Americans alike during the war, and at its end they still did not have the answers.

The Japanese saw a fundamental connection between domestic social order and the new Asian order, of which China formed a vital part. It was not simply, or even primarily, that the Japanese economy required control over the resources and markets of the China mainland. On December 3, 1941, the supreme headquarters in Tokyo stated that the Japanese army of occupation should strive to develop north China's natural resources and make the region self-sufficient.[5] The raw materials and foodstuffs would be used primarily by the Japanese in China, not at home, which was understandable, given the anticipated shortage of shipping. It also meant that Japan's presence in China could not be justified in traditional economic terms. Earlier the argument had been, especially by left-wing writers, that China was providing work opportunities for thousands of Japanese who would otherwise be unemployed. That may have been valid before 1941, but after the outbreak of the Japanese-American war, unemployment ceased to be a major problem. With the expansion of the armed forces and the need for increased munitions production, there was if anything a shortage of manpower, causing the government eventually to import unskilled laborers from Korea and Taiwan. Most able-bodied Japanese men were either in the armed forces or working, and a steadily increasing number of women were recruited into the work force.[6] Under the circumstances, there was a noticeable drop in the number of Japanese going to China for employment.

China's meaning for wartime Japan was more ideological than economic. Japan's continued hold on China symbolized its determination to shed its Western orientation and identify itself with Asian destiny. In a radio broadcast in July 1942, Okumura Kiwao, assistant director of the Office of Information, declared that the war against China, which had begun in 1937, had prepared the country internally as well as militarily for the Pacific war. Japan's political and economic life, he asserted, had been purged of liberalism and Marxism, and the nation had awakened to its Asian identity. The Japanese government was now solidly grounded on the institution of the emperor rather than on selfish party politics, and the country's economy, instead of being patterned after the unlimited and disorganized capitalism of the West, was systematically controlled to serve the greater interests of the nation. Thanks to the struggle with China, Japanese society had been transformed. Therefore the new order of Chinese-Japanese cooperation, the external counterpart to the new order at home, must be firmly established. By the same token, the war in China would not end until Western influences were driven out of Asia. The Sino-Japanese war had become part of the Japanese-American war, and both must be fought by a people determined to create an entirely new society. Only by redoubling their efforts to bring China under their influence would the Japanese be able to win the war against the Anglo-American nations and to reconstruct their society on the basis of entirely new, anti-Western, principles. Japan, in restructuring the world, must insist upon its definition of Chinese-Japanese relations, and the Japanese people must accept the economic and ideological orientations that would be compatible with the war effort.[7] Thus for Japan's leaders, the Japanese presence in China represented the sociopolitical system they were seeking to establish.

This was particularly true of the military, who were more than ever the embodiment of Japanese society. The nation was reorganizing itself in order to reorganize the world, and in both efforts the role of the armed forces was crucial. It may be, as Alfred Vagts has observed, that "old-style officer methods and ambitions" had remained strong in Japan during the interwar years, whereas the armies and navies of most other countries had shunned politics.[8] But unlike other countries, where "wartime civilian militarism" enhanced the role of civilian governments at the expense of professional soldiers and admirals, in Japan the military enjoyed near autonomy in making strategic decisions. The supreme headquarters, comprising the top leaders of the general staffs of the two services, had been established in 1937 and remained the exclusive seat of power regarding military and strategic questions. The civilian government had no influence on those decisions.

The link between the cabinet and the supreme headquarters was the liaison council, instituted in 1940, in which the prime minister, foreign minister, service ministers, and finance minister met representatives from the supreme headquarters. The records of the council's meetings indicate, however, that the military never gave up their jealously guarded autonomy on strategic issues. Not even Prime Minister Tōjō, who had spent his entire career in the army, was permitted to attend supreme headquarters deliberations. Civilian authorities could attempt to influence military decisions only through the emperor. By conferring with the officials of the Imperial Household Ministry and those who had daily access to the Palace, they could communicate their views to the emperor. Even then, however, their views might not carry any weight, because the emperor tended to take a narrow view of his authority and did not want to create a constitutional crisis through acting boldly on his own.

Such undisputed authority in military hands, however, had drawbacks. The military had become the single most powerful entity in the nation, the symbol as well as the agent of the new order. Its privileged position was justified by the magnitude of the task, but the task was never clearly defined. To be sure, the new order in Asia was to reflect the new order at home, but the external objective tended to be less important than the military's power in Japanese society. On the other hand, ultimately its status would reflect its success abroad. If the military did not succeed, its power in Japanese society might be seriously undermined.

The tangled story of the occupation of China was a perfect illustration. After the Pacific war started, the army tried to clarify its objectives in China. "A new China [would] serve as an essential wing of the new order in East Asia," declared General Okamura Neiji, commander of the North China Area Army.[9] Army strategy following Pearl Harbor was to "take positive measures to bring about the submission of the Chiang regime and to cooperate with Germany and Italy in order to bring Britain to its knees, thereby causing America's loss of will to continue the war."[10] Annihilation of Chiang Kai-shek's resistance was considered the key to achieving what the army believed to be a realistic objective, a quick stalemate in the war with the United States. If successful, these strategies would enable the Japanese to remain predominant in the western Pacific and on the Asian continent; the new order would be achieved by dividing the Pacific and expelling Anglo-American influence from the Japanese-dominated half.

To bring that about, the anti-Japanese forces in China must be destroyed. Thus strategy and ideology were unified in the Japanese army's call to the Chinese to cooperate in fighting against their common foes, Chinese and Anglo-American. As the public affairs department of the North China Area Army stated in a memorandum on December 3, it was important "to impress the Chinese strongly with the idea that the United States and Great Britain were the common enemies of Japan, Manchukuo, and China."[11] Five days later, as war broke out between Japan and the Anglo-American powers, the army adopted an "outline of principles for ideological warfare on the occasion of the war against the United States and Britain." It reiterated the idea that the war was "a struggle between new order and old order, a sacred war for liberation of Asia." Japan, Manchukuo, and China must cooperate in building the new East Asian order. Japanese propaganda reminded the Chinese people that the war had been provoked by the Anglo-American nations, which for centuries had invaded and exploited East Asia. The disastrous fate of the European countries that had relied on these powers for protection should serve as a lesson to all Asians not to trust the Western democracies, which cloaked their selfish ambitions under fine-sounding slogans.[12]

These ideas became an integral part of the war effort. It was more than ever imperative to create new arrangements in Asian countries that would contribute to the dissipation of Anglo-American influences. China, in particular, would have to develop a new framework of social relations, both between Japanese and Chinese and among the Chinese. However, the army of occupation was able to come up with only stale ideas and strategies. The above-cited December 3 memorandum stressed calling on the Chinese in north China "to eliminate the Chungking regime and the Communist party, both of which cater to America and Britain," promoting "spontaneous and positive cooperation by the Chinese in the occupied areas," and "dividing the allegiances of people in enemy territory." Attaining such ambitious goals would require a massive reorganization of Chinese society, going beyond the handful of pro-Japanese elements and reaching out to other groups to co-opt them, to provide them with a stake in the new developments, and to divide them against themselves to eliminate extremist elements.

The Japanese army was not unaware of these needs; General Okamura recognized the importance of dealing with recalcitrant Chinese at three levels: through the armed forces, the government, and mass organization. The last was the most crucial in view of the Chinese Nationalists' and Communists' skill in organizing mass movements against Japanese imperialism. To combat such movements, Japan had to mobilize the Chinese masses, and quite predictably, the Hsin-min Hui became the instrument. The society was to reorganize and engage in intensive local propaganda and organization. Its regional branches were instructed to work energetically for mass movements in support of Japanese policy against dissidents. In every *hsien* (county) the Hsin-min Hui set up organs to teach villagers how to defend their communities against hostile forces. In some areas, it was hoped that the "self-defense" forces would not only maintain law and order but would also wage a counteroffensive against Communists and other partisans.[13]

Suzuki Yoshimichi, the retired army general who was chief adviser to the Hsin-min Hui, boasted in August 1942 that the society had a membership of 3,500,000, in contrast to the Chinese Communist party, which had only 40,000 members. According to an official report at the end of that year, the organization had 13,490 branches. Still, these figures accounted for only 3.6 percent of the entire Chinese population of north China, and the hope was that it would eventually embrace the entire population. At a meeting of the Hsin-min Hui in October 1942, the leaders explained that its campaigns were intended to help build a new China on the basis of a "radical culture," by eliminating the evils of communism,

Anglo-Americanism, and feudalism. In order to do this, various youth organizations were amalgamated into a new "North China Hsin-min Youth Corps."[14]

These efforts indicate that the Japanese army was quite aware that only through mass organization and mobilization would it be possible to develop a new China oriented toward cooperation with Japan. But would a new China acquiesce in Japan's military presence in, and economic domination over, the country? It would have been naive to think so, given the long history of Chinese resistance to Japanese imperialism. Ironically, those Chinese who joined and worked for the Hsin-min Hui may have done so primarily to preserve the social status quo and to perpetuate their vested interests. In many communities, joining the Hsin-min Hui was the only means of ensuring law and order. The alternative was continued resistance to Japan and consequent warfare. The Hsin-min Hui at least gave village leaders a political superstructure and arms to cope with problems of security and stability, as well as a voice in decision making.

In 1942 such collaboration was not automatically penalized by the anti-Japanese forces within China. According to a Japanese intelligence report, the Communists tried to neutralize collaborators by assuring them that they were still considered loyal Chinese, even though they were in the Japanese camp. Moreover, the Communists planned to infiltrate the Hsin-min Hui and other organizations both to obtain secret intelligence and to prepare for an eventual revolt against Japanese authority. A Japanese officer later recalled that the Communists were extremely adroit in countering Hsin-min Hui efforts to mobilize the masses. Communists and their sympathizers occupied important positions in Hsin-min Hui branches, and sometimes engaged in bribery and corruption to turn the people against the organization. They became teachers to propagate anti-Japanese ideas. To break the Japanese blockade of the Communist areas and to obtain much-needed foodstuffs and other goods, the Communists often infiltrated Hsin-min offices in the border areas. In that way they could join the food distribution network in occupied north China.[15]

Even if the Japanese had been able to contain these subversive activities and rid the occupied areas of radical dissidents, they still would have had to cope with the people's awakened political consciousness. Ironically, if the Japanese efforts to organze a new society in China had been more successful, the Chinese would have been more resistant to Japan's continued presence. In time the Japanese would have had to face the consequences and redefine their relationship with the host population. In fact there is little evidence that the Japanese in north China became any more conciliatory toward the Chinese after Pearl Harbor than they had been in the past. Army documents reported that the Japanese in China continued to view themselves as masters and the local populace as inferior beings. The Japanese civilian population in north China numbered roughly 400,000 in 1942, mostly merchants, students, and entrepreneurs who took advantage of the Japanese army's presence and their traditional extraterritorial rights to acquire riches quickly. An army memorandum of January 15, 1942, noted that Japanese residents were pursuing their material objectives through "individualism, utilitarianism, hedonism, and utopian humanism." Having been immersed in the colonial atmosphere, they lacked patriotism. Far from promoting cooperation with the Chinese, they regarded them merely as objects of exploitation.[16]

A few Japanese recognized that such a state of affairs totally belied the spirit of Asian solidarity against Western imperialism. Nashimoto Yūhei, who was an economic advisor to the North China Political Affairs Committee, wrote in his memoirs that he was constantly working with Chinese leaders to improve economic conditions in north China on the basis of equality between Chinese and Japanese. But he was helpless against the vested interests of both Chinese and Japanese who did not want to give up their privileged positions in society and government. The army of occupation continued to control the railway, banking, and most industrial establishments, and the Japanese were ultimately protected by the military presence.[17] The more the Japanese paid lip service to the new Asian order, the more impatient the Chinese grew with the obvious gap between rhetoric and performance. In a truly new order, Japan would relinquish its privileged status and develop a new system of relations with the Chinese. In short, there would be no new Asian order without a new order in China.

The dilemma was clearly felt by the Japanese diplomats in Nanking, the seat of the nominally independent government of Wang Ching-wei. Although it had been recognized only by the Axis powers, it had all the appearance and pretensions of a national government: a cabinet, various agencies, and diplomatic representatives abroad. This fact was of some importance because Japan dealt with the area nominally under Nanking's control not as an occupied territory like north China, but as an independent state, at least technically. However, the Nanking government did not possess the most obvious symbol of sovereignty, its own military force. The headquarters of the Japanese expeditionary force was in Nanking under the command of General Hata Shunroku, who saw Wang and other Chinese officials almost daily, rather than waiting for the Japanese embassy to take the initiative. It was Hata, not Hidaka Shinrokurō, chargé d'affaires, who first informed Wang Ching-wei of the outbreak of war against the Anglo-American powers.

The coming of war should have provided an opportunity to bring Nanking-Tokyo relations a bit closer to the professed ideal of cooperation, and Japan's diplomats tried to do so as best they could. They reasoned that the surest way to obtain full Chinese cooperation in the war efforts would be to demonstrate Japan's genuine dedication to pan-Asianism and its willingness to bring China into full partnership against common foes, although naturally that would entail restoring more rights to the Chinese government. As Hidaka wired Tokyo on December 21, 1941, Japan should make it clear to the Chinese that "this war is a war for Asian liberation." Since Japan was fighting for that goal, it must, Hidaka declared, promote Chinese sovereignty and independence.[18] More specifically, such a policy would mean reducing the expeditionary forces' restrictions on Nanking's freedom and eventually restoring to China the rights of a sovereign nation.

As in north China, this policy would have been a logical extension of the rhetoric of pan-Asian order, but in Nanking its implementation would have involved serious negotiations with a recognized government for revision of many existing arrangements. Because of military needs, that would be a formidable task, as was demonstrated when the Japanese supreme command vetoed Nanking's declaration of war against the United States and Britain. Although the Wang regime had no armed forces to back up its words, the declaration would have given the regime greater prestige; it would have been a full-fledged ally of Japan, an independent belligerent, not a puppet of a conquering army. The regime could then assert greater authority in the internal affairs of occupied

China and, as Japan's co-belligerent, could look after its own interests at a peace conference. (Chinese officials remembered that in the First World War, by joining the war on the winning side, China had been represented at the peace conference as a victorious power.) For all these reasons Wang and his officials wanted to declare war and to support Japanese war efforts. The Japanese military, however, preferred Nanking to be officially neutral so that there would be no significant change in Japan-Nanking relations. Rather than having Wang Ching-wei raise an army to join the war effort, Japan wanted him to continue as a figurehead over a land that was a major source of supply for the Japanese forces.[19]

It was ironic that the Chinese collaborators were not allowed by the self-proclaimed "liberators" to declare war on their allegedly common foes, because that would have curtailed the freedom of action of the "liberators." In such small ways, the Japanese from the very beginning revealed their disregard for their own rhetoric when it interfered with their military objectives. Barring active military cooperation with Nanking, Tokyo might have responded to Hidaka's pleas by helping it improve political and economic conditions in the areas under its control. Inflation, monetary chaos, and shortages of goods were plaguing the region, almost all because of the Japanese troops' claims on food, shelter, and services. The economic blockade set up by the occupation army was an enormous obstacle to the flow of goods, and the presence of a large foreign army inevitably invited black-marketing and profiteering by both Japanese and Chinese merchants. Chinese youths not connected with the government "had no place to go," Wang told Shigemitsu Mamoru, who was appointed ambassador to Nanking in February 1942.[20] Their frustration and anguish were the biggest problem faced by Chinese authorities collaborating with Japan. It was absolutely essential, Wang told Shigemitsu, to improve the livelihood of the people in pacified districts so that the areas under Nanking's jurisdiction would develop as a model of peace and prosperity through Chinese-Japanese cooperation. Otherwise, the Chinese occupied areas would have no incentive to actively support Japan, and those outside would merely laugh at so blatant a betrayal of the slogans about the new order.

Shigemitsu fully agreed, but he could do little to help promote political and economic stability so long as the war in China went on. The lot of the Chinese, whose loyal support was desperately needed for Japan's war against the Western powers, would not improve until Chinese-Japanese hostilities ended and the Japanese forces were reduced or eliminated, but the hostilities would not end until one side or the other won. The Japanese army had to pacify the country before paying more attention to the welfare of the Chinese people, but the army had not been able to achieve that in four years, and there was no assurance that they could do so while engaged in a fierce combat against powerful Western arms.

The only plausible way out of the dilemma would have been a peaceful diplomatic settlement of the Chinese-Japanese conflict. That the Japanese were interested in this alternative was revealed in 1942 when they talked of a "total peace" in China. The idea was that somehow Japan should encourage peace sentiments among all factions in China and coalesce them under a unified authority, presumably of Wang Ching-wei's. Because Nanking's authority was recognizably limited and most of the hinterland was engaged in anti-Japanese resistance, the best way to enhance Nanking's prestige and weaken the resistance would be to work for a cessation of hostilities and then credit Nanking with the peace.

This was a colossal task, but in the initial enthusiasm following the Pearl Harbor attack, some Japanese and their Chinese collaborators believed the time was opportune for initiating peace moves throughout China. This would entail some contact with the Nationalists in Chungking. As a group of Nanking officials told Japanese diplomats in December 1941, Japan's initial victories had shaken some Nationalists, and Japan should take this opportunity to further peace with them.[21] In February 1942 Ambassador Shigemitsu and Ch'en Kung-po, a high Nanking official, agreed that Nanking should send emissaries to Chungking to probe peace possibilities.[22] Wang Ching-wei supported these overtures, provided they were coupled with some genuine efforts by Japan to improve conditions in areas under its control. Chungking's potential moderates, he told Shigemitsu in May, would not work for peace unless the suffering of the people in occupied areas was alleviated. Otherwise they would have no incentive to join the peace movement, for they might suffer the same fate as those other Chinese.[23]

It was obviously logical to try to stabilize conditions throughout China by political means. If successful, the policy would isolate

Communists and other extremists, detach most of the country from the Japanese-American war, and strengthen the pro-Japanese Nanking government. In that case there might be hope for a genuinely pan-Asian crusade against the United States and Great Britain. Of course, the Japanese would have to offer sufficient concessions to the Chinese, not simply in the occupied areas but also in the hinterland. The most crucial issue was Japan's military presence. So long as it persisted, there was little reason to expect that Chinese leaders in Chungking and elsewhere would be interested in bilateral negotiations. Given the Japanese army's reluctance to make changes even in Nanking, it would certainly not be willing to reduce its forces significantly to placate the Nationalists.

There is evidence that at least some Japanese, including former Foreign Minister Matsuoka Yōsuke and General Ishihara Kanji, believed that the most practical way to break the impasse in China was by dealing with Chungking rather than Nanking. Those two men, the architects of Japan's Manchurian policy during the 1930s, recognized the folly of fighting both the Chinese and the Anglo-Americans; they wanted to concentrate on the latter by yielding to the former's wishes.[24] These men, however, had lost their power, Matsuoka having been ousted from office and Ishihara being in virtual exile as commander of the Sixteenth Division in Kyoto. They spoke for the outsiders in wartime Japan, visualizing that a new situation in China would produce corresponding changes in Japanese politics. They knew that making significant concessions to Chiang Kai-shek's followers and reducing military forces in China would have serious domestic repercussions in Japan, but these were not unwelcome to them. Indeed, they insisted that only by drastic reordering at home could Japan expect to win the war for a new order abroad.

The Japanese military in China, obviously, were adamantly opposed to such a course. Although some of them recognized the tactical advantage of maintaining contact with Chungking, they never systematically cultivated ties with it. Thus, in early May, when Nanking sent a secret peace emissary to Chungking with the endorsement of the Japanese embassy and the expeditionary army, the army did not coordinate its military operations with the move. In June the Japanese army carried out an offensive against Chungking's forces in southeast China, thus nullifying this and similar peace moves initiated by Nanking.[25]

What stands out in Japanese policy and strategy in China immediately after Pearl Harbor is that the beginning of the American war actually made little difference. Japan had the choice, as had become clear by 1941, of either continuing to dominate China militarily or of returning to the pre-1931 arrangements in which it would promote its interests in China in the framework of co-operative competition with other industrialized countries. Neither alternative implied full Chinese-Japanese cooperation against the West, and yet that was the vision that informed the spirit of the war against the United States and Great Britain. That the Japanese almost totally failed to translate that spirit into reality indicated not merely the practical difficulties, but more fundamentally the weakness of their commitment. In reality, the situation was even worse, for Japanese strategy called for subjugating the Chiang Kai-shek regime as a precondition for victory over the Anglo-American powers; the Chinese war would continue simultaneously with the Pacific war. Eliminating Chiang would, it was believed, force the United States and Britain to give up their resistance to the new pan-Asian order. But that strategy amounted to fighting the Chinese in the name of pan-Asianism. Such rhetoric made little difference in the Chinese theater of war. The conflict went on unchecked, even as the Japanese were finding it necessary to divert their resources to the Pacific Ocean.

INTERESTINGLY enough, American relations with China after the outbreak of the Pacific war were no less confusing. United States policy had consistently opposed the new Asian order the Japanese were allegedly constructing; according to the American perception, Asia should be an arena for Western political and economic activities as much as for the development of non-Western peoples. A Japan-dominated Asia would combine the vast resources and population of the region against the rest of the world, a prospect that held frightening implications. The fear of pan-Asianism as a corollary of the Japanese war was widespread. The Japanese, a State Department memorandum noted in January 1942, professed to save Asians "from the white man's economic exploitation and soul-corroding material civilization, and to let them flower and return to their original virtues under the benevolent protection of the Emperor."[26] Japanese strategy was seen as turning Asians against white countries; Japan's victory would surely mean the exclusion of Western influence from the area. Thus in January 1942, on the eve of the battle of Singapore, an officer of the Far Eastern division of the State Department wrote that the impending conflict was "more than a focal point in military strategy—it is a symbol—a symbol of power, the determination, and the ability of the United Nations to win this war." Japanese seizure of Singapore would mean that "the prestige of the white race and particularly of the British Empire and the United States" would suffer throughout Asia.[27] The purpose of the Pacific war, in this perspective, was to prevent such a development. The Anglo-American powers must combine their resources against the Japanese in a test of strength, the outcome of which would determine the shape of the Asia-Pacific region for years to come.

But where did the Asians themselves, above all the Chinese, fit? If the Japanese war was seen in the context of future Anglo-American interests, there was no ready answer. The fate of the Asians was distinctly secondary to the survival of the British empire and American power. Theoretically, Britain and the United States should be able to cope with the Japanese challenge in the traditional framework of rivalries among advanced, industrial nations. How the rest of Asia behaved was, as in the past, relatively unimportant. And yet Japan's rhetorical device of calling the war a pan-Asian conflict had practical as well as symbolic significance for the Allies. As the above memorandum noted, a Japanese victory in Singapore would "give considerable impetus to any movement in China favoring a settlement with Japan." The faith of those Chinese who had supported the Japanese would be reaffirmed, and others would lose confidence in the staying power of the white nations. Since Western prestige in Asia depended as much on psychological as on physical factors, their loss of face would do irreparable damage.

In February, when Singapore did fall, Ambassador Clarence E. Gauss reported from Chungking that the Chinese press viewed the event as a failure of Allied strategy and morale. Westerners seemed to be weak and irresolute, a far cry from their pretensions as masters over the Asian races.[28] French and Dutch authorities in Asia were also worried about the implications of Japanese advances for Chinese attitudes toward Westerners; after the war there might be a Chinese "invasion" of European colonies.[29] The West might become isolated and eventually be expelled from Asia, not simply because of Japanese attacks but also because of cooperation, explicit or implicit, by Chinese and other Asians with Japan.

How to prevent such a combination of Asian peoples was thus a serious question, both strategically and politically. How could the United States and Britain ensure that China and the rest of Asia would resist Japan without provoking their assault upon the West? How could they be persuaded to help white countries fight an Asian nation? In retrospect it appears that the fear of a pan-Asian combination against the West was vastly exaggerated. Certainly there was no likelihood of Chinese collaboration with Japan unless the latter renounced its continental expansion; in that case Japan would be reverting to the pre-1931 path of cooperation with the industrialized West, thereby mitigating the possibility of an exclusive Asian bloc. The fact that such fears were expressed reflected the West's insecurity about its position in Asia as well as about the behavior of Asians. And undoubtedly the pan-Asianist rhetoric and Japanese attacks upon the colonies strengthened these impressions. It is not surprising, therefore, that after Pearl Harbor, American officials seriously sought to work out a strategy for deflecting Asian political consciousness from anti-Western channels.

First it was considered necessary to demonstrate, to Asians and to Americans themselves, that the Western presence in China and in Asia had been qualitatively different from that of the Japanese imperialists. In the memorandum of January 23, 1942, the Far Eastern division of the State Department asserted, "Wherever the American, British and Dutch flags fly in the Orient all men, regardless of race, are equal under the law." This was contrasted to areas under Japanese rule, where native and local residents had been ruthlessly exploited. In Manchuria, for instance, they "have been reduced to virtual slavery and they now compare themselves with mules whose masters work them from daybreak to nightfall with just enough food to keep them alive and working." The old Chinese colleges and universities had been destroyed, and at the new universities, "the chief subjects of lectures are totalitarian economic control, state capitalism, Japanese political concepts, and mystical Pan-Asiatic nonsense." In other areas of China as well, the Japanese were "reducing inhabitants to serfdom and destroying their minds and bodies. In these areas the administration, the wealth, and the important properties of the inhabitants have passed into Japanese hands, while the output of the fields, of the factories, and of the mines has become the exclusive property of the Japanese state."[30] There was substance to these accusations, as there was to the view expressed in another State Department memorandum, that "the stubborn resistance of the Chinese . . . destroys Japan's claim that she comes to emancipate either China or Asia!"[31]

Officials were not content with such comfortable generalizations, however. For even as "40,000,000 Chinese, including many of the intellectual and educated classes, [have] fled to free China to escape the 'benevolent' rule of the Japanese," the above memorandum continued, one could not be absolutely sure, especially in the early stages of the war, that an important segment of the Chinese leaders and population would not be attracted to the idea of pan-Asian order. The fall of Singapore seemed to increase that possibility, because it symbolized the collapse of Western prestige in Asia. It also necessitated strategic reorientation by the Anglo-American powers, which were now forced to concentrate on the defense of India and Ceylon in the west and the Pacific islands in the east. China was even more cut off from the outside world than it had been before 1941, which might encourage Chinese separatism and defeatism and generate a lack of trust in Western countries. Already at the beginning of 1942 Chiang Kai-shek was complaining to Roosevelt that he considered "himself entirely out of touch with the main decisions of strategy, which profoundly affect China's future. Whether an offensive will start from Australia, whether it is considered feasible to hold Burma, what steps are taken to protect the Indian Ocean route, what air forces will be sent to India, Burma and China, on all these vital questions his role is that of an occasional listener."[32]

His complaints were justified, for the United States failed to establish any agency in Asia even remotely resembling the Combined Chiefs of Staff in Washington, where top American and British strategists continually exchanged information and worked out plans for victory. Their close collaboration resulted, predictably, in an Atlantic-first strategy. In the early months of the war, Combined Chiefs of Staff memoranda seldom mentioned China; the strategists were far more concerned with Europe, the Middle East, and above all with the survival of the Soviet Union against persistent German attacks. The United States navy, to be sure, often expressed its preference for a Pacific-first strategy. This was supported by influential segments of the Republican party and by the mass media, because it would give America a virtually free hand to avenge itself on Japanese treachery. However, China did not figure prominently in naval strategy; the war against Japan was viewed as essentially a classical bilateral conflict between two navies. In any event, the Roosevelt-Churchill conference of December 1941–January 1942 decided on a counteroffensive first against Germany, where Anglo-American-Soviet cooperation would be the key to success. The Chinese theater of war would not be fully integrated into the main military effort.

These developments confirmed that America's policy was oriented toward Europe, leaving Asia outside. But that position was patently inadequate, because the United States *was* engaged in an Asian war and had to obtain the support of the Chinese and other Asians. Having no coherent approach to the region was tantamount to leaving Asians to their fate, just as the Japanese were vowing to turn them against the West. The only plausible way out of this dilemma was to promise the Asians a brighter future if they resisted Japanese pressures than if they succumbed to them. The United States might thus be able to compensate for the lack of a more vigorous policy. Some such rationale explains the rather precipitous interest shown by Washington officials in the idea of China as a great power.

President Roosevelt first clearly enunciated the idea of China as a great power in conversations with Soviet Foreign Minister V. M. Molotov and Ambassador Maxim M. Litvinov, in late May and early June 1942. Discussing the future of the colonial areas, Roosevelt remarked that "the white nations . . . could not hope to hold these areas as colonies in the long run." But since they would not yet be ready for self-government, it would be best to set up an international trusteeship to be administered cooperatively by "the four major nations," which included China along with the United

States, Britain, and the Soviet Union. These four would undertake police activities in the postwar world "as guarantors of eventual peace." They would become world "policemen."[33]

It should be noted that Roosevelt's inclusion of China among the big four was a corollary to his vision of the future of the colonies. Neither he nor other officials in Washington advocated immediate independence for these lands; rather, they wanted to ensure the colonies' pro-Western orientation while helping them work toward eventual independence. In Roosevelt's thinking, peace and stability in these regions was a primary responsibility of the great powers. China would be expected to collaborate with the other three in supervising the development of the colonies. In return for being granted the status of a great power, China would have to assume responsibility for peace in the less advanced areas, especially in Asia. Roosevelt was convinced that such an arrangement would be acceptable to the Chinese. In fact he first broached the trusteeship concept to the Russian visitors as Chiang Kai-shek's idea, although there is no evidence that Chiang had originated the idea. By coupling China's great-power status with the postwar scheme for the colonial areas, Roosevelt ingeniously hit upon a policy that could persuade the Chinese to continue their war against Japan and to maintain their Anglo-American orientation after the war.

This design had the virtue of rhetorical coherence and served the immediate purpose of quieting China's fears that it was a minor partner of the great Western powers in the struggle against Japanese militarism. Chinese leaders could say that they were being taken into the confidence of the United States government and that they would play a crucial role in the international order after the war. This was in line with China's aspiration to be, in the words of Chiang Kai-shek, "one of the greatest and strongest nations" in the world.[34] But the United States rhetoric was vague on specifics, and Americans found the task of implementing a grand design as frustrating as the Japanese. For instance, Roosevelt sent General Joseph W. Stilwell to Chungking at the beginning of 1942 as a gesture of goodwill, a demonstration that the United States was taking the Chinese theater of war seriously. However, Stilwell soon discovered how difficult it was to effect cooperation between the two countries. There was something anomalous about America's recognizing China as a great power and at the same time providing an

American general as chief of staff for the Chinese commander-in-chief. Chiang Kai-shek was constantly irritated by the suggestion that he needed a foreigner's counsel regarding strategic decisions, and personality differences between the two men did not help.

But the real problem lay in the domestic repercussions of Stilwell's presence in China. Although Roosevelt talked of that country as a great power, he was aware of its political instability. As he told Molotov and Litvinov, there "was still a question-mark" as to whether a unified central government would ever be set up in China.[35] Certainly during the war Chinese society and politics did not seem as stable and organized as they should be. Could there be substantial cooperation between such a country and the United States? It was one thing to talk of American-Chinese collaboration in the abstract, but quite another to follow through its implications. Ultimately that vision would have to be translated into the realm of internal political forces and social orientations. In America the idea was universally accepted because it was painless to do so; no groups or interests had a stake in opposing the idea. Even so, Republican critics of the Roosevelt administration later used the China issue for partisan ends, asking, for instance, why the United States was not doing more to assist the Chinese forces or to coordinate strategy against Japan.

At this time, however, it was in China that domestic politics was more gravely tangled up with the promise of great-power status. General Stilwell firmly believed that he was to make China a stronger and better-disciplined country so that it could exercise leadership in postwar Asia. But any such scheme involved him in complex Chinese politics, for the military strengthening of a country that lacked administrative unity was itself a political act. He could choose either to work closely with Chiang Kai-shek and his trusted generals, to the exclusion of other centers of power, or he could insist on training and equipping all Chinese forces that were willing to fight against Japan. The Kuomintang leadership of course wanted Stilwell to adhere to the first alternative, whereas Communist and other dissident groups wanted a more equitable distribution of American aid and a more representative form of government for a country that would be a partner of the United States. In this sense, the American rhetoric of supporting China as a great power paradoxically served to deepen the rift among various groups in that country, undermining the very ideal of a strong and unified China.

The Chinese situation had, of course, existed for decades, but now it had serious implications for United States policy, for it was more difficult than ever to envision a systematic approach. How could America define and develop a coherent policy toward a country whose internal politics intruded at every turn? The problem might not have been so baffling and frustrating if American officials had been able to agree. Unfortunately, by the beginning of 1942, a sharp division was developing within the United States government regarding Chinese politics, in particular the Kuomintang-Communist struggle for power. Ambassador Gauss, General Stilwell, and some diplomats in Chungking were more and more critical of Chiang's leadership; they did not feel that America's support of China as a major ally automatically meant accepting Kuomintang rule as it existed. They were taken aback by Chiang's bold request in early 1942 for a $500 million loan from the United States, considering it unnecessary and extravagant. Gauss thought that the request was clearly intended to cover up the Nationalists' inept handling of the war and inflation and to help them consolidate their hold on the country's economy and war machine. Stilwell criticized Chiang for not distributing American aid goods equitably among all military units. From these points of view, the United States government would be making a mistake by dealing with the Chungking regime as the sole source of legitimacy in Free China.

Other Americans, however, opposed such views. Stanley K. Hornbeck, political advisor to the secretary of state, believed that the United States should assist cooperative and friendly Chinese, and in his mind this meant Chiang and his followers. To criticize them would be to rebuke these very leaders who were committed to wartime and postwar collaboration with the United States.[36] Other Americans in China more openly promoted the cause of the Kuomintang, including General Claire Chennault, commander of the Fourteenth Air Force, which was delivering goods over the Himalayas to Chungking, and Captain Milton Miles, head of the Naval Group China (NGC), organized in early 1942 as a secret liaison between the Chinese government and the United States navy. Chennault and Miles, who were convinced that the Nationalists should be encouraged and supported as America's allies, represented the air force and the navy, which tended to be at cross purposes with the army, represented by the more critical Stilwell. Rifts and tensions among the Chinese reverberated among the Americans in Chungking, creating an incoherent picture of wartime China.[37]

This lack of consensus made it extremely difficult for the United States to develop a consistent policy toward China. Realizing the ideal of cooperation with the Chinese was as frustrating to American officials as it was to the Japanese, and for basically the same reasons. The vision of China's postwar greatness, though shared by all American officials, was not a sufficient guide to policy regarding factional disputes in that country, just as the idea of pan-Asian order gave the Japanese little help in devising a workable approach to the various Chinese groups.

The confusion in American policy toward China is even more striking when contrasted to the official United States attitude toward Japan. As mentioned earlier, numerous analyses written soon after Pearl Harbor pointed to the inherent structural and ideological weaknesses of the Japanese policy that had led that country to act irresponsibly. Japan's aggressiveness was attributed to the emperor system, ethnocentrism, "Japanese philosophy," and the like. But the situation was not as hopeless as these memoranda seemed to indicate; coupled with denunciation was the inference, as one State Department official put it, "that if lasting peace is to come to the Pacific following this war, Japan's national philosophy must change."[38] Since "lasting peace" in the Pacific was obviously a goal that the United States was fighting for, it followed that Japan's "national philosophy" not only must but *could* change.

How would that be possible? Given the view that Japanese aggression and imperialism were but external manifestations of the national character and tradition, it would seem preposterous to suggest that such behavior could be ended by anything but a fundamental transformation of Japanese ideas and institutions. Some observers in fact asserted that after Japan's defeat only a revolution would ensure democratization and a peaceful attitude. For instance, in the February 1942 issue of *Asia* magazine, Nathaniel Peffer warned that Japanese behavior could not be explained in conventional terms; rather, the aggressiveness sprang from "the character and outlook of the ruling class, the military caste, and the submissiveness of the rest of the Japanese nation."[39] The implication was that a wholesale transformation of the Japanese polity and even national character would be required before peace and security could be restored in the Pacific.

Few officials, however, were going that far. When they talked of the need for "change," they were optimistic that the pernicious features of Japanese society and politics could be eradicated without completely putting an end to the Japan that existed. On the contrary, by "change" they often meant a return to the past, which was recalled as having been more peaceful and friendly toward the United States. That such a past had existed was a key assumption as Washington's officials began formulating their views on the future of Japanese politics and of U.S.-Japanese relations.

John K. Emmerson of the Far Eastern division wrote, "The materials, the inventions, the ideas, the sympathetic suggestions for the creation of a peaceful Pacific—all these have gone to Japan from America. With them in her possession, she has professed peace and treacherously planned for and waged war."[40] The point was not so much that Japan had inevitably risen in revolt against America as that there had been a peaceful pattern of giving and receiving across the Pacific. As Emmerson explained, for eighty-eight years, between 1853, when Commodore Matthew C. Perry "opened" Japan, and December 1941, "Japan and the United States remained at peace." During this entire period, the Japanese "gorged themselves on Western learning." The United States aided Japan's industrialization and educational development, and "Japanese-American friendship seemed a possibility." This era ended "because Japan set out on the path of the conqueror, rejecting the ways of peace which would have given her an honorable place among the nations of the world." But the very fact that there had been a long tradition of trans-Pacific communication and cooperation was the key to exploring future prospects, according to Emmerson. Recalling that tradition sustained American optimism about the future. It would be possible to change Japanese behavior, because the nation had been in the past pro-American and a factor for peace in the Pacific. In other words, the conflict between the two countries was not an inevitable cultural clash. Once Japan was defeated and its militarism discredited, it was assumed, it should not be difficult to restore the framework of friendly and cooperative relations between the two countries.

What is striking about these ideas is their specificity about

Japan's domestic politics. For instance, Hornbeck, certainly no friend of Japan or the emperor system, privately admitted that "while the Emperor is the symbol of the state and the repository of national authority," he should be distinguished from the military leadership. He surmised that after the military were discredited, the emperor would claim the people's allegiance and survive as their leader.[41] The reason for Japan's aggression was not the emperor system itself but the system's abuse by military extremists.

Actually, as Emmerson noted, some prewar leaders who had been close to the emperor had opposed militarism. "There are those in Japan," he wrote in January 1942, "who do not subscribe to the philosophy of life which has in recent years led their nation down a path of aggression and destruction of the rights of peoples. The future hope of Japan will rest with new leaders and with a changed philosophy to arise when peace again prevails upon the Pacific. And this can be accomplished through defeat of Japan's war effort and the inevitable repercussion in Japan and on the Japanese mind of such defeat."[42] Although Emmerson spoke of new leaders, he had in mind those leaders of the 1920s—politicians, businessmen, scholars—who had opposed militarism and who could be expected to guide postwar Japan along more peaceful paths. Although no names were mentioned, these men were not untried new faces but restored old faces, so it was possible to visualize postwar Japanese politics with some degree of specificity. Already it was quite evident that the United States would be able to develop a coherent approach to Japan more easily than China. The United States and Japan, it could be argued, had only to resurrect the interdependent world of the 1920s to restore peace between them, whereas there had been no such history with China.

The fact that the United States was treating China as an ally made it paradoxically more difficult to develop a vision of cooperation with that country than to prepare for postwar reforms in Japan, which was an enemy to be defeated. State Department officials had a remarkable opportunity to plan for surrender terms and postwar arrangements precisely because they played almost no role in the actual conduct of the war. It is interesting to note in this connection that the Advisory Committee on Postwar Foreign Policy, established within the State Department in February 1942, produced far more policy studies and recommendations about Japan than about China.

Its members—including politicians, scholars, and journalists who were invited to participate in its activities—were free to try out any number of schemes for the future of U.S.-Japanese relations, whereas they found the Chinese question far more frustrating.

The political problems subcommittee of the Advisory Committee was one of several subcommittees, the others being on economic reconstruction, economic policy, territorial problems, and security problems. At the August 1, 1942, meeting the subcommittee first took up the general East Asian problem. Under Secretary of State Sumner Welles, chairing the session, observed that "Japan should not start off the new era with territories obtained through its aggressive action." There was virtual consensus on the point. Specifically, this meant that the United Nations would deprive Japan of Taiwan, Korea, and the Mandate islands. However, the participants were not sure if some other territories should be taken away. They were inclined to let Japan keep Okinawa and the Kuriles, but concerning Sakhalin, Hornbeck remarked, and no one else disputed, that "since the Russians were among the United Nations, the territory would probably go to them." Although nothing definite was concluded on this point, the subcommittee members agreed that the territorial question would be fairly straightforward, with the Allies justified in acting to ensure their security after the war.

More complex was the issue of Japan's survival after its defeat. Senator Tom Connally pointed out that while "he despised the Japanese and would love to crush them," defeat and territorial losses would not solve their population problem. Anne O'Hare McCormick of *The New York Times* agreed, saying, "If we were to put Japan back into a small space, we would have to take cheap Japanese goods. We would thereby force them to industrialize to a great extent and would have their problem of over-industrialization on our hands." American labor, Hornbeck added, would never agree to the influx of cheap Japanese goods. Still, it would be dangerous to let Japan shift for itself after the war. Some scheme for international cooperation ought to be worked out within which the Japanese problem could be handled. As Benjamin Cohen pointed out, "It was important that the aftermath [of the war] should not be a kind of isolationism of the Far East region . . . [All] countries—East and West—had a common interest in their economic connections."

Although this kind of thinking was still vague, postwar Japan was being visualized as a nonaggressive, noncolonial country whose survival would hinge upon the establishment of an economically interdependent world. It was not clear how the Japanese, a "very aggressive" people, according to Hornbeck, would fit into such a scheme. But it was taken for granted that somehow their aggressiveness would diminish once they were thoroughly defeated, their overseas territories mostly taken away, and their population problem taken care of through some global framework. While lacking precise definition, the vision at least had a focus. Most important, no one at the August 1 meeting raised the question of Japan's domestic politics. That did not mean that the members were not concerned with punishing the militarists and their collaborators; the important point is that they apparently did not consider the country's domestic political conditions a major obstacle to their vision.

This was in sharp contrast to their discussion of China; no matter what aspect of postwar U.S.-Chinese relations they took up, the issue of China's internal politics was raised. When Under Secretary Welles mentioned the possibility of setting up a regional trusteeship in parts of Asia under the supervision of China, the United States, and the Soviet Union, Senator Warren Austin reminded the members that "[for] some time the four hundred million people of China would not be able to sustain the ideal government they seek. A vast chasm existed between the leaders and the masses, so that he could not hope for the immediate feasibility of the theories we were thinking of." Isaiah Bowman, in connection with Welles's inclusion of China and the Soviet Union among the trustee powers, asked "whether the communist influence in China had declined in the last four years." This was obviously a key question, but Maxwell Hamilton, chief of the State Department's Far Eastern division, merely answered, "that would be a long story." The matter was not pursued further, and it is not surprising that a much less coherent picture of postwar China than of Japan emerged from this discussion.[43]

Lacking a clear-cut idea of the current state and future prospects of Chinese politics, American officials found the task of clarifying a long-range policy toward China quite frustrating. Hornbeck, the one official who spent much time speculating about the future, wrote in July that of the four nations that were likely to dominate the world "for at least two decades after this war is ended," Great Britain "will be the most conservative and the most aggressively minded, in the fields both of international politics and of international economics." Neither Russia nor China would be "strongly rivals of or competitors with the United States." Consequently, America's wartime strategy and diplomacy should be to put these two countries "in debt to us." Such a situation "would make us secure in the Pacific and would tend to strengthen us for and in any critical controversies which might develop between us and the British."[44] But such a formula immediately gave rise to a question: how could the United States hope to befriend both China and the Soviet Union in view of those countries' known hostility toward one another? Equally important, how could there be U.S.-Chinese-Russian cooperation when Kuomintang-Communist antagonism inside China was intensifying? As Hornbeck noted in another memorandum at this time, "We may find before the war is over that the Chinese will not be affiliates of ours . . . [and] find the balance of influence tilted heavily in favor of 'Bolshevik' concepts as compared with Anglo-Saxon or American concepts."[45] Hornbeck's fears of the diminution of "Anglo-Saxon" influence in Chinese politics and his simultaneous advocacy of an entente among America, China, and Russia against Great Britain, say something about the conceptual difficulties confronting even a knowledgeable official. China's extremely fluid internal situation made it impossible to predict the shape of U.S.-Chinese relations after the war.

Another point that must be made is the lack of precedent. Full U.S.-Chinese or U.S.-Chinese-Russian cooperation had never been the basic framework of international politics in Asia. Until the American alliances with Russia and China in 1941–1942, alliances, ententes, and cooperation had almost always been among the industrial powers, as exemplified by the arrangements of the 1920s. Although the domestic situations of the industrial countries differed considerably, on the whole they reflected the growth of cities, unions, the professions, and other aspects of modern society, with an increasing tendency toward large-scale organization. There was a degree of interchangeability among the individuals and social components of these countries, and one could assume some sense of shared outlooks and interests. Their rivalries and competition could be defined through the mutually comprehended framework of tariffs, armament, and rates of exchange. International relations in this sense existed largely among the advanced, Western countries, including Japan. Although its history and culture set it apart from Western countries, Japan's society was characterized by the same features of modern development that were found in the West.

A remarkable development after 1939, and particularly after 1941, was that international politics came to embrace many different types of society, so that the more or less traditional rivalry between the great-power groups (Germany, Japan, and Italy against Britain, France, and the United States) was no longer confined to them. In fact, the very outcome of that rivalry seemed to hinge on events elsewhere: in the Soviet Union, China, and the largely underdeveloped regions of Asia, Africa, and Latin America. This totally novel situation created a sense of uncertainty about the shape of the postwar world. How could the underdeveloped, non-industrialized, noncapitalist countries of the world contribute to postwar peace and security in cooperation with the advanced, industrialized West? That was one of the fundamental questions of the war.

The Americans (no less than the Japanese) had a feeling of frustration about formulating a workable scheme of cooperation with China during the war. There was a record of past economic interdependence and political cooperation between Americans and Japanese, and, as even Japan's militant fanatics admitted, the society had been permeated by American influence. The same could not be said of China. Nevertheless, officials in both Tokyo and Washington continued their heroic efforts to integrate China into their respective schemes of new order in East Asia.

EVEN MORE BAFFLING, for both the United States and Japan, was the question of the colonial region in the southwestern Pacific and Southeast Asia. The war had come about because of the Japanese assault upon American and European possessions in Asia and the Pacific, and the point of no return was reached in July 1941, when the Japanese decided to occupy southern Indochina. These moves might have been viewed in the framework of traditional power politics as one colonial power trying to aggrandize itself at the expense of another. The war between Japan and the Anglo-American nations could have been just another chapter in their quest for raw materials and natural resources. The Japanese never disguised the fact that their primary interest lay in obtaining the rich resources of the colonial region. The difference this time was that in trying to achieve this goal, they were engaged in an expulsion of Westerners from Asia. Somehow the Japanese believed that the presence of Westerners was incompatible with the aim of acquiring these resources. The rhetoric of pan-Asianism provided a ready-made rationale for such action. At the same time, however, this rhetoric required something more substantial than defeating American and European armed forces. The Japanese had to develop a vision of the new Asia that they were purportedly constructing. The course of the war demonstrated how difficult it was to give specificity to such a vision and how tempting to be content with taking the place of the Western colonial rulers. The more the Japanese spoke of a new order, the more evident it became that this order was little different from the existing colonial systems.

Attempts at ideological justification began as soon as the war came. On December 12, 1941, the government announced that the Anglo-American war would henceforth be called a Great East Asian war "because it is a war for the construction of a new order in East Asia." It entailed the "liberation of East Asian peoples from the aggression of America and Britain," which was to lead to "the establishment of a genuine world peace and the creation of a new world culture."[46] Such an assertion justified the war in historic terms. Far more than a conventional struggle for reasons of security, aggrandizement, or national honor, it was a necessary step in creating the new order, built on the foundation not of Western dominance but of a reawakened Asia. Eliminating Anglo-American influences from Asia was but a preliminary stage for a wholesale assault upon the West and for a complete transformation of international relations.

Such rhetoric was calculated to appeal to the Japanese people, whose sacrifice would be needed to prosecute the costly war. They had to be told that they were engaged in a historic mission, that justice was on their side, and that the nation would ultimately benefit from the expulsion of Western power and vested interests from the resource-rich areas of Asia. This line of argument was also used to justify continued suppression of Western influences in

Japan. As Okumura Kiwao, assistant director of the Office of Information, stated, Japan must get rid of the pernicious influences of Western liberalism, democracy, and internationalism and create a world more in tune with the Japanese traditions of harmony, purity, and selflessness. The whole of Japanese history had in fact prepared the nation to lead the new order. The Japanese people, therefore, must continue their struggle against Western ideas, goods, and tastes, and purify national life.[47]

This kind of propaganda facilitated the silencing and often imprisonment of scholars, journalists, and others suspected of being tainted with Anglo-American liberalism. It also rationalized censorship, economic control, and the curtailment of cultural entertainment. As a wartime slogan put it, "Luxury is our enemy." Craving material comfort was an Anglo-American vice, and the Japanese could win the war only by accepting austerity. Lest this policy cause widespread deprivation and alienation, the government assured the people that liberating the colonial areas, which abounded in mineral and food resources, would enrich Japan. For too long, the Europeans and Americans had exploited these areas for their own self-interest. The time had come for the Japanese to lead in developing the region economically for the benefit of all Asia.

The concept of Asian economic development was no Japanese innovation. It was as orthodoxly Western as liberalism or democracy, the targets of Japanese propaganda. As noted in chapter one, Japanese spokesmen were not opposed to industrialization and economic development, but they insisted that Western domination and colonialism had stifled Asian development. Japanese policy would be different, aimed at "the discovery, growth and development of industries that are best suited to individual regions and of resources that are most abundant in them with a view to effecting mutual assistance and cooperation," in the words of Suzuki Yasuzō, a respected political scientist.[48] The stress was on mutual dependence, cooperation, and harmony. As Prime Minister Tōjō stated in the Diet on January 21, the fundamental principle of the new order in East Asia was "coexistence and coprosperity."[49] The phrase had been used earlier by no less a pro-Western statesman than Shidehara Kijūrō in the 1920s. But whereas for Shidehara the idea denoted interdependence among equal sovereign states, for Tōjō and his followers it meant overcoming unrestrained marketplace competition and integrating the parts into a larger whole. The various parts of Asia would contribute to the welfare of the whole region according to their geographical conditions and special circumstances. The result would be a harmonious development of the whole, free from Western domination and from unrestricted competition. Japan, of course, would make a unique contribution of capital, technology, and above all spirituality, a product of its history.

To construct this vision of a new order in the colonial region, even in part, would require substantial systematic planning for the administration and economic development of each area. Plans would have to be made for settling Japanese technicians, engineers, skilled workers, teachers, and other personnel in all parts of the projected new order, as well as for coordinating their efforts with those of the native populations. The impact of these projects upon Japan and other Asian societies would have to be weighed, and most important, provision be made for the future, when Western interests would be gone and the indigenous peoples would take matters into their own hands, with or without Japanese guidance. All this planning would have required an enormous expenditure of time and energy by Japanese officials when they were preoccupied with the war against the Anglo-American powers.

It is indicative of the superficiality of the whole concept that the Japanese failed almost completely to devise a coherent scheme for Southeast Asia and the southwestern Pacific. On the eve of Pearl Harbor, there was virtually no blueprint for the administration and development of the region. To be sure, in October 1941 the Planning Board had established an East Asian office to survey climate, natural resources, and ethnographic data in Southeast Asia. Along with Tōa Kenkyūjo and various private research agencies, it did collect valuable data, primarily from Western sources; in fact these agencies' activities consisted mostly of translating from Western languages. As a 1943 Planning Board memorandum admitted, the majority of information concerning Asia had been "derived from existing enemy sources."[50] The lofty calls for a new Asian order concealed a huge intellectual void. The situation did not improve after Pearl Harbor, although there was now a better opportunity to survey the area firsthand. The Home Ministry, the Finance Ministry, the Ministry of Agriculture and Forestry, and the Ministry of Commerce and Industry all dispatched their officials to the occupied areas. Private organizations did likewise, Tōa Kenkyūjo, for instance, sending more than eighty staff members to Java, Sumatra, Burma, Hong Kong, and elsewhere to survey political, geographical, economic, religious, and social conditions. All these activities, however, were carried out at the request of military authorities, and thus the degree to which they were able to establish a coherent scheme for the region hinged on the planning and strategy of the armed forces.[51]

The military had developed few new ideas, however. Available evidence indicates that it was only in February and March 1941 that a small group of General Staff officers began a study of occupation policy for Southeast Asia. The study was completed in late March, but no action was taken in view of the ongoing negotiations in Washington, and it was not shown to the navy or to the Planning Board. The document is nevertheless of considerable interest, as it provides evidence of the army's thinking about the new order before the war. Over two hundred pages long, the study emphasized practical strategic considerations in occupying the Western colonial areas. The purpose of military occupation, it asserted, was to restore law and order in each occupied territory so that it could provide natural resources for Japanese armed forces. This meant that military authorities would not encourage indigenous movements for autonomy or drastically modify the existing administrative apparatus. Instead, Japanese forces would aim at "reestablishing" former colonial governments. Japanese would simply replace Westerners and administer the lands with the aid of local personnel who had worked for colonial regimes.[52]

This document was rescued from oblivion in November, when the Tōjō cabinet and the military recognized the need for establishing guidelines for occupying other Asian lands, now that the prospects for peace appeared slim. On November 15 the cabinet–supreme headquarters liaison conference approved the principles contained in the March study, and five days later it adopted the policy that the occupied areas were to be administered by Japanese military personnel, "making use of existing organs of government as much as practicable." This meant, of course, perpetuating colonial regimes, merely replacing Europeans and Americans with Japanese administrators. The liaison conference reiterated that the aims of the military occupation would be to acquire speedily raw materials for national defense and to enable the forces of occupation to be self-sufficient. This policy might cause suffering to the native populations, but they would have to accept that burden. They should be "guided in such a way as to develop trust in the Imperial army," but they should not be encouraged to seek premature independence.[53]

This was about all that the Japanese military did to prepare for administration of the colonial areas, a far cry from the ideal of establishing a new order in Asia. There was little in the above plans to transform the region or to distinguish Japanese policy from those of the Western colonial powers. The only difference was that Japanese, rather than Westerners, would be the rulers. Americans, British, and Dutch personnel in the colonies were to be induced to cooperate with Japanese military rule, and if they resisted, they were to be expelled. Existing German and Italian rights would be protected, but they would not be expanded. Western vested rights and interests would presumably be replaced by Japanese, but that would require sending merchants, businessmen, industrialists, and engineers from Japan. To select such personnel and establish guidelines for economic development of the region, the Planning Board on November 26 created a committee—known as the sixth committee—consisting of top officials of various ministries. Before anything specific was done, however, war came. That these efforts constituted the sum total of Japanese planning on the alleged new order only a few days before the commencement of hostilities says something about their commitment to the idea. When war actually broke out, they were utterly unprepared. After December 8 the sixth committee speeded up their planning and selected the first groups of civilians who would engage in economic activities, but in the meantime the armed forces occupied and administered the various areas.[54]

Because there was no comprehensive blueprint, Japanese civilians in the colonial areas, numbering close to ten thousand at the end of 1942, often had to operate under conflicting policies of local commanders. They were given little idea of how to conduct their affairs other than by serving the immediate needs of the forces of occupation. This state of affairs led some officials in Tokyo to recognize the need for a central planning agency for the occupied areas that would prepare for the new Asian order. Instead of being created before Pearl Harbor, this agency was contrasted as an ad hoc response to the haphazard nature of military government, when officials belatedly recognized the need for a cabinet-level organ for colonial affairs. Not surprisingly, the initiative came from civilian officials in the Planning Board and the Ministry of Colonial Affairs. But the ad hoc nature of the proposal was betrayed when they noted that the major goal of the new organization would be "to carry out the establishment of a great East Asian order properly and expeditiously so as to enable all regions of Asia to concentrate their resources on the strengthening of [Japanese] fighting capabilities." This was clearly a proposal for Asian regionalism, led by Japan. As Prime Minister Tōjō stated at a meeting of the Privy Council, to win victory over America and Britain, Japan must compel all parts of East Asia, whether autonomous or occupied, "to unite with Japan and contribute their respective resources to Japan."[55]

What is interesting is not that such a proposal was made at this time, but that it met with some fierce opposition inside Japan's corridors of power. Tōjō was being logical in a sense when he proclaimed that since Japan was engaged in a war, its Asian policy should serve military and strategic purposes. Creating a new ministry with sole authority over the region was the least the country should do. Nevertheless, he was criticized by some privy councilors as well as by Foreign Minister Tōgō Shigenori. The Privy Council included ex-diplomats such as Ishii Kikujirō and Ogata Yūkichi, as well as former financial leaders like Fukai Eigo, who were openly dismayed by the proposal, considering it a mistake to separate Asian countries from others. They were moreover concerned that the ministry would become the symbol of Japanese policy in the region, an agency to compel Asian peoples to cooperate in constructing the new order. If they became disillusioned and dissatisfied, the whole structure would be jeopardized.

Tōgō's opposition to the new agency was undoubtedly derived from bureaucratic rivalry; the proposed ministry would have sole jurisdiction over Asian affairs, taking away some of the functions of the Foreign Ministry. But there was more to his opposition. Like the privy councilors, he thought an East Asian ministry would represent a point of no return in Japan's determination to separate the region from the rest of the world. It would be particularism in the extreme, making it more difficult than ever to come to terms with the Western powers. He believed that Japan should, on the contrary, be making plans for terminating hostilities; although the country was engulfed in emotional hatred of the enemy and excitement over initial victories, it would be foolish to assume that this state of affairs would last forever. The Foreign Ministry should at least start considering ways to end the war, but such a task would be much more difficult if policy toward Asia, where the war was being waged, were the sole responsibility of the new ministry.[56]

Opposition to the new scheme was so intense that Prime Minister Tōjō felt his very authority was at stake. It should be noted that the crisis in Japanese leadership first arose before the war began turning badly for the country; it derived from the lack of consensus within the government about how far the country was willing to go to establish its particularistic Asian empire. The issue should have been faced before the decision to go to war, which, after all, had been sanctified in the name of new Asian order. But that rhetoric had hidden a serious division among the leaders about the content of the new policy and the means for carrying it out. To put it simply, the debate on the East Asian Ministry was between advocates of a completely new system of Asian international relations and the victims, as Tōjō scornfully called them, of "the old idea that Japan should deal with all countries as equals."[57]

In the end Tōjō won, basically because his opponents shrank from causing a political upheaval so soon after the outbreak of the war. As Kido Kōichi, lord privy seal, recorded in his diary, they were unwilling to persist in their opposition at the expense of "political change." They decided that Tōjō should not be forced from power, so Tōgō resigned as foreign minister.[58] But unhappiness remained in ruling circles, centering around the Privy Council and Kido, who were only half-convinced of the wisdom of Tōjō's policy. But they feared domestic turmoil even more. Thus they gave in, and the East Asian Ministry was established on November 1, amalgamating work that had been carried on in various agencies. But the new ministry was never able to carry out its mission, for by late 1942 the United States had launched its counteroffensive, attacking Japanese-controlled islands and ports one after another, and sinking and disabling Japanese ships, which were of vital importance as carriers of goods and manpower. Japanese forces were continually put on the defensive. The East Asian Ministry could not enjoy the luxury of working out a long-range policy for occupied areas. Instead, because these areas would be subjected to vicissitudes of warfare, the policies must be a function of strategic needs, not a reflection of a comprehensive design.

These events were not entirely unexpected. The Japanese had never underestimated enemy strength, and they had anticipated an American counteroffensive against the southwestern Pacific. What was more significant was their lack of understanding about the relationship between the new Asian order and Japanese political and economic structures. There is little evidence that the officials had anything but makeshift ideas about the problem. They assumed that the economic exploitation of the area would be in the hands of Japanese businessmen and industrialists, as in Manchuria and north China.

Prime Minister Tōjō established four guidelines for the development of occupied areas: Japan must secure resources that were essential for the prosecution of the war, prevent natural resources from reaching the enemy, ensure self-sufficiency for its armed forces throughout Asia, and try to get existing business enterprises to cooperate with the war effort. To provide initial capital and facilitate monetary transactions in the region, the government established a South Asia Development Corporation, and the army and navy appointed several prominent businessmen as advisors on Asian development. In February 1942 an advisory commission for East Asia was created with thirty-seven initial members, most of whom had been active in business enterprises in China and Manchuria.[59] Government and business would continue to cooperate with business interests supplying the bulk of manpower and capital in Southeast Asia. These programs revealed the assumption that little would change in Japan as a result of southern expansion during the war. As the political scientist, Suzuki Yasuzō, one of the more sophisticated supporters of the war, wrote, the country had not restructured its domestic systems in accordance with "the great project for leadership and construction" in the whole of Asia. Its economic organizations and bureaucratic systems had not changed much, and the people were still pursuing private profit and acting as if a free enterprise system still prevailed. Not only had the selfishness, waste, and corruption of a capitalist economy not disappeared, they seemed to be increasing.[60]

Suzuki also noted a curious fact: whereas domestic reconstruction had accompanied mobilization and warfare in Germany, Italy, the Soviet Union, China, and even the United States and Great Britain, nothing of the sort seemed to be taking place in Japan. The cabinet system of government remained unchanged; political parties continued to exist, and private interest groups had not become unified for the prosecution of the war. Above all, the country lacked "a powerful, political force" exercising leadership, articulating new ideals, and putting them into effect. Government, politics, and society had not become one, as they had been in so many other countries. Japanese government, to be sure, had grown increasingly totalitarian, and the nation had been mobilized since 1937. But the coming of war in 1941 had not brought about further qualitative changes. Bureaucratic control of business was tightened, but mostly through soliciting the cooperation of industrialists. Private economic activities were increasingly regulated, but the responsibility for carrying out wage and price controls, establishing distribution networks, and procuring labor remained mostly in the hands of businessmen who did not, as their counterparts did in other countries, enter the public service for the prosecution of the war. They expected regulations to be removed as soon as the war was over and free-enterprise capitalism to again be the dominant mode. The government, on its part, frequently called for citizens' voluntary cooperation, stressing the difference between it and the more stringent controls exercised by the German, Soviet, and other governments.[61] Few considered that Japanese society would have to be totally and irrevocably transformed. Under the circumstances, it was not surprising that the setting-up of the East Asian Ministry made little difference in wartime Japanese policy. It was more the expression of an intention rather than a workable blueprint. As of late 1942 the alleged objective of the war—creation of a new order in Asia—was no more within reach than it had been.

IRONICALLY, Washington was doing more planning for the colonial areas than Tokyo. Almost all American officials realized that the Japanese assault meant the passing of an era in Southeast Asia and the southwestern Pacific. This realization compelled them to consider seriously the future of the region after the war. Their interest was more intense than that of the Japanese, probably because they had the luxury of time to speculate on its future, quite apart from the exigencies of the war.

Officials in Washington and among the other United Nations had little doubt that Southeast Asia and the southwestern Pacific would eventually be liberated from Japanese occupation, mainly because of the area's strategic significance. Since Japan was helping itself to the region's oil, rubber, tin, and other resources and denying them to the West, it was extremely important to retake these lands. The Japanese shipping that carried those vital resources would have to be destroyed. Thus in the middle of 1942 campaigns were launched against Japanese ships and bases in the Pacific to destroy the logistical basis of the Japanese empire and eventually to drive Japanese forces out of the occupied areas.

On the face of it, the sea battles had all the marking of conventional warfare. From the very beginning, however, it was recognized that something more than traditional strategy was involved. As Maxwell Hamilton, chief of the division of Far Eastern Affairs of the State Department, succinctly pointed out in a memorandum on January 6, 1942, the Japanese war had unusual political and psychological significance because it involved so many colonial populations:

> In connection with the war effort of the United States and the other United Nations, it is very important that the loyalty and wholehearted support of the native people of Far Eastern areas be enlisted. Early Japanese successes will inevitably discourage certain elements among these peoples and will create an atmosphere in which dissident elements can and probably will merge and increase in strength. Japanese propaganda can be counted upon to emphasize heavily the exploitation by Western powers of Far Eastern peoples. It is believed that every feasible effort should be made to counter that propaganda and to create a situation which would serve to cut the ground from under such propaganda.[62]

This and numerous similar memoranda written early in the Asian war expressed the awareness of factors that were not present in the European theater. It is true that the Russo-Japanese War

(1904–1905) had been viewed by some in racial terms, as the struggle of an Asian country against a European power. But that war had not involved colonial peoples except tangentially; neither Japan nor Russia, while fighting in Manchuria, espoused the cause of Chinese freedom even in rhetoric. The Japanese-American war, on the other hand, involved the mass of Asians physically and mentally, and Japanese propaganda was incessantly talking of Asia's liberation from the West. That actual Japanese policy fell far short of propaganda did not diminish the importance of the new phenomenon from the United Nations' point of view. For this reason, officials in Washington considered it imperative to frustrate Japanese attempts to turn the indigenous sentiment against Japan's Western enemies. The Western nations would have to expose the superficiality of Japan's pan-Asianism and the actual cruelty of its rule over occupied areas, and also show the colonial peoples that their future would be much brighter if they cooperated in getting rid of the Japanese invaders.

Like the Japanese, American officials had to start from scratch in devising a policy toward the colonial region. United States policy in Asia, no less than Japanese policy, had been primarily a matter of relations with the industrial and colonial powers. Unlike the government in Tokyo, however, officials in Washington were able to undertake comprehensive and systematic studies on the colonial question through the State Department's Advisory Committee on Postwar Foreign Policy. Because it was not concerned with the actual fighting, it had the leisure to consider plans for the future. It drew on the expertise of State Department officials as well as of academicians, journalists, and politicians. Various private organizations such as the Council on Foreign Relations and the Institute of Pacific Relations also set up study groups to deal with the question. Although their ideas were not necessarily reflected in the Roosevelt administration's official policies, these organizations provided much more opportunity for mature deliberation than was possible in wartime Japan.

However, it was one thing to have institutions for study and planning and quite another to develop a workable scheme for Southeast Asia and the southwestern Pacific. One problem was that officials and planners had to reckon with the strong current of opinion in favor of liberating the colonial peoples. It is doubtful that the majority of the American public paid much attention to the political issues of the war. As John Morton Blum has noted, most saw the war as one of revenge for the Japanese attacks, to be fought, won, and gotten over with as expeditiously as possible so that they could go back to their normal peacetime pursuits.[63] A significant minority, however, was becoming quite excited and articulate about America's aims in the colonial region. Pearl S. Buck, for instance, spoke for those Americans with a strong interest in Asia's future in the March 1942 issue of the *Asia* magazine, declaring that the United States should make clear its "determination for real democracy for all peoples." She noted the gulf "between our belief in democracy for all and our practice of democracy only for some." Japanese propaganda was dangerous because it was directed at "persons who have had unfortunate experiences with English and American people." Indeed, "the tinder for tomorrow" was that "the white man in the Far East has too often behaved without wisdom or justice."[64] In another article, entitled " 'Freedom for All'," published in *Asia* in May, Buck asserted,

> This war is at the same time a dozen civil wars, an interracial war, and an international war of the widest scope yet known . . . It seems to me there is a password and the password is freedom for all. If a man believes in and fights for freedom for all he is the ally, whatever his nation or race. If he is fighting for the freedom of a group, be that group national or racial or political, then he is the enemy. . . . [Freedom] for all must be established as a principle for all or it will be lost by all.[65]

Similar views were expressed by other writers. Perhaps the most influential in early 1942 was Walter Lippmann, who wrote after the fall of Singapore that the Western nations "must now do what hitherto they lacked the will and the imagination to do: they must identify their cause with the freedom and the security of the peoples of the East, putting away the 'white man's burden' and purging themselves of the taint of an obsolete and obviously unworkable white man's imperialism. In this drastic reorientation of war policy, the leadership of the western nations must be taken by the United States."[66]

Such an idea, a call for a novel definition of America's war aims, going beyond the Atlantic Charter, had the virtue of simplicity. Although that declaration, and the subsequent declaration of the United Nations in January 1942, had mentioned "the right of all peoples to choose the form of government under which they will live," Buck, Lippmann, and others were pressing the administration to enunciate a Pacific charter telling the Asian and Pacific peoples that the United Nations were fighting to liberate them from colonial rule, whether Japanese or European. The idea could be a revolutionary one, not only for those peoples but also for Americans. As Buck mentioned, discrimination against minorities in the United States undermined the efforts to counter Japanese propaganda. If Asians were to be free, it followed that all minorities in America would also have to be treated equally, an idea that most white Americans in wartime would not have accepted. If they had considered its domestic implications, they would therefore not have supported a Pacific charter. On the other hand, the concept of Asian liberation was inherently anti-British and could appeal to segments of American society that resisted close wartime collaboration with Great Britain. By talking of anticolonialism, proponents of Asian freedom could play upon that sentiment. Still, it is doubtful that anti-British feeling was strong enough to create a powerful public clamor for liberation of the European colonies in Asia.

Officials in Washington were aware of these viewpoints, as expressed in the mass media, and also they were sensitive to the feelings of America's European allies. In obtaining their support in the war, the United States had not insisted on colonial liberation. In fact the State Department had explicitly stated that it would support the return of all colonies to a free France.[67] Nevertheless, all shared Maxwell Hamilton's concern that Asians would interpret inaction by the United States as lack of interest in their welfare. They would have to be placated and assured that the United Nations contemplated something other than a return to the prewar status quo in Asia. The problem was to define specifically what that would mean. Above all, American officials needed basic principles for visualizing postwar arrangements in the Asia-Pacific region. What should be the future of Europeans in Asia? Having lost the prestige on which their power had depended, as the Australian minister in Chungking remarked, could they expect to regain their influence and again engage in business enterprises that would be essential for maintaining the supply of oil, rubber, and other vital resources after the war?[68] Or should Americans take the place of the Europeans? Was the United States prepared to be the major economic and military power in the region after Japan's defeat? What would be the relationship between American policy and the interests and aspirations of the native populations? What were these aspirations, and how could they be channeled into peaceful, constructive paths?

These complicated questions of fact and interpretation required a framework of policy for dealing with specific situations. One framework that American officials came to accept in 1942 was that of trusteeship. As noted earlier, that scheme was presented by President Roosevelt to Foreign Minister Molotov and Ambassador Litvinov in June. His reasoning was that each colonial area "would require a different lapse of time before achieving readiness for self-government," although, as he told them, "a palpable surge toward independence was there just the same, and the white nations . . . could not hope to hold these areas as colonies in the long run."[69] The significance of the trusteeship idea was twofold. First, as discussed in connection with policy toward China, it involved the concept of big-power collaboration to police the world, which Roosevelt believed was the best way to ensure stability and peace. Second, by definition, trusteeship meant that the local populations were not ready for immediate independence. They would have to be nurtured and given administrative experience before they could be entrusted with their own affairs. What was not altogether clear, however, was the role of the colonial powers in the transition period. Great Britain, as one of the "four major nations" that would be trustee powers, would presumably retain a degree of control over its colonies. To insist on more radical steps would be unrealistic in view of the British government's unwillingness, as revealed, for instance, when Churchill and Roosevelt met in Washington at the end of 1941, to consider the demise of the empire.

More complicated was the question of the Dutch East Indies, the major target of Japanese expansion because of its rich mineral resources. The Japanese in occupied areas there were replacing the Europeans in administrative and business positions. Before the war the United States had not really had a coherent policy toward the Dutch colonies, so officials had to start afresh in considering alternatives. Shortly after American consular officials were evacuated from the Indies to Australia in mid-March 1942, before the Japanese occupation, the State Department instructed them to file detailed reports on such matters as "general behavior of the native population, including fifth columnist activities, if any, during and immediately preceding the invasion and the reaction of the natives to such scorched earth measures as may have been undertaken. Best estimate as to the extent to which natives will voluntarily cooperate with the Japanese."[70]

The reports from Melbourne that arrived several weeks later were not at all reassuring. Consul General Walter A. Foote wrote that the people of Java were "not politically minded and, therefore, think only in terms of rice and fish and cheap gadgets. In brief, they are, with very few exceptions, completely apathetic towards the outcome of the war." They would welcome the return of Dutch rule if the Japanese occupiers failed to provide them with food. Otherwise, it would be difficult for the Dutch to regain their prewar status, for "the white race lost face which will be most difficult to regain." The situation elsewhere in the Indies was much the same. Many native leaders, on the other hand, had told Foote that they desired "to become a part of the possessions of the United States." Consul Thomas S. Horn concluded his report by saying, "In my opinion the majority of the native population will voluntarily cooperate with the Japanese, perhaps chiefly for the reason that Netherlands colonial policy has never sought effectively to incorporate the native into the Netherlands body politic . . . Most of the natives of the Netherlands Indies are pacific, tractable, conservative and little inclined towards political activity on a national scale." The theme that the natives would collaborate with the Japanese because of their lack of political awareness was repeated by other consuls who had served in the Dutch East Indies. Vice Consul V. Lansing Collins wrote, for example, that "the average native cares only for his house and enough rice and fish to live on, and he does not care particularly who happens to be his master, provided his simple requirements are met." Consul Jesse F. Van Wickel reported, "If they get enough food, and it is well known that they can subsist on relatively small quantities of rice, tubers and fish, then the natives will continue their normal mode of life" under Japanese rule.[71]

This information, it may be pointed out, did not differ significantly from what the Japanese knew. They, too, viewed the native peoples as pacific, particularistic, and not politically aware. The Japanese colonial regime, like the Dutch, was built upon that passivity, and both aimed at exploiting the country's rich natural resources without disturbing the social system. In such a situation, American officials could not be very optimistic about obtaining local support against Japanese rule or about a rapid change in the country after the war. Trusteeship under the circumstances would be very difficult to carry out.

Although Under Secretary Welles declared at a State Department meeting that "the period of European domination of every individual Oriental people should be stopped," he and those who shared his view had to face reality as reported by knowledgeable consuls.[72] It was agreed that after the war the Dutch would be entrusted with administering their former colonies. At a meeting of the political problems subcommittee on August 15, Welles stated that both the Dutch and the British should be allowed to continue administering their colonies but that the governing countries must act on behalf of an international organization.[73] This was in line with Roosevelt's trusteeship principle. Whereas Roosevelt's main interest was big-power collaboration, however, Welles stressed internationalization, with trusteeship arrangements carried out under the auspices of a world organization to be set up after the war.

In 1942 the United States policy was a far cry from the idea that the end of the Asian war "should see the end of European domination there," as Welles had once said. Instead, the colonial question would be dealt with through the principle of international organization and cooperation, which would be strengthened by the trusteeship scheme. As expressed clearly in a study paper presented to the territorial problems subcommittee, international supervision of former colonies "would give substance to the international organization that is already being created through the machinery of the United Nations." Moreover, the scheme would provide the best guarantee for the security of the Pacific region. The paper went on to state that trusteeship arrangements would "require continued collaboration by the United Nations, and offer bases from which they could police the Pacific and prevent future aggression by Japan."[74] The idea of establishing bases all over the globe opened the way for Roosevelt's conception of the big powers policing the world. It also led to the idea emerging in 1942 in American military circles of "strategic areas." According to this notion, some territories were of such strategic importance that the great powers could justify administering them as military bases. More specifically, the United States might assume responsibility for the security of the Pacific Ocean by keeping some captured and recaptured islands after the war. In time this view was to result in an unambiguous call for retention and control of the islands by United States forces.

An alternative scheme that emerged at this time was the concept of regional authority, a framework for having some sort of supranational authority supervise a region without completely destroying the colonial structure. In Asia and the Pacific, a regional council deriving its authority from Britain, the United States, and some European powers, might be responsible for orderly development and security in the entire region, while each colonial power retained control over its internal affairs. That idea was fully developed by British officials by the end of 1942, but they had not yet exchanged views directly with the Americans. Still, it was an alternative somewhere between a trusteeship scheme within the framework of a new world organization and the "strategic bases" concept.[75]

In these proposals for the future of Southeast Asia and the southwestern Pacific, it is clear that no sharp break from the past was contemplated. Sumner Welles, to be sure, spoke for one official current of thought when he declared that "the principles of the Atlantic Charter were applicable to the Far East as well as to Europe."[76] But, as noted in chapter one, these principles were basically Wilsonian internationalist notions, harking back to the diplomacy of the 1920s. They were grounded on the view of an economically interdependent world in which each region tended toward greater development, prosperity, and peace. Benjamin Cohen observed that "it was important to emphasize continually that political independence does not mean economic isolation. We must always keep making the point—and sincerely—of the genuine interdependence of all countries."[77] The theme of economic interdependence coupled with political autonomy went back to the 1920s, and Cohen and others were convinced that the world—under American leadership—should go back to the peaceful international system of that decade. They were not arguing for a radical restructuring of the system. In the post-1919 world the advanced industrial powers had tried to cooperate to promote their mutual economic interests and to develop other regions of the globe, so it was not surprising that in their discussion about the future of the colonial areas, officials stressed similar themes. Their trusteeship scheme, their faith in an international supervisory organ, and their interest in developing the natural resources of the colonial region—these were not revolutionary ideas. Rather, they were essentially "metropolitan" conceptions, part of the perspective of the advanced (and colonial) powers.

The foregoing suggests that the clash between Japan and the Anglo-American countries in the colonial areas had not yet forced either side to consider seriously the relationship between the war and the future of the indigenous colonial peoples. They found it easier to view the whole question in terms of relations among the metropolitan powers. In a private memorandum written in September, Hornbeck observed:

> If Japan is permitted for several years to consolidate her position in eastern Asia and the western Pacific, few indeed of the many Occidental persons who are now at Japan's mercy will survive with physical and/or mental health; Japan will have developed the resources now at her command, will have established industrial plants at strategic points, will have fortified various strategic bases, will have indoctrinated the peoples of Asia with ideals inimical to the interests of the Occident and hostile to the presence of Occidentals in the Orient and will have strengthened her position enormously for the ultimate showdown with the United Nations.[78]

This indicates a well-defined commitment to preserving the prewar structure of Asian politics within the framework of Wilsonian internationalism, not a concern with abstract rights and freedom for Asians. In other words, despite the rhetorical war between Japanese and Americans, and although some spokesmen were advocating "freedom" for all Asia, both countries wanted to maintain stability in the region and use its rich resources, not transform its structure. Ironically, this common interest in time made Japanese-American reconciliation easier. Because the Japanese failed to effect radical rearrangements in the colonies, Americans could assume that it would be possible to go back to the principles of the 1920s once the Japanese were expelled. The Japanese in turn were to find it more advantageous to exploit the region's resources in cooperation with, rather than in opposition to, other industrial countries.

AMERICAN-JAPANESE clashes in China and the rest of Asia revealed the persistence of the orientations and strategies of the 1920s, but in one respect at least the war was altering the nature of international politics in the Asia-Pacific region. The change was in the role of the Soviet Union. Russia had not been fully incorporated into the Asian international system after 1917, and although in 1933 the United States recognized the Soviet regime, by then Japan had left the League of Nations and begun its unilateral action to dismantle the system. Throughout the twenties and thirties Russia had never been part of a multilateral scheme for economic development or for collective security.

By 1942, however, both Japan and America understood that after the war the Soviet Union would be a major factor in the Asia-Pacific region. It was evident then, as it is clear now, that the course of the war as well as the future shape of the world hinged on the outcome of the German-Soviet fighting close to Leningrad, Moscow, and Stalingrad throughout 1942. The outlook for Russia was bleak, with those cities on the brink of German conquest, Allied North Seas convoys almost completely destroyed by German raiders, and the cross-Channel invasion of France postponed by Churchill and Roosevelt. Soviet defenses appeared ready to collapse completely, and the German forces seemed about to turn to the oil fields in the Caucasus, thus establishing themselves as masters over the Black Sea–Caspian Sea region and threatening the oil-rich Middle East and farther east. Combined with Japanese successes in Southeast Asia, this might mean, according to one scenario, that the Axis powers could establish control over the enormous stretch from the eastern Mediterranean to the western Pacific. Because the German offensive was compelling the Soviets to divert more of their Far Eastern divisions to Moscow, the Russian defense against Japanese forces in Northeast Asia would be that much less effective. Thus Japan could concentrate on conquering China and the rest of Asia without having to maintain a substantial force against Russia. The Anglo-American countries, in turn, would have to ship available tanks, aviation fuel, and ammunition to help the Russians, thus lessening their counter-offensive capabilities in the Pacific. The resulting respite could give Japan sufficient time to organize the newly acquired territories into a gigantic bloc of enormous strategic and economic significance.

To speculate on such a scenario allows one to comprehend the pivotal importance of the Soviet Union in both the European and Asian theaters of the Second World War. That events did not follow the scenario also attests to the fact that the successful Russian resistance in late 1942 marked a decisive turning point of the war. Starting with the encirclement and destruction of 300,000 German troops in Stalingrad, the fall and winter of 1942–43 brought an end to Hitler's dream of Slavic and Caucasian empire along with any possibility of a separate peace between Germany and the Soviet Union. The German forces were now put on the defensive, and the Russians pursued them, determined to avenge the destruction of their homeland, their villages and families. Chances for German-Japanese strategic collaboration, never very great, all but disappeared, and Japan again had to consider the possibility of conflict with Russia even as it had to defend its southern empire. Whether or not war actually came, the Soviet Union would be a major power in Northeast Asia.

Actually, Russia's reemergence as an Asian power had been virtually assured when the Japanese decided to strike south and maintain the Russian neutrality treaty at the same time. The new Asian order expounded by most Japanese spokesmen after Pearl Harbor did not call for absorption of Siberia and other Russian territories. For instance, in a speech before the Diet in March 1942, Tōjō announced Japan's intention to "deal a decisive blow" to the Anglo-American powers and to establish a new world order in cooperation with Germany and Italy. Not a single mention of Russia was made in the speech, either in the original draft or in the version approved for delivery after some revision at a meeting of the liaison conference.[79] In August the north China expeditionary force asserted that a new order would never be established until "we eradicate Anglo-American ideas that still cling to us like fleas." Again, nothing was said about the dangers posed by Soviet ideology.[80] While Western liberal ideas of freedom, democracy, peace, and material comfort were being harshly criticized in official and private publications, little was said openly about the Soviet Union. To be sure, the government's anticommunist policy was continued, especially in the wake of the sensational discovery of the Sorge spy ring just before the war. Thirty-five Japanese and foreigners in the country were arrested between October 1941 and June 1942 for alleged intelligence activities on orders from the Comintern.[81] But Tokyo's authorities did not wish to create a mass commotion against Russia. Although sensitive about communist propaganda and possible Comintern activities, in public they played down the danger of Soviet communism. Certainly few of them considered the destruction of Russia a prerequisite for the construction of an Asian empire.

This policy reflected their conscious decision not to be drawn into the German-Russian war, although some, especially in the army, continued to insist on an offensive in Siberia in coordination with German campaigns in European Russia. To prepare for such a contingency, the supreme command in Tokyo established, in the middle of 1942, two new area armies under the Kwantung Army's jurisdiction.[82] But they never saw action. If Russia had had to fight Japan in Siberia, it would have kept there the divisions that were being sent to defend Moscow, creating a chain of events detrimental to the United Nations' war efforts. But that Japanese strategy also would have necessitated greater American military involvement in the Pacific, and the Japanese would have had to decide whether they could carry on a two-front war. The overwhelming sentiment among civilian and military leaders in 1942 was that they could not. Instead, they reaffirmed their stress on a southern strategy.

More important, they sought to use political, diplomatic, and economic means to detach the Soviet Union from the Anglo-American camp. Already in January, the liaison conference had agreed that "we should maintain peace between Japan and the Soviet Union and try to prevent the establishment of closer ties between it and the Anglo-American powers. If possible we should try to drive a wedge between the two."[83] The first objective was the easier to pursue. Japan could try to maintain an uneasy peace with the Soviet Union by not provoking it and by giving the impression of strict adherence to the neutrality treaty. Japanese officials repeatedly communicated to the Russians their intention to do so. In return, as Foreign Minister Tōgō told Ambassador Constantin Smetanin on January 23, they hoped that the Russian government would reaffirm the spirit of the treaty. In mid-April Ambassador Satō Naotake told Foreign Minister Molotov at Kuybyshev, to which the Soviet government had been removed, that the two countries should try not to provoke one another into a hostile relationship.[84] Both Smetanin and Molotov assured the Japanese that the Soviet Union fully intended to continue the policy of neutrality.

The second objective, that of dividing Russia from the Anglo-American powers, necessitated an overall strategic concept of the global war. Japanese officials held to the view, as a policy paper stated, that "cooperation among America, Britain, and Russia, unlike that between the first two, is unnatural and contains many contradictions."[85] It did not seem possible that two such different socioeconomic systems could cooperate effectively. But the European war indicated that the capitalist and socialist countries were capable of tactical military cooperation, and they might even collaborate in Asia, for instance by Russia's offering its Siberian bases and airfields to United States armed forces. Obviously, that must be prevented. It was far from clear, however, how Japan could separate Russia and the Anglo-American nations. Ambassador Satō thought that the best way was to placate the Russians by settling such issues as the future of oil and timber concessions in North Sakhalin. In a fourteen-page telegram to Tokyo on June 30, 1942, Satō argued that while German forces were fighting Russians in the west, the Japanese, instead of attacking Russia from the rear, should consolidate their southern empire and exert pressures upon India. Should Japan achieve mastery over the Indian Ocean, it could then create a liaison with a victorious Germany in Iran, which would probably signal the end of the war. In the meantime, it was imperative to avoid provoking Russia because that would detract from the main goal of solidifying control of Asia and the Pacific. By maintaining "a superficially friendly relationship" with the Soviet Union, he reiterated, Japan could hope to complete its conquest of the south and be in a position to undertake an offensive in India and Iran. The first priority was to "forget about small differences and try to harmonize feelings" between the Russians and Japanese by offering timely concessions on the North Sakhalin and other questions. By establishing an impregnable southern empire, Japan would ensure a stable relationship with Russia, whereas failure to achieve its objectives in the south would invite Russian and Anglo-

American intervention. Thus logic dictated a policy of tactical amity with the Soviet Union.[86]

Satō's opinions were based on the assumption that Germany and Russia would conclude their fighting fairly soon, with Germany emerging victorious in Europe. Japanese officials in Tokyo, however, were less optimistic. Already in March the liaison conference was frankly admitting that "the course of the Russian-German war is not proceeding as we expected." If the spring war proceeded in Russia's favor, there was a danger that the Soviets might strengthen their ties with the United States and Britain and even join with them against Japan.[87] Should that happen, Japan would obviously be faced with a two-front war before there was time to consolidate the empire in the south. To avoid that possibility, some officials, notably Foreign Minister Tōgō, began urging that Japan should try to arrange a truce between Germany and the Soviet Union. The reasoning was quite simple; since Russia was the key factor in the global war, it was in Japan's interest to maintain a peaceful relationship with it. By bringing the German-Russian war to an end, Japan would gain Russia's gratitude and release German forces for use against the Anglo-American enemies. In the meantime, Japan could concentrate on its southern war. But Tōgō recognized the importance of timing. Japanese initiatives for a truce on the German-Russian front would work only while the Soviets were on the defensive; otherwise Russia would have little incentive to befriend Japan and alienate America and Britain. Thus in early March the foreign minister decided to call for swift Japanese action.[88]

In addition to tactical considerations, Tōgō may have been thinking ahead to the end of the Asian-Pacific war. According to his postwar memoirs, he was convinced that the most expeditious way to end the hostilities in the Pacific was to make use of the fact that Japan was not at war with the Soviet Union, which, theoretically at least, could mediate between Japan and its enemies. It would, of course, be imperative not to provoke Russia and instead to create conditions favorable to mediation, so the idea of a German-Russian truce through Japanese good offices naturally came up.[89] If his scenario worked, it would be followed by steps to detach the Asian war from the European war, bringing the situation back to what it was in June 1941, before the German invasion of Russia. If that could be done, Tōgō thought, Japan should be able to conclude its belligerent relationship with the United States and Britain, which might lead in turn to restoration of a more normal pattern of diplomacy among the advanced industrial powers.

In retrospect, the idea that amity among the capitalist countries might be restored through the good offices of the Soviet Union is rather grotesque. Relying on Russia would inevitably enhance the Soviet position and power not only in Asian international affairs but also in Japanese politics. How such a development could be considered compatible with the vision of restabilized relations with America and Britain is difficult to explain, but Tōgō persisted in believing in this equation. In 1942, however, few shared his long-range vision of restored peace. Continued war with the Anglo-American powers was taken for granted, and policy concerning the German-Russian war was debated in that context. The sentiment among Japan's military leaders was not to act for the time being, until the outcome of the German offensive became clearer. In July, when Berlin proposed that Germany and Japan undertake a joint strategy against the Soviet Union, Tōgō seized the opportunity to again suggest peace moves between those countries. But the liaison conference decided to reject the German proposal without committing Japan to a possible mediation attempt. As Satō Kenryō, chief of the military affairs division of the War Ministry, explained, the time was not yet ripe to depart from the policy of avoiding war with the Soviet Union and cooperating with Germany and Italy. The German government was told, therefore, that Japan must concentrate on its war against the Anglo-American powers, which would be jeopardized by a premature offensive in the north. Diverting Japanese military strength to the north would create a situation favorable to the enemy not only in Asia but in Europe as well. Japan's contribution to Axis strategy lay not in joining German forces against Russia, but in establishing a firm base in south Asia, thus denying its resources to the enemy and weakening their strength.[90]

This litany of conventional wisdom was becoming less and less appropriate in the second half of 1942 as the effects of the Russian resistance to Germany began to show. The Germans assured Ambassador Ōshima, on a tour of the Ukraine in August, that their offensive would be successfully consummated by winter, but Tokyo remained unmoved by continued pleas for cooperation against Russia.[91] On November 7 the liaison conference discussed "the evaluation of the world situation" and came to a rather somber assessment. The Anglo-American nations were likely to mount a counteroffensive, which would reach a climax toward the end of 1943 and would include aerial attacks on Japan proper and the occupied territories. As part of this strategy, the United States and Britain would cooperate with Russia not only against Germany and Italy but also against Japan. Although the opening of the second front in Europe was likely to be delayed by Allied shipping shortages, the Anglo-American powers would secretly try to establish bases in eastern Siberia, and there was no assurance that the Soviet Union would refuse to provide them. China, in the meantime, would strengthen its ties with Russia and count on increased shipments of goods from America and Britain. The German offensive against the Soviet Union was ending in a stalemate, the conference reported, and there was no immediate prospect of German victory in the Caucasus or in western Asia. Germany might even try to initiate peace talks with Russia and England. After the second half of 1943 the enemy's strength and resources would begin to outstrip those of the Axis powers. It was even possible that the Anglo-American powers would terminate hostilities with Germany and Italy so as to concentrate on the Pacific theater. If Soviet leaders thought that the war was going in favor of their allies, they might join them in an offensive against Japan.[92]

This assessment, just eleven months after Pearl Harbor, was realistic and accurate, on the whole. It shows that in Japan's highest councils there was growing pessimism about the prospects for success, although the leaders did not think that they should give up and seek a peace. The whole nation was too committed to the war to consider such an abrupt shift. Nevertheless, few spoke of victory over America and Britain. The liaison conference report on the world situation concluded that if Japan were able to "destroy enemy forces in appropriate times and places" as they undertook a counteroffensive, then it would be able to "cause their loss of fighting will." The Japanese then "will have achieved [their] war objectives." Nowhere were the "war objectives" specified, but it was clear that they did not include total victory over the Anglo-American powers. Rather, they were purposely left vague so that the Japanese could

later say that they had achieved those goals even though they had
lost the fight. In any event, November 1942 marks the time when
the Japanese leaders recognized the need to go beyond existing
strategies to prevent the collapse of their position. New efforts were
to be undertaken in all areas, including domestic politics, to bring
the war to some conclusion. The story of the Japanese-American
war after November 1942, in that context, was one of Japan's effort
to terminate it on the best possible terms.

One constant theme was Japan's willingness to allow Russia to
have enhanced power and prestige in Asia. The decision to refuse
Germany's request for joint action, Ambassador Satō's call for concessions, and Foreign Minister Tōgō's proposal for mediation between Germany and Russia all indicated the shared perception that
whether they liked it or not, the Japanese would have to live with
a strengthened Russia in the north. No matter how the war ended,
it appeared to be a foregone conclusion that the Soviet Union
would become a major Asian-Pacific power. To that extent postwar
Asian politics would differ from the situation in the 1920s. It remained to be seen how the Japanese would fit this new development
into their overall scheme for the future.

AGAIN, AMERICAN thinking was running parallel to Japanese ideas.
American officials and strategists were fully aware that if the Allies
were to defeat the Axis, Soviet survival in Europe and Asia was
crucial. The grand strategy throughout 1942 was predicated upon
the need to give Russia as much assistance as possible in various
forms. As a study prepared for General George C. Marshall noted,
"an offensive against Germany" and "diverting action in the South
Pacific" were both important.[93] The offensive was not put into
effect immediately, as the United States and Britain decided first to
launch their invasion of Morocco and Algeria in November, but
diverting actions were carried out in various parts of the Pacific
Ocean. In addition, there were chances for joint American-Soviet
operations in Northeast Asia. Much, of course, depended on whether
war broke out between Japan and the Soviet Union. A memorandum
prepared in May for the army chief of staff noted, "Japan possesses
the capability to attack Soviet Russia within the next eight weeks.
Such action by Japan, though not without danger to herself, appears a sound and logical military move, and entirely in accord with

the wishes of her principal ally, Germany." This was an accurate assessment, as was the point that Japan's attack on Russia depended on a speedy conquest and fortification of the southwestern Pacific and south Asia.[94] While there was skepticism within the chief of staff's office that such a scenario would occur, the military intelligence division nevertheless noted in May that Japan would "successfully conclude" its operations in the south and that action against Siberia "can and will be initiated by the 15th of June."[95] Even though nothing happened, the operations division asserted in mid-June that a Japanese assault on Siberia "at any time is possible and an attack prior to October 1 is likely." The conquest of the area had long been one of Japan's basic objectives, and the naval and shipping situation seemed extremely favorable to Japan in 1942, whereas the Russian position was much weaker.[96]

American officials feared that a successful invasion of Siberia would not only establish Japan's preponderance in the Pacific region but would weaken Soviet resistance to Germany in the west. Although the Japanese in the end gave up any idea of attacking Siberia, strategists in Washington felt that every effort should be made to ensure Russian survival in Asia as well as in Europe. One of the earliest and most comprehensive studies on the subject was a war plans division memorandum of March 8, entitled "An analysis of the lines of action open to the United States for the rendition of assistance to Russia in the event of hostilities between Russia and Japan in the spring of 1942." It noted that the United States could come to the aid of the Soviet Union in three areas. First, airplanes and other supplies might be delivered to Siberia by a northerly sea route, air transport across the Bering Strait, the Trans-Siberian Railway, or across central China and Outer Mongolia. But, the memorandum pointed out, none of these possibilities was feasible when the Russians were struggling for survival on the western front. Second, American forces might be brought to eastern Russia to reinforce the Soviet contingents carrying out an offensive against Japan. But to transport American troops to Siberia would be a nearly impossible task because there were no railways or other forms of communication between the Bering Strait and Siberia. Any offensive against Japan would be "entirely out of the question" until American forces captured and established bases on the Kurile islands and Sakhalin.

If these two alternatives were ruled out, the only other viable strategy, according to the memorandum, was to create "a diversion by offensive operations in other theaters designed to contain Japanese forces in areas distant from the Siberian front." Specifically, the United States could initiate offensive operations from India, from Australia, or northwest from the New Caledonia–Fiji area. It was this last strategy, an offensive through the Micronesian and Melanesian islands, that the war plans division recommended as the best alternative at this time, because there would be comparatively little Japanese resistance and the Japanese navy would progressively deny the support of aviation based on the islands. This strategy would steadily reduce the naval power of Japan and "thereby restore our control of the oceans and remove the threat of the British Empire being dismembered by Japanese."[97]

Thus, even as the Japanese were deciding to concentrate on a southern strategy before undertaking operations in the north, the Americans were concluding that it would be best to meet Japan in the Pacific Ocean rather than in Northeast Asia. The above memorandum, in fact, accurately predicted that a Pacific strategy against Japan would prevent the Japanese from attacking Siberia and "encourage Russia to direct all of her resources toward successful resistance of the Germans instead of dissipating her strength in anticipation of difficulties with Japan in Siberia . . . The most valuable assistance which can be rendered to Russia is to contain Japanese forces, mainly her air force, in the South Pacific and the sooner our action clearly indicates to Russia that we shall do this the greater advantage she can gain from that assistance." Because of such reasoning, the United States adopted a Pacific counteroffensive, thus dooming Japanese hopes for a quick consolidation of their Pacific empire.

At the same time, Japanese calculations for persuading the Soviet Union to stay clear of Anglo-American connections in the Asia-Pacific region were also doomed to disappointment. Although American strategy was to concentrate on the south, officials in Washington never gave up the idea of eventual cooperation with Russia against Japan. In March they wrote of a joint operation in Siberia and of "a more complete military collaboration between the United States and the U.S.S.R." against Japan.[98] President Roosevelt assumed that sooner or later Russia would join the United States and Great Britain in the Pacific war. As he wrote to Joseph Stalin on June 17, the United States was pledged to come to Russia's aid in case of war with Japan. To prepare for that eventuality, Roosevelt proposed that the two countries exchange detailed information concerning their joint operations against Japan.[99] No such exchanges actually took place, but President Roosevelt continued to prod the Russians to construct airfields in Siberia for use by American as well as Soviet aircraft.

It was considered merely a matter of time until the Japanese-American war involved the Soviet Union. The obvious implication was that at the war's end Russia would be one of the victorious nations in Asia as well as in Europe. Although at the end of 1942 ultimate victory was only dimly foreseen, a United Nations victory appeared to mean that the Soviet Union would be a major factor in international relations. As noted earlier, Roosevelt had already articulated the idea of the four major powers, including Russia, policing the world. When the State Department's political problems subcommittee turned to Asian issues at its August 1 meeting, the members assumed that after the war Sakhalin island would revert to Russia, although they were not sure of the future of the Kuriles. Eleven days later the subcommittee drafted a memorandum reiterating that "conditions may favor some form of assignment of Southern Sakhalin to the Soviet Union."[100] Identical language was used in other subcommittee papers from that time until well into 1943, providing the basis for subsequent American policy on territorial dispositions after the war. Soviet repossession of South Sakhalin, with or without the Kuriles, would considerably strengthen its position in the northwestern Pacific.

In October the political problems subcommittee adopted the idea of a tripartite trusteeship for Korea, under the United States, China, and the Soviet Union. It also specified that "the North Pacific Region" would come under a regional supervisory council made up of those countries. A south Pacific regional council, consisting of Australia, New Zealand, China, Britain, the Netherlands, the Philippines, and the United States, was to supervise affairs in Indochina, Burma, Malaya, and Ceylon.[101] Although Russia was not envisaged as a major southern power, there was little doubt that it would be entitled to a share of power and responsibility in the postwar international system. According to a memorandum drafted in November by the security subcommittee of the Advisory Committee, immediate steps had to be taken "to bring about an agreement among the United States, Great Britain, the Soviet Union and China for the purpose of establishing a common policy and effective machinery" for dealing with postwar security.[102] The idea was further elaborated by the special subcommittee on international organization, which was created within the political problems subcommittee. At its meeting of November 27 the new subcommittee agreed that "an Executive Committee of the four powers would be created, as a part of a more generally representative Council" of a future international organization, "to handle security matters including those relating to disarmament of aggressor nations and world-wide limitations of armaments."[103]

It was symbolic but hardly surprising that on the first anniversary of Pearl Harbor the security subcommittee declared that "the governments of the United States, Great Britain, the U.S.S.R. and China should agree to collaborate in the development of a permanent system of organized peace . . . Unless they can agree on a common policy now when their very existence is at stake, it is all too likely that they will not agree later on when that threat has been lessened or temporarily removed."[104] It was no less symptomatic of the problems and challenges that would face such four-part collaboration that the same committee, only ten days later, noted that "up to now, the Soviet authorities have maintained great reticence concerning even the general principles upon which they hope to see peace established."[105] The United States was willing to have Russia play a major role in the postwar world, so it seemed crucial to devise ways for the two powers to cooperate after the defeat of the Axis nations. The trouble was that such cooperation had never existed in the past. The Soviet Union had been largely kept out of East Asian international relations, which had been defined in terms of associations among the advanced industrial countries. For a while after American recognition of the Soviet Union in 1933, there had been a possibility of a power-political arrangement to maintain a balance in Asia, but it had never been more than a possibility for the rest of the decade. It was only the outbreak of the second global war that brought Russia back into a Western system of states, and few in the West knew what to expect of the Soviets after the war. It was imperative, as the above memorandum by the security subcommittee pointed out, "to make every effort at the present time to secure some clarification of Soviet policy, so that security planning can be studied in a somewhat more realistic atmosphere."

Here again one should note the contrast between the be-wilderment about Soviet policies and intentions, on the one hand, and the feeling of certainty about Japan, on the other. The latter's postwar disposition was much easier to visualize because that country had once been a fully integrated member of the Asian international system, whereas Russia had not. To the extent that State Department planners were envisioning a return to the international economic system of the 1920s, they could conceive of Japan fitting into the scheme. It would be a different matter with Russia and China.

Thus the idea of big-four collaboration, although it sounded plausible and logical, was an untried equation, requiring a sense of mutuality and interdependence that had not existed earlier. Even more important, it was far from clear how such a scheme would work, given the political and social conditions in Russia and China. There were too many uncertain features about both societies to enable observers to feel confident about the domestic underpinnings of four-power collaboration. Could there really be such collaboration while Russia was in the throes of convulsion brought about by the war, where only a few years earlier bloody purges had taken place, and where various nationalities appeared to be loosening their ties to the government? It would be desirable from the American point of view to encourage the more moderate and liberal forces in Russia so that the two countries' cooperation would not simply be a matter of expediency. But how could the United States encourage these tendencies in the midst of war? The question of the substantiality of American-Russian cooperation preoccupied American officials throughout the war. Like the Japanese, the Americans recognized that the postwar world would somehow have to come to terms with Russia as a major power, but that Russia would also have to come to terms with the world.

THE YEAR 1942 revealed to both Japan and America that it was extremely difficult to break with the past and plan for an alternative future. It was much more comfortable to remain within the framework of familiar ideas and time-tested definitions of interest than to contemplate an unknown future with all its domestic implications. John Morton Blum has shown that even as the war was bringing about mass production, mass consumption, and mass employment, thus putting an end to the depression, Americans continued to hold an idealistic image of the past. They visualized the postwar future as a return to the pre-1929 norms of prosperity, competitive free enterprise, individualism, and a sense of American uniqueness and superiority.[106]

The Japanese, on the other hand, were suffering from mass dislocation, deprivation, and dehumanization. Yet for this very reason they had a nostalgic vision of the brief prewar period—now gone for so many years—when they had enjoyed a degree of economic well-being and political freedom. They were being told by their leaders to forget about these Western vices and look ahead to a more glorious future. But that future was no more articulated for them than it was for Americans. Certainly the government and the military were not thinking of a wholesale transformation of Japanese society. Instead, they were demanding national sacrifice in the name of an Asian order built upon the foundation of Japan's "spiritual culture," in the words of a Tokyo Imperial University professor.[107] The idea of constructing a new world by returning to traditional cultural essences was patently unworkable; the war required greater efforts at industrialization and urbanization, efficiency, productivity, and utilization of resources, as well as scientific and technological innovations, than ever before. To that extent, the very act of fighting obliterated differences between nations. By December 1942, when Japanese leaders realized that the war was not going well, they had good reason to wonder about the merits of a future that hardly resembled the alleged purity of Japan's imperial past. In time they recognized that they were fighting for the preservation of a social order at home that had been largely defined, not in terms of a premodern and pre-Westernized tradition, but in terms of a more recent past when Japanese and Westerners had belonged to the same universe.

REDEFINING
WAR AIMS

3

THE FIRST anniversary of the Pearl Harbor attack was not a very joyous occasion for Japan's wartime leaders. In November 1942, they had admitted that the war was not going well, either for their country or for their German allies. On December 10, at a liaison conference in the presence of the emperor, Prime Minister Tōjō recognized the generally accepted fact that the United States and Great Britain were "now jointly undertaking counteroffensive operations." In particular, he noted the grave difficulties in the south Pacific theater. Chief of Staff Sugiyama candidly explained that the enemy had an advantage over Japan in shipping and aircraft. The ongoing struggle over Guadalcanal and other islands in the Solomons would be decided by the combatants' concentrations of troop strength and equipment. But troops had to be transported by ships, and America's submarine attacks and their speedy construction of airfields in the islands made it extremely difficult for Japanese forces to establish a beachhead. The Japanese army and navy needed far more ships than had been anticipated because so many were being sunk or damaged by enemy attacks. The only way to increase military shipping was to divert those civilian and commercial ships that were to carry goods from the conquered territories to Japan proper and to occupied China. To reduce commercial tonnage would seriously jeopardize the national economy, cause additional hardships to people at home, and play havoc with the scheme, admittedly ill defined, for establishing an economically interdependent East Asian bloc. But given the unexpectedly swift and successful American counteroffensive, there was no choice but to divert the bulk of available shipping to military use. Otherwise, Sugiyama insisted, the nation would lose the Solomons and the New Guinea area, outposts of the alleged coprosperity sphere. Such losses could be followed by defeats in the Marshall and Caroline islands, and even Japan itself might become a target of enemy bombing. The strategic perimeter connecting Burma, Sumatra, and Java would be endangered, and in the north the Aleutians could be retaken by the enemy. Chief of Naval Operations Nagano Osami agreed with this grim prognosis and reemphasized the critical importance of ships for the war effort.[1] Even so, the realization that adequate shipping was unavailable led to the inevitable decision, on December 31, to give up Guadalcanal, reflecting the recognition that the nation must drastically curtail its ambitious strategy for a new order.

This realization forced Japan's leaders to clarify their war aims. Although efforts had been made to define specific war objectives, the initial sweeping victories after Pearl Harbor and the changing military circumstances after mid-1942 had given the Japanese little time to develop a systematic vision of the world for which they were fighting. After December 1942, however, political and diplomatic offensives were to be carried out simultaneously with military campaigns because it was crucial to have the cooperation of all Asians in the struggle against the Anglo-American powers. Earlier Japan had controlled Asian lands through military rule, but henceforth they would try to establish a partnership with the Chinese and other Asians. As Japan's military position deteriorated, the assistance of these countries was more desperately needed.

This readjustment strategy had two important implications. First, it necessitated working out a specific blueprint that would be acceptable to all Asians as a basis for cooperation with Japan. The Asians would have to be drawn more systematically into the Japanese war effort. In China as well as in Southeast Asia, Japan would have to concede much more and in some cases promise greater rights than in the past. Above all, the Japanese would have to clarify their alleged new order, which had remained the basic rhetoric of the war. They would have to say what that vision would do for Asians, and how it differed from that offered by the Western nations. Second, devising this blueprint would involve a shift in the balance of decision making within Japan. The military would need the assistance of civilian bureaucrats and nongovernment personnel in working out a political strategy toward Asia, and these people in turn would insist on a greater say in military matters and a degree of independence from military influences. In other words, the structure and content of wartime leadership would have to change.

The story of Japanese war policy during 1943 can best be understood in such a framework. It was not that the leaders gave up the war as totally hopeless, or even that Prime Minister Tōjō and his supporters were willing to contemplate a negotiated settlement. But the growing importance of political questions meant that Japan's war aims had to be redefined and that those who undertook the task would gain a measure of influence. Depending on how that was done and what leaders emerged, the nature of the war would change. As it changed, chances of accommodation with the United States and Great Britain might become greater. The events of 1943 in fact did show a great deal of similarity in the views of Japan and of its enemies, and in some important respects their policies were converging.

It was seen in chapter two that even in 1942 there were some common elements in the Japanese and American approaches to wartime China. They both found it difficult to bridge the gap between rhetoric and performance, between the vision of a new China and the realities of China's domestic society. When Japan and the United States redefined their military strategies in 1943, their views of China were even closer. Japanese policy toward China was forced to change because of setbacks in the southwestern Pacific in 1942. Destruction of Japanese shipping meant that not enough supplies and foodstuffs from the south seas were available to the Japanese forces in China. Moreover, increasing numbers of troops stationed in China had to be diverted to the Solomons. Under the circumstances, a military offensive against Chungking had to be put off indefinitely.

It was against this strategic reorientation that Japan's leaders, meeting in the presence of the emperor on December 21, 1942, adopted "the fundamental guidelines for dealing with China in order to complete the Great East Asian war." The "great departure," as the new policy was described, consisted of three major elements: a declaration of war by the Nanking government against Japan's enemies; the strengthening of that regime; and the restoration of

some rights to China. Wang Ching-wei had, from the very beginning, wanted to join Japan as an ally in the war to enhance his
regime's prestige and compel the Japanese to treat it with greater
respect and justice. For that very reason the Japanese had been
opposed to Wang's regime declaring war, but the same factors now
induced them to seek Nanking as an ally. Obviously, that decision
reflected their desperation about the entire war and their recognition that while focusing on the war in the Pacific, Japan should
begin seriously formulating its political objectives. Thus Nanking's
cobelligerent status was not intended for military purposes; its actual
contributions to the American war would be minimal in any event.
Rather, it was a political step to demonstrate Japan's aims in China.
As the above "guidelines" noted, Nanking's declaration of war would
make Japanese-Chinese cooperation a reality. The Wang regime
would become a truly independent government, no longer a Japanese puppet. Japan would reduce its control over internal Chinese
affairs in areas under Nanking's jurisdiction and desist from interfering with Chinese administration, domestic politics, and civil
affairs. However, Japan would continue to control military and
strategic issues concerning China. Prime Minister Tōjō apparently
felt that the new policy, with this large exception, would indicate
Japan's good faith. As a first step, he wanted to drastically reduce
the number of Japanese advisers in China, leaving the administration of civil affairs to its own officials.[2]

As a logical extension of the policy of placing China on some
footing of equality, the "guidelines" called for giving up the various
privileges that Japan had enjoyed under the unequal treaty system.
First, Japan would relinquish its concessions and settlements in
China; second, it would renounce the special administrative rights
within the legation quarters in Peking; and third, it would set up
a joint committee with the Chinese (Nanking) government to
arrange for the retrocession of consular jurisdiction to China. These
steps would bring to the areas of China under Nanking's control a
measure of sovereignty and independence. They were precisely the
points Wang Ching-wei had insisted on in 1939 in return for a
peace settlement with Japan. The fact that the Japanese were now
willing to contemplate them revealed not simply their desperation
about the war against the Anglo-American countries, but more
important, their willingness for the first time to draw up a blueprint

for the future. They were ready to define the kind of China and the Japanese-Chinese relationship they wanted. This, their first list of war objectives concerning China, would, it was hoped, undermine Chungking's propaganda that Japan was fighting for its own imperalistic aggrandizement and would win the support of the Chinese masses, even those outside of Nanking's authority. It was even possible, according to Tani Toshiyuki, who had replaced Tōgō as foreign minister, that these gestures might impress all other Asians with Japan's sincerity and fair-mindedness.[3] In sum, the new policy would define Japan's vision of the ultimate consequences of the war.

The government announced the new China policy with a fanfare at the beginning of the year 1943. On January 9 the Nanking regime declared war against the United States and Britain, and Tokyo expressed respect for the principle of Chinese sovereignty and independence. Prime Minister Tōjō reiterated Japan's intention to treat the new China as a member of the greater East Asian order so that together the two countries could rid Asia of Anglo-American enslavement and construct a new order.[4] These proclamations were designed to demonstrate Japan's commitment to Chinese independence as an essential part of the war effort. The Chinese people, according to this logic, should actively cooperate with Japan rather than continue to resist, which would benefit only the Anglo-American imperialists. Such rhetoric had always been present in Japanese propaganda, but the new policy was more specific and included relinquishing some Japanese rights. It was presented as an alternative to Japanese military domination of China. With the Chinese regaining a measure of autonomy and sovereign rights, the Japanese could hope for a political settlement of the Chinese war and concentrate on the struggle against America and Britain.

The supreme irony of the situation was that the allegedly new Japanese formula, designed to bring about cooperation between the two countries against Anglo-American domination, closely resembled the policy that the United States and Great Britain were announcing. They too had decided to promise restoration of sovereignty to China so that the Chinese people would redouble their efforts against Japanese imperialism. While Japanese and Americans were bracing themselves for conflict in the Pacific, they were thinking along parallel lines about China—although obviously "China" meant different entities to them. At least in formulation, the policies of both countries went back to the days of the Washington Conference, when they had pledged to restore sovereignty to China. The pledge had been carried out only partially—most notably by returning tariff autonomy to China in principle—but now, in the middle of the war, both Tokyo and Washington found it advisable to push ahead with what was essentially a liberal reformist program, looking to a relationship of mutuality and equality between China and the great powers.

In that sense, the Japanese rhetoric of cooperation with China against the Anglo-American countries was misleading; restoring partial sovereignty to China would not turn that country against the United States and Great Britain, especially when the latter were also advocating Chinese sovereignty. Rather, the Japanese were recognizing that it was futile to force the Chinese into a new Asian order; they would have to be induced to join it voluntarily. But voluntary participation was the traditional pattern of international relations among independent states. Therefore, a more independent China could presage, not an anti-Western, pan-Asianist regional system, but a return to the 1920s framework of international relations, which would negate the very rationale for fighting the Anglo-American powers. This was the dilemma; Japan's leaders felt constrained to find a reason for continuing the war, but their war objectives provided a less and less substantial justification for it.

It was one thing to redefine Japan's war aims; it was quite another to accept the inevitable inference that this was tantamount to giving up the grand design for Asian empire, that there was little point in continuing the war. Although they ultimately came to that realization, for the time being the Japanese leaders were more interested in using the new policy to turn the tide of war in their favor, so they were impatient with its meager results. At a meeting of the liaison conference on February 27, when Prime Minister Tōjō asked the participants' views on the effectiveness of the new China policy, no one responded in an encouraging manner. They shared the feeling that the gesture of goodwill might have been too late and of little practical value. The liaison conference approved a position paper on the international situation conceding that Chungking apparently had not abandoned hope of victory. The Nationalists, whom the new policy was to have induced to come to terms with Japan, would probably turn to the United States and the Soviet

Union for assistance, offering in return bases from which to launch aerial attacks on Japan proper and Burma. Moreover, the Anglo-American powers would do everything possible to keep China in the war. Army and navy officials attending the conference pointed out that these powers might even shift their strategic emphasis to Asia, where the United States would actively cooperate with the Soviet Union against Japan. The only hope lay in a long-drawn-out war that would damage American and British morale.[5]

Such a gloomy assessment was a far cry from the calculated optimism of the new China policy. The fact that the Japanese were hoping for a stalemate, not because of the new policy in China but because of a hoped-for decline of morale in America and Britain, indicates impatience and a serious lack of self-confidence. With those feelings it was not surprising that the Japanese soon lost interest in carrying out the new guidelines with vigor. Although the expeditionary army was under orders to adhere to the guidelines, Japanese army officers in China were on the whole cynical about the new policy, regarding it as an expedient means to salvage the situation after the failure of military campaigns against Chungking. According to an imperial order issued at the end of February, the expeditionary force was to engage only in limited military action to preserve law and order in the occupied areas and to prevent the enemy air force from attacking Japan proper; the Japanese army, however, was no longer to administer these areas. Civilian administrative, commercial, transportation, and other matters were to be carried out by Chinese, assisted by Japanese officials of the East Asian Ministry. Specific requests from the army to Chinese officials were to be made through Ministry personnel.[6]

Although these directives, aimed at reducing Japanese control over Chinese domestic affairs, were fairly specific, immediate results could not be expected. Inevitably there arose the question of where to find qualified Chinese officials to take the place of Japanese personnel. In the area under Nanking's jurisdiction there was an acute shortage of persons willing to fill the void, for that implied collaboration with Japan. The majority of well-trained Chinese officials and administrators had forsaken Nanking, and, according to a report by Minister Tajiri Aigi in June, most of the Chinese who had replaced Japanese local administrators were unskilled, incompetent, and corrupt.[7] He thought that the local populace in such communities actually preferred the Japanese to these officials and that replacing the former with the latter had only alienated the people from Japan and the Nanking regime. The result was further antagonism toward Japan and conditions of lawlessness and uncertainty, a situation conducive to anti-Japanese partisan activities.

In the economic sphere, too, the new policy was confusing, because few Chinese officials were willing to or capable of taking action to stabilize prices and relieve food shortages, chronic problems that were exacerbated by the policy of issuing paper notes for Japanese purchases. The contradiction of reducing the number of Japanese officials while supporting the still huge Japanese army was all too evident. As Ambassador Shigemitsu Mamoru reported from Nanking, most Chinese cared little for politics; all they were concerned with was food. But they were ill prepared to tackle the problem by themselves. Many Japanese economists and experts remained to work on price stabilization, food distribution, and similar issues, thus undermining the plan to reduce the Japanese presence.[8] From any angle one looked at the situation, it was obvious that the new policy was not yielding the expected results.

The situation was even more grievous in north China, the region of maximum Japanese influence. The policy of restoring sovereign rights would remain hollow unless carried out in this area. Thus the supreme headquarters took pains to ensure that at least administratively, north China would merge with the rest of "new China," losing its particularism under Japanese control. The North China Political Affairs Council, hitherto the main administrative organ in the area, was not abolished, but its decisions were to be reported to the central government in Nanking. Whereas up to that time the Hsin-min Hui flag of five colors had been the official emblem of the Council, under the new policy the Council was to use the blue-and-white flag of the Nanking government. This was the same flag as that used by the Nationalists at Chungking, but with the addition of a small triangular flyer with characters designating "the construction of the nation on the basis of peace and anti-communism." Now this flyer was to be removed, and the whole of occupied China to come under the same flag as the Kuomintang-dominated areas. In the meantime, the Hsin-min Hui decided to transfer most of its offices and functions to Chinese members. Most Japanese personnel were removed, and the Hsin-min Hui began to collaborate actively with the East Asian Association, an organization in the Nanking area in which Wang Ching-wei had taken an active part. Wang now became honorary chairman of the Hsin-min Hui, and various ideological and propaganda activities hitherto confined to areas under Nanking's jurisdiction were allowed to move northward.[9]

These were largely symbolic and superficial changes, which would not have brought about a new climate in north China even if they had been fully implemented. The Japanese army of occupation and its civilian personnel had developed such vested interests in the region, however, that it proved nearly impossible to replace them with Chinese. Moreover, as in the Nanking area, there was an acute shortage of qualified and willing people to replace Japanese authorities in maintaining law and order. The army of occupation had employed Japanese civilians as liaison personnel between army intelligence and the local Chinese government. With the inauguration of the new China policy, both the army intelligence organ and the liaison function were abolished, and some of the liaison personnel became advisors to the Hsin-min Hui's local branches. Actually, however, the same individuals continued to operate under different titles rather than being replaced by Chinese. As General Hata Shunroku noted after an inspection tour of several provinces, it was impossible to withdraw Japanese personnel totally and speedily; they had been involved in security matters, and their withdrawal without replacement by adequate Chinese would only invite insecurity and disorder. "The new policy seems to be turning north China into an arena of active Communist machinations, and the north China expeditionary army is genuinely concerned," he wrote. Under the circumstances, he saw no alternative to keeping most of the Japanese civilians in local administrative offices to help the Chinese fight dissident elements and maintain a semblance of law and order.[10]

To make the matter worse, some Chinese in north China had a vested interest in the continuing presence of the Japanese armed forces, with whom they had worked closely, and they were reluctant to submit to Nanking's authority as required by the new policy. When Prime Minister Tōjo visited Nanking in March, he heard complaints from Wang Ching-wei that the North China Political Affairs Council under Chu Shen was acting even more independently than before.[11] From Chu's standpoint, however, the anti-Japanese guerrillas in north China were an acute problem; the "north China committee to exterminate Communists," which he created in late March, was the major organ to mobilize the region against the guerrillas. At every administrative level officials were appointed to fight against Communists. The Hsin-min Hui, the only civilian organization with branches in all parts of north China, became, not surprisingly, an important arm of the new committee. As a result the region remained virtually autonomous.[12]

The Japanese also continued to control north China's economy. Although the new policy presumably indicated readiness to reduce such control and eventually hand it over to Chinese, the idea of self-sufficiency was not abandoned. The Japanese army needed the region's footstuffs and mineral resources, so the role of Japanese personnel could not be drastically curtailed. "In order for our army to be self-sufficient," a directive of the expeditionary force stated, "it is of basic importance to placate the people and to obtain their friendly and positive cooperation." More specifically, the army must make sure that there was no Communist interference and that landed interests did not exploit the peasants and workers who were supplying goods to the Japanese. But it was difficult to leave these tasks to Chinese. Army personnel had to oversee the harvesting and collection of grains and to supervise inspection, confiscation, and other measures to ensure against bribery, inefficiency, and low productivity.[13]

Again the Hsin-Min Hui continued to play a role, mobilizing people to blockade anti-Japanese regions and providing informers to report lack of cooperativeness by the Chinese. In June the association resolved to cooperate with the government's food policy by making sure that food was marketed at prescribed prices, by discouraging speculation and hoarding, and by trying to bring about general price decreases.[14] Two months later, when Wang K'o-min, replacing Chu as head of the Political Affairs Council, initiated a movement "for the construction of a new north China," food production, price stability, and other economic factors were considered the keys to success. Provincial and lower-level officials were all exhorted to cooperate with Japanese military and civilian personnel in promoting the movement, and especially with the Hsin-min Hui, "the only mass organization," in mobilizing the people. The Hsin-min Hui was invariably involved in these various activities. "In order to oppose and destroy the mass organizations that have been created by Communists," the expeditionary army noted in a pamphlet, "it is imperative to turn to Hsin-min Hui branches to carry out the new people's movement and to expand their spheres of activity." The Hsin-min Hui was regarded as a "revolutionary" organization, the last hope for providing a "revolutionary" solution to the myriad problems in north China.[15]

Paradoxically, to the extent that the new efforts were successful, they made north China even more separate from the rest of the country than before. No matter what the actual achievements—and in some areas the threat of Communist guerrillas declined noticeably in 1943—vigorous enforcement of these measures could only result in a "new north China" as an autonomous entity and the perpetuation of existing trends, with Japanese armed forces and civilians and their Chinese collaborators retaining power. Four hundred thousand Japanese military and civilian personnel still presided over a hundred million Chinese in the northern provinces. Despite the nominal restoration of sovereignty to China, the actual implementation of the new policy worked to the detriment of Chinese unity and independence. The paradox was further accentuated by the fact that although Japan was making the gesture of giving up its vested rights, its military superiority remained. As the diarist Kiyosawa Kiyoshi noted sarcastically, Wang Ching-wei and other collaborators could claim victory in regaining these rights, although they had done nothing but submit meekly to Japanese power.[16] The result was a pervasive sense of unreality about Japan's policy. China was gaining "sovereign" rights under duress, but there was no diminution of Japan's involvement in its internal political and economic affairs, ostensibly to make that sovereignty a reality. Nonetheless, the new policy was remarkable as a statement of Japan's war aims, a basis for discussing a possible end to the war.

That such a possibility would sooner or later have to be discussed with the Nationalists in Chungking, and even with the Communtsts in Yenan, was never very far from Japanese consciousness. Although the new policy explicitly stated that for the time being Japan should strengthen the Nanking regime and not attempt a deal with other factions, that possibility could reemerge if the situation in the Nanking-controlled region became less than satisfactory.

However, the Chinese Nationalists and Communists, who viewed the new Japanese policy as a sign of weakness, were now even less likely to be receptive to Japanese overtures. The Nationalists virtually ignored Japan's gestures toward restoring rights to China; actually, they may have preferred to keep north China and Nanking separate, because the merging of Peking and Nanking, as implied by the new policy, could consolidate Wang Ching-wei's authority, making it more difficult for the Nationalists to undermine it.

More important, on January 10, 1943, the United States and Great Britain gave up extraterritoriality and other treaty privileges in China, thereby lessening the impact of Japan's action. Chiang Kai-shek, while maintaining complete silence on the Tokyo-Nanking agreements, hailed the Anglo-American action as a victory for China. "Today marks a new epoch in China's history," he said the day after the signing of the treaties; "today Britain and America have lighted a new torch to guide man's progress on the road to equality and freedom for all peoples." Now, he declared, "we are on an equal footing with Great Britain and the United States." He exhorted his countrymen to continue working hard to deserve that status, for they could no longer blame the country's weakness on the unequal treaties.[17] The problem from now on, Chiang told a group of youth leaders in late March, was for all people, especially the young, to strive for self-strengthening and self-discipline to eliminate the enemy's violence and complete the construction of the nation. As if in response to occupied China's stress on "the new people's" (hsin-min) principles, he recalled the revolutionary tradition of Sun Yat-sen and stressed that China's cultural heritage was essential to national reconstruction, a theme he had enunciated in China's Destiny. The life of the nation was eternal, he said, and the Chinese must complete the revolution and reconstruct national life on the basis of the heritage and Sun's principles. Victory was almost in sight, but it would be a glorious moment for the nation only if the people further purified their personal lives and sacrificed themselves to national objectives.[18]

The last point was a veiled reference to the ongoing struggle with the Communists, who also denounced Japan's new policy. They planned to take advantage of the likely reduction in Japanese personnel by infiltrating occupied areas and causing further disorder. As the Japanese army's determination to increase productivity and efficiency in the occupied areas was causing greater hardship for Chinese in the border areas, the people's dissatisfaction could be easily turned into enmity toward the Japanese. Those who were not already working for anti-Japanese organizations were recruited to become secret agents of the Communists; Japanese prisoners of war continued to be reeducated; and antiwar groups made up of Japanese dissidents in China operated in close cooperation with the Communist party.[19] The inevitable outcome was the growth of Communist influence in north China just when Nationalist prestige was at its height following the new treaties with the Anglo-American powers. It was not surprising, then, that the Communists increasingly denounced Chiang's exhortations to the Chinese people to rally around the Kuomintang as the custodian of traditional culture and the embodiment of Sun Yat-sen's principles. The Communists called for democratizing Chinese politics to obtain the support of all groups and individuals in the struggle against Japanese imperialism. The upshot was that both Nationalists and Communists reemphasized their determination to oppose Japan, just when Japan was trying to redefine its objectives in China to frustrate anti-Japanese movements there.

The dissolution of the Communist International in May further exacerbated the situation, both in internal Chinese politics and in Japanese strategy. The worldwide revolutionary organization broke up in belated response to the wartime situation, which had made obsolete the Comintern thesis that the global proletarian struggle against imperialism should be directed from the center. Instead there was perceived a need for a new popular front, a grand coalition of Soviet workers with those in the United States, Britain, and elsewhere and with the forces of resistance and national liberation in fascist countries and occupied regions. It was agreed that workers in each area should be given greater autonomy, because conditions differed from country to country. The abolition of the Comintern would thus provide flexibility in dealing with international events. In China this step justified Moscow's severance of official connections with the Chinese Communists and endorsement of the Nationalist regime as the legitimate authority of Free China. This did not mean that Moscow abandoned all support of the Communists but that the Soviet leaders thought it made more sense to work with, not against, Chungking in the struggle against Japan.

Although the new policy must have been caused by concern with stable Chinese-Soviet relations, which were essential to the protection of Russia's Far Eastern interests after the war, the dissolution of the Comintern also had repercussions in Chinese domestic politics. It emboldened the Kuomintang to strive for control over the Communists. Soon after the Comintern was dissolved, Chiang Kai-shek sent emissaries to Yenan to demand the ending of Communist autonomy in border governmental and military affairs and their submission to the Nationalist government. In July military pressure on the Communist areas was increased, and two months later the Kuomintang's central executive committee resolved to resist the Communists' separatist activities and to call on them to cooperate in carrying on the war and unifying the country. The committee granted Chiang Kai-shek supreme authority, naming him president of the government, commander-in-chief of the armed forces, and chairman of the party.

But the Communists refused to submit to his power. They rejected all the Nationalists' demands and instead called on them to fight the Japanese rather than using their forces to encircle the Communist areas. Mao Tse-tung denounced Chiang as a fascist and accused him of having undertaken no democratic reforms. The Communists presented themselves as the champions of democratic principles, and in various communities under their control they reorganized the government, established schools for spreading democratic ideals, and implemented economic measures such as rent reduction, wage increases, progressive taxes, and land reclamation. By the fall of 1943 the Communists were more visible than ever as the major force opposed to Japanese aggression in China. As General Okamura Neiji conceded in September, they were enlarging their influence through stepped-up activities and massive propaganda campaigns.[20]

Against this background the Japanese leaders once again decided to approach the Nationalists at Chungking. Given the frustrating results of the new policy in the occupied areas and in response to the stiffening attitude of both the Nationalists and the Communists, the Japanese inevitably questioned whether restoring sovereign rights would have any meaning unless it was applied to the whole of China, not simply to areas under Japanese control. To the extent that the new policy was a statement of Japanese war objectives, it made more sense to deal with all Chinese groups. But the serious rift between Nationalists and Communists meant that the Japanese could not negotiate with them both simultaneously. In 1943 the Japanese were inclined to approach the Nationalists first, in part because the Communists appeared more unyielding; their influence and strength did not seem easy to overcome except by continued military pressures. The Nationalists, on the other hand, seemed to be amenable to political arrangements if Japan offered attractive terms. Although these terms had already been spelled out in the new China policy, Tokyo's leaders, especially the army, were willing to go beyond them if Chungking responded earnestly and agreed to terminate the hostilities.

The culmination of this line of thinking was the statement of yet another set of principles as a framework for peace with China. On September 18 the liaison conference endorsed the idea of resuming talks with Chungking, to be initiated through the Nanking government. Three days later the conference specified the basic terms for peace for both Nanking and Chungking, including withdrawing all Japanese armed forces from China and giving up the right, provided for in the Boxer protocol, to station troops in the Peking-Tientsin region. In addition, Japan would abolish the special arrangements it had established in parts of China for controlling security and economic matters. The two countries would develop resources in cooperation, respect each other's sovereignty and territorial integrity, undertake close economic collaboration, and jointly contribute to peace. These principles would establish a perpetual peace between the two countries—if the Nationalists would accept them. As a precondition for peace, they would have to agree to cease hostile action and to expel the Anglo-American forces from China.[21]

In retrospect it seems fantastic that the Japanese leaders even considered such an unrealistic approach to Chungking. Certainly the Nationalists would never have accepted the preconditions until the Japanese had taken steps to reduce their forces and vested rights in the country. Nonetheless, the terms are of interest as an indication of the belief of Tokyo's leaders that a rather sweeping definition of war aims would provide the rationale for Japan's eventual acceptance of peace. This factor grew in importance. Along with the Great East Asia Conference, the decisions of September 1943 prepared the Japanese psychologically and intellectually for accepting defeat in the war by saying that the objectives they had fought for had been achieved. For the time being, however, Japan's leaders stressed the tactical importance of offering concessions to China to detach it from the Anglo-American powers. As Foreign Minister Shigemitsu explained, "The only country with which there is a possibility at present of terminating hostilities is China; with the other enemy powers it is impossible to conclude the war now. Moreover, Japan's position will improve enormously if the China problem can be settled; otherwise, it will only worsen."[22] Prime Minister Tōjō agreed, explaining at a meeting of the Privy Council, "Earlier we had the need to control China, but now the important thing is to appease its people." If Chungking were willing, Japan would "join hands" with it to concentrate on "the destruction of America and Britain."[23]

This formula was implicit in the pan-Asianist doctrine that had provided the rationale for the war against the Anglo-American powers. Now the Japanese leaders were taking the formula a step beyond mere rhetoric to see if it could serve as a basis for peace with China. That peace, it was thought, would be a prerequisite for the ultimate showdown with the Western nations. Such conception, however, proved to be faulty on two counts. First, the new propaganda offensive aimed at Chungking contained elements that were essentially similar to those being presented by the United States and Great Britain, which also stressed Chinese sovereignty and international mutuality. The wartime press of unoccupied China constantly repeated the refrain that China, the United States, and Britain were united in their pursuit of identical goals and that the three could never be separated.[24] If Japan were now to approach Chungking in the name of those goals, then it might lead to a general peace in Asia, but certainly not to the creation of a Japan-China bloc against the West. In fact, peace with China would be accompanied, if not preceded, by peace with the Anglo-American nations. If all the belligerents were professing their adherence to similar policies, there would be little point in continuing their fighting. Instead, they could come together on the basis of those objectives. This was the second aspect of the new Japanese policy toward China that eventually doomed it to failure. Redefining war aims in time brought into question the pan-Asianist rationale of the war and induced the Japanese—excepting a few who chose death over acceptance of a Western-imposed peace—to reorder priorities in their domestic and external affairs to allow restoration of normal relations not only with China but primarily with the Western countries.

SOME OF THESE dilemmas also were evident in the application of the new China policy to the rest of Asia. To the extent that Japan was now proposing to settle the war in China under new principles so as to concentrate on the Anglo-American enemies, it made sense to further clarify policy toward the other Asian countries. The Chinese must be convinced that they were Asians and should fight for an autonomous Asia, instead of being used as an instrument of Western ambitions. But such an appeal to Chinese sentiment would be convincing only when the Japanese had an overall program for Asia. Calling the war a Great East Asian war indicated that the Japanese were committed to a new order, but they had spelled out few specifics. For this reason, it was natural that the fresh approaches to China in 1943 were coupled with a readiness to come to terms with conditions in Southeast Asia and to go beyond the existing arrangements of military occupation.

Already on January 14, 1943, the liaison conference had adopted a policy statement regarding the future status of the occupied areas, which were to be divided into two categories: those to be incorporated into the Japanese empire and those to be made independent. The first category embraced those regions and countries that were absolutely essential for Japanese strategy and those in which the native population had no capacity for self-government. The second consisted of countries whose independence was a practical possibility that would contribute to the war against the Anglo-American enemies. At that time only Burma and the Philippines were included in this category, but the liaison conference noted that other countries would be added when feasible.[25]

Such a policy was hardly a major departure, and without doubt strategic and tactical considerations played a part in even this degree of concession to Asian nationalism. Nevertheless, the decision is of interest as marking the point when civilian officials, especially in the Foreign Ministry, began to assert their role in wartime policy. While the armed forces were almost exclusively concerned with obtaining Burmese collaboration against British forces by granting them at least nominal independence, Foreign Minister Shigemitsu and his aides were more interested in the political implications of the strategy. They reasoned that by taking the initiative in Burma, Japan would have an impact on neighboring India, encouraging the movements against British colonialism there. If successful, Japanese action in Burma would be the beginning of a new relationship among Asian countries. Although the military would grant concessions only if it were strategically sensible and would wish to retain a Japanese presence after independence, the civilians insisted on solidifying ties with Asians even at the expense of military considerations. If Asia were really free and interdependent, they argued, Japan would have achieved its objectives, even if its armed forces were no longer in command throughout the region. Such a concept of Asian regionalism, although still extremely abstract, was not incompatible with American and British conceptions.

For some time, however, any convergence of views by the belligerents was obscured not only because they continued to fight, but also because the Japanese civilians had to accommodate military wishes. Thus at the liaison conference of March 10, the government and military leaders worked out a compromise policy toward Burma. In accordance with Foreign Ministry views, they agreed that an independent Burma was to be "founded on moral righteousness" and to "contribute to a new world order." However, the new Burmese government would have some Japanese advisers, would conduct its foreign affairs "in close cooperation" with Japan, and would "promise complete military collaboration" between the two countries. These restrictions were the price the Japanese supreme command exacted from the civilians and from the Burmese for independence. Prime Minister Tōjō persuaded both sides to accept the compromise, and on March 18 Ba Maw, head of the executive administration in Rangoon, was invited to Tokyo for consultation. He accepted the principles and conditions of the March 10 decision and agreed with the emperor that the Burmese people seemed ready to work with Japan in constructing a new nation based on moral precepts.[26]

Ba Maw returned to Rangoon after a month's stay in Tokyo and on August 1 issued a declaration of independence. This interesting document declared that the independence and salvation of Burma lay in Asia's liberation and in cooperation with Japan.

The new nation would gladly join the new order in East Asia, which aimed at coalescing Asia's "resources, intentions, and activities" to contribute to a new world order based on "justice, peace, and prosperity."[27] Such expressions were borrowed from Shigemitsu's concept of Asian order, stressing its universalistic aspects and making it almost indistinguishable from wartime Allied pronouncements. Unfortunately this universalism was compromised immediately after Burmese independence by a treaty of alliance between Japan and Burma, pledging strategic, political, and economic cooperation against the Anglo-American powers. They were to work together "for autonomous development of the East Asian countries on the basis of coprosperity, and for construction of a rising greater Asia." The military had at first insisted on the phrase "coexistence and coprosperity," in an obvious attempt to preserve the framework of policy that had brought about Japanese domination over Asia. Shigemitsu, who drafted the treaty, was adamantly opposed to such phraseology, instead preferring words like "mutual benefit" and "reciprocity." From his point of view, the treaty marked a new departure in Japanese relations with the rest of Asia based on the principle of mutuality and equality. His draft also included a provision that the two governments should whenever necessary "consult with representatives of other Asian countries." Such a provision, Shigemitsu thought, would further broaden the framework of Japanese-Asian relations and prevent other countries from regarding the independence of Burma as a mere military expediency. But this was exactly how the Japanese military viewed Burmese independence and the new treaty, and they vehemently opposed Shigemitsu's draft, calling it old-fashioned, an attempt, in fact, to resurrect a mechanism like the League of Nations. In the end, another compromise was reached, with the treaty of alliance referring to the principle of "coprosperity" rather than "coexistence and coprosperity," and to "close mutual cooperation" rather than "consultation" among Asian countries.[28] Such squabbling over words may appear trivial, but it foreshadowed the open collision within Japan's ruling circles between exponents of two different conceptions of Japanese-Asian relations, with obvious implications for Japanese-Western relations.

The exponents of new objectives were at least partially successful in applying their ideas to other parts of Asia. The Philippines were perhaps the simplest case, because the United States had already promised them independence, and even the Japanese military recognized the propaganda advantages of speedily granting it, provided, of course, that independence would not damage military and economic "cooperation" with Japanese armed forces. On January 14 the liaison conference agreed that Japan should express its readiness to grant independence to the Filipinos "when they have made substantial efforts to render hearty cooperation" to Japan.[29] In May Prime Minister Tōjō, on a visit to Manila, intimated that the islands would gain "early independence" and asked the Filipino leaders to organize a preparatory commission. On June 26 the liaison conference sketched specific guidelines that were quite close to those for Burma. The independent Philippines were to be a member of the East Asian coprosperity sphere, to have Japanese advisers, to provide necessary facilities for Japanese armed forces, and to cooperate closely with Japan in diplomatic affairs.[30] Again there was a compromise between Shigemitsu's idea of incorporating an independent Philippine republic into a regional system based on mutual cooperation and the army's concern with preserving Japanese strategic advantages.

In one respect, however, the policy differed from that toward Burma. Whereas Burma was to declare war on the United States and Britain upon obtaining independence, there was no such stipulation with respect to the Philippines. This reflected the view, shared by Japanese civilians and military, that Japan should not give the impression of granting independence to the Filipinos merely so that they would join in the war effort. They were willing to accommodate the wishes of José Laurel, elected by a national assembly in September as the first president of the republic, and his colleagues that for reasons of social stability the country should not become formally involved in the American war. Even Japanese military observers conceded that pro-American sentiment persisted in the islands, where the majority seemed to believe in America's ultimate victory. Involvement in the war would further divide opinion and might even bring about a civil war if there were a military draft. Instead, Japan simply granted the Philippines independence and arranged to use the country for its own military purposes to minimize its disadvantages in the southwestern Pacific.

Shigemitsu and other Foreign Ministry officials believed that

Burmese and Philippine independence should be followed by similar steps in other parts of Asia. During 1943 the Foreign Ministry gradually persuaded the rest of the government and the supreme command to grant at least a measure of sovereignty to Malaya and Indonesia. Thus by June the liaison conference adopted a directive specifying that local personnel in Java should be employed in administrative offices and that similar steps should be taken in other areas "in accordance with the capabilities of indigenous populations and local circumstances."[31] The only tangible evidence of this policy was the setting up of local consultative councils and a central advisory council in Java, although these were seen by Shigemitsu and others as a step in the right direction. But they were convinced that Japan would have to do much more to check its military reverses and arrive at some workable formula for terminating hostilities.

At a meeting of Japan's top leaders on September 30, 1943, in the presence of the emperor, Shigemitsu was able to push his ideas further. There was a candid and open exchange of information and ideas in light of the recent military setbacks which, Tōjō conceded, were likely to be followed by intensification of the enemy offensive. Under the circumstances, he said, Japan must prepare for a decisive moment in the war by making increased shipping tonnage available for military use, augmenting the armed forces, and uniting all Asians. Everything must be done to defend the core of the Japanese empire, now more narrowly defined. Termed "the absolute national defense zone," it included Japan proper, the Kuriles, the Bonins, the west-central Pacific (that is, the Marianas and the Carolines), most of Indonesia, and Burma. This zone was more modest than the coprosperity sphere envisaged during the euphoric moment after Pearl Harbor. But even this shrunken area was in danger, Tōjō reminded the conferees, unless the nation stepped up war production, won battles, and made diplomatic efforts. General Sugiyama agreed, saying that the defense of this region would require at least 55,000 aircraft, whereas Japan was producing only about 18,000 annually. An "evaluation of the world situation" submitted to the meeting explained that in aircraft and other types of production the enemy, particularly the United States, enjoyed absolute superiority. Moreover, the American people, who were "adventurous, positive, and full of initiative," continued to be firmly united in support of the war. The American air, sea, and land forces would further expand in 1944 and after. In cooperation with Britain, the Soviet Union, and Nationalist China, the United States would probably crush Germany and Japan within a year and establish "a world order in which it would occupy the central position." Even if they did not attain an early victory, the Americans would try to end the war and implant their influence in Allied as well as enemy countries.[32]

This pessimistic outlook gave Shigemitsu an opening to push for acceptance of his ideas. Only by clarifying its war aims, he asserted, would Japan be able to obtain the support of its own people and of Chinese and other Asians. Not enough had been done to inform these countries of the war aims, and their cooperation was essential both for solidifying Asian ties against the enemy and for "establishing a basis for national expansion after victory." Japan was fighting for "liberating great East Asia from the yoke of the United States and Great Britain, constructing a new and just Asian order through voluntary cooperation of Asian peoples, and bringing about Asian stability and prosperity on the basis of equality and mutuality." This was not very different from earlier wartime pronouncements, but there were subtle differences. A January 1942 policy statement by Prime Minister Tōjō, for instance, had referred to establishing a "new order of coexistence and coprosperity on the basis of moral righteousness," but that new order was to "have Japan at its core" because it was derived from "the great ideals which existed when the nation was founded." Other Asian countries and peoples were "to be allowed to find their respective places" in such an order. The stress was evidently on Japanese hegemony.

By September 1943, however, Shigemitsu was willing to talk of "voluntary cooperation" among Asians and of Japan as an equal partner in the creation of a stable, prosperous, interdependent Asia. Thus stated, his perception was not drastically different from wartime pronouncements by the American government, as Shigemitsu was apparently becoming aware at this time. This may explain his insistence that those objectives should be enunciated throughout the world, so that people everywhere would recognize the similarity between Japan's goals and those of its enemies.

To be sure, Shigemitsu contrasted Japan's "justifiable war aims" with the Anglo-American powers' feeble "excuses" and reiterated the goal of liberating Asia from their "yoke." He also mentioned the possibility of taking advantage of what appeared to be a growing rift between the United States and Great Britain on one hand, and the Soviet Union on the other. As he said, the three powers were strange bedfellows, and their talks concerning postwar matters were likely to run into difficulties. The Russians appeared determined to establish a basis for controlling Europe. Although this did not necessarily mean that the Allies' wartime cooperation against Germany would break up, Shigemitsu believed that if Japan took hostile action against the Soviet Union, it might consolidate their ties. Instead Japan should offer the Russians inducements, for instance retroceding fishing and mining rights in North Sakhalin, thus giving them no excuse for abrogating the neutrality pact. This argument, based on power-political reasoning, confirmed the Japanese leaders' interest in working for a German-Soviet rapprochement and for continued peace between Japan and Russia. There is no doubt that by supporting such a policy, the foreign minister gave the impression of siding with the Soviet Union in its potential conflict with the Anglo-American powers. Later in the war Shigemitsu viewed Russia as even closer to Japan in orientation and national interests than to those powers. All of this, however, may have reflected his search for a point of contact with one or more of the enemy camp so that Japan would not be totally isolated in the world arena.

There is little doubt that at this time the Foreign Ministry's chief concern was to enunciate Japanese war aims, as was shown by the Great East Asia Conference in early November. The idea of such a conference with Japan's Asian friends and allies was implicit in Shigemitsu's statement at the September 30 meeting, calling for an enunciation of war objectives. But it also appealed to the military and political leaders, who were eager to have some visible evidence of pan-Asian cooperation against the enemy. The liaison conference agreed in early October to use the meeting to declare the Asian countries' "firm resolve to continue the war and to establish a great East Asian coprosperity sphere."[33] The Foreign Ministry was determined to clarify the meaning of the war as much for the benefit of the Japanese as for wartime propaganda purposes. When a joint declaration, to be issued at the end of the conference, was drafted by the Tokyo government, Shigemitsu was particularly insistent on removing any impression of particularism and substituting a more universalistic statement. As approved by the liaison conference on October 23 and as adopted by the Asian conferees on November 7, the declaration of the Great East Asia Conference enunciated five doctrines:

> 1. The countries of great East Asia will cooperate together in order to secure the stability of East Asia and establish an order based on the principle of coexistence and coprosperity.
>
> 2. They will respect their mutual autonomy and independence, extend aid and friendship to each other, and establish an intimate relationship throughout East Asia.
>
> 3. They will respect their respective traditions, promote each people's creativity, and enhance the culture of the whole East Asia.
>
> 4. They will closely cooperate according to the principle of mutuality, plan their economic development, and promote the prosperity of East Asia.
>
> 5. They will maintain friendly relations with all nations, abolish systems of racial discrimination, undertake extensive cultural exchanges, voluntarily open up their resources, and thus contribute to the progress of the entire world.[34]

This declaration was to Japan what the Atlantic Charter was to the United States and Great Britain. Foreign Ministry officials were keenly aware of the parallel, and in fact Kase Shun'ichi, the foreign minister's private secretary, had the Allied statement by his side when he drafted the Asian declaration. Many Japanese newspapers observed that it was an answer to the Atlantic Charter. Kiyosawa Kiyoshi, the diarist, noted sarcastically, "It is Japan's tragedy to have had to draft a declaration which is similar to the Atlantic Charter, granting all peoples their independence and freedom."[35] He clearly recognized that Japan's rhetoric was becoming more universalistic and less pan-Asianist, thus negating the very basis of the war started in the name of Asian solidarity. If, as it seemed to him, the two sides had parallel and almost identical principles and goals, why should they persist in fighting? Kiyosawa correctly noted that the answer lay in domestic Japanese leadership. Only when the leaders closed the gap between their universalistic principles in world affairs and their suppression of those principles at home would the war come to an end. Shigemitsu observed after the war that the declaration of the Great East Asia Conference contained "many ideas common to the Atlantic Charter."[36]

Observers like Shigemitsu and Kiyosawa were right; the Tokyo declaration was an undeniable replica of the Atlantic Charter. The charter's emphasis on self-determination and autonomy, equal access to the world's markets and raw materials, economic prosperity, international cooperation for economic development, and "freedom from fear and want" found close parallels in the East Asian declaration, although freedom of the seas and abandonment of the use of force were not mentioned directly in the latter, nor was the Asian statement's particular emphasis on "culture" echoed in the Atlantic doctrine. The significance of the Asian declaration to those who signed it was that they were applying those universalistic principles to East Asia, a region which had been "enslaved" by "the unceasing aggressiveness and exploitation" of the Anglo-American nations. From their point of view, the Atlantic Charter was a self-serving document to perpetuate Anglo-American dominance throughout the world, whereas the Tokyo doctrine would liberate Asia from Western ambitions and then establish a world order according to these principles. If true to their words, the Japanese would have to not only expel the West from Asia but also dismantle their own regime of domination. No one foresaw that as an immediate prospect, so the Great East Asia declaration remained a statement of ideals, just like the Atlantic Charter. In that sense, too, the gulf between the two was narrow, for the United States and Great Britain were just then defining a new policy toward the colonial areas to implement some of the charter's ideals in Asia. In essence, both sides recognized the need for some modification of the existing arrangements along the lines of mutuality, cooperation, economic development, prosperity, autonomy, and self-determination, ideals that went back to the shared Wilsonian internationalism of the 1920s.

By the fall of 1943 Tokyo's leaders were indicating that first their perception of war aims and then their self-perception might change and that in time the ideological and psychological gaps between Japan and the United States could narrow. Eventually the Japanese would realize that there was a tension between the two countries' military, power-oriented relations and their nonmilitary relations. Perception of this tension was necessary before they would resolve to terminate the hostilities. The story of the remainder of the war from the Japanese side is of the gradual dawning of this realization and of efforts to bring about necessary domestic changes to prepare for an end to the war. As Kiyosawa recognized, there would be much domestic struggle before Shigemitsu's scenario could be worked out. The Great East Asian declaration was as much for domestic as for foreign use, to give the Japanese people a clearer conception of the war aims. It was no accident that around this time Shigemitsu and other leaders began emphasizing that Japan had defined its war aims, whereas the enemy had only the fuzziest notion of what their war was all about.[37] They may have hoped to impart to the Japanese people the impression that once the enemy understood Japan's war objectives—and, like Japan, subscribed to them—peace could be restored, regardless of the vicissitudes of war. This was perhaps too subtle a strategy to work in wartime Japan, but at least it was worth trying. In retrospect it can be seen that Shigemitsu and others were preparing themselves and the nation for accepting defeat by calling it a victory for certain universalistic principles.

THE AMERICAN AND British leaders were also beginning to formulate guidelines for ending the hostilities. The year 1943, to be sure, opened with President Roosevelt and Prime Minister Churchill meeting in Casablanca, where they discussed the policy of unconditional surrender to be applied to the Axis powers. At the press briefing afterward, Roosevelt declared that the "elimination of German, Japanese, and Italian war power means the unconditional surrender of Germany, Italy, and Japan." Many factors went into this announcement, including the need to assure the Russians that the Allies would not agree to a negotiated settlement with Germany and the determination to avoid repeating the experience after the First World War when the truce was complicated by Germany's prior acceptance of the Fourteen Points.[38] Roosevelt undoubtedly believed this was the best formula for continuing to mobilize popular support for the war. It gave the impression of inter-Allied solidarity because presumably the United Nations would persist in their war efforts until the enemy was totally destroyed; only then would they discuss terms of peace and the shape of the postwar world.

The announcement may have discouraged the American people from speculating about the victorious powers' postwar dispositions, but it did not stop deliberations within the government about peace aims. Postwar planning committees within the State Department were not dissuaded by the president's announcement, and in fact their planning was stepped up because the tide of war seemed to have turned after the Russian counteroffensive. The British were also beginning to study armistice and postwar problems, and in March 1943, Washington and London began exchanging views on these matters, particularly the occupation and military government of Germany.[39] By August the British government had established a committee on armistice terms and civil administration, as well as a post-hostilities planning subcommittee within the cabinet. Shortly thereafter, in September, came the Italian armistice, which almost totally disregarded the unconditional surrender doctrine. According to the plans reaffirmed at Casablanca, the United States would continue to bear the major responsibility for the war in the Pacific, so it is not surprising that the government stepped up its efforts to outline a prospective peace with Japan. In so doing, American officials developed ideas that closely approximated those of some Japanese leaders.

Throughout 1942, as indicated earlier, the State Department had discussed the disposition of Japanese territories as well as the nature of Japanese domestic politics. The deliberations continued in 1943, but they became more specific as Japanese advances in the Pacific were definitely halted and as United States forces recaptured Japanese islands and sank Japanese ships one after another. By the fall American officials had identified the issues about which decisions must be made before terminating the war and had established a policy framework for discussing such issues.

In May 1943 for the first time the United States government held extensive discussion concerning the treatment of Japan after the war. The security technical committee, organized within the security subcommittee of the postwar policy committee in December 1942, provided a good setting, for its members included the research staff of the State Department as well as army and navy representatives. The committee chairman, Grayson L. Kirk, president of Columbia University, remarked at its meeting of May 7 that officials had been almost exclusively concerned with postwar European security problems. But the time had come, he said, to raise the question of "what type of over-all security organization was desirable in the interests of political stability and international security in the Pacific area?"[40] It was assumed, as it had been throughout 1942, that Japanese militarism would be thoroughly crushed by the end of the war and Japan deprived of its overseas empire, but that defined only one area of postwar arrangements in the Asia-Pacific region. Kirk and other committee members recognized the need to explore in greater detail the whole international system as well as each component's domestic orientations. Indeed, Kirk was reiterating the familiar view that "political stability" and "international security" were interdependent, that there could be no stable peace without stable domestic conditions, and vice versa. The task before the committee and before the government was to define such interdependence and the political and economic patterns for each country in Asia and the Pacific that would contribute to, and be reinforced by, stable international relations in the region. How could the world regain the stable relationship between domestic cultural factors and external power considerations that had been shattered during the 1930s?

The committee seriously debated Japan's place in such a context. One extreme view was presented by Captain H. L. Pence of the navy, who argued that Japan should be destroyed both as a power and as a culture. The Japanese, he said, were "international bandits and not safe on the face of the earth." The only way to ensure peace was to destroy them; "Japan should be bombed so that there was little left of its civilization, so that the country could not begin to recuperate for fifty years." Such drastic measures, he insisted, were necessary because this "was a question of which race was to survive, and white civilization was at stake." "We should kill them before they kill us," he asserted, even going so far as to call for "the almost total elimination of the Japanese as a race." Pence believed that there was little in Japanese culture that was worth saving or that would generate international peace and friendship. The Japanese had "accepted Western civilization only recently and should not be dealt with as civilized human beings. The only thing which they would respect was force applied for a long period."[41] Because Japanese domestic conditions had created the country's aggressive behavior overseas, the only way to eliminate the threat would be to destroy it entirely or possibly to turn it over to China. In either case, Japan as a culture and as a power would cease to exist.

This argument ran counter to the thinking of some State Department officials who believed, as noted in chapter two, that Japanese society was not totally to blame for the emergence of militarism and imperialist aggression. In their view some forces in Japan were still oriented toward cooperative external relations and liberal government and economic policies at home. The war, in other words, should be seen as a subversion, not an expression, of Japanese cultural aspirations. Exponents of such views assaulted Pence's extremism and successfully persuaded most members of the committee to consider not the elimination or subjugation of Japan but measures to make the Japanese more peaceful and cooperative. As Kirk observed at the meeting of May 19, the measures taken by the victorious powers "should not be such as to permanently destroy Japan's willingness to cooperate."[42] The assumption was that most, if not all, Japanese were "willing to cooperate," and the problem was to consider specific ways in which cooperation would take place.

The spring meetings of the security technical committee took up such issues as the treatment of the emperor and the militarists after the war, Japan's economic future, and the occupation, all in order to clarify the question of postwar Japanese cooperation. Joseph Ballantine represented a majority opinion when he remarked that Japanese imperialism was a product of the militarists, who should be distinguished from businessmen and others. It should be sufficient to punish the militarists to ensure the people's cooperativeness. In time the businessmen should be restored to positions of influence so that the country could again establish peaceful economic relations with other nations.

In considering "how far the list of war criminals should be extended," as Kirk put it, officials inevitably faced the problem of how to treat the Japanese emperor. Although no censensus emerged at this time, official thinking was indicated in a May 25 memorandum drawn up by Cabot Coville of the State Department. According to him, the Japanese were "peculiarly and sentimentally responsive to generosity and indications of respect," and, therefore, the Allies would be able to attain their desired objectives in Japan if they dealt generously with the emperor. "The survival of the emperorship would be a potential asset of great utility," he wrote, "as an instrument not only for promoting domestic stability, but also for bringing about changes desired by the United Nations in Japanese policy." Like Kirk, he was linking domestic stability with international security, arguing that the emperor provided a useful link; in his words, a nonmilitaristic government in postwar Japan would be able to carry out reform measures more effectively if it spoke "in the name and with the authority of the emperor."[43] Although there was no extensive discussion of the Coville memorandum or the emperor question in general, it can readily be seen that Coville's views were in agreement with the State Department's stress on stability as a key to peace. The emperor could serve as an expression and instrument of stability, to rally reform-minded forces within Japan to reconstruct the country along peaceful paths. To deal harshly with the emperor would be to tamper with traditional institutions and time-honored symbols, which would cause greater chaos in the country, a condition not conducive to fulfilling Allied objectives. The emperor, in other words, should be allowed to continue as a manifestation of Japanese culture, not as an embodiment of aggressive military power.

Washington's views about Japan's postwar economy were similar. Since few agreed with Captain Pence that the whole country should be eliminated, it followed that Japan would have to be allowed some sort of economic existence after the war. This was important, as Ballantine said, because Japanese attitudes would "depend on whether they felt that they were given justice in the economic field." More specifically, American officials recognized that after their overseas territories and spheres of exclusive economic control were taken away, the Japanese would be more dependent than ever on foreign trade. To pay for food and raw materials, they would have to sell manufactured goods abroad. If they were denied access to overseas markets and supplies, Ballantine warned, their "desire for revenge" could become stronger. To ensure a reformist, stable, and cooperative regime after the war, Japan should be permitted to enter international economic transactions. This was what Kirk meant by "the future reintegration of Japan on a basis of equality," in essence harking back to the Wilsonian rhetoric. Just as Wilson in 1918 had envisioned defeated Germany's reintegration into an economically interdependent world order, some American officials in 1943 spoke of reintegrating Japan into an international economic system that would not only ensure global cooperation, prosperity, and peace, but would also sustain stable and nonextremist forces within each country. The linkage between domestic and external orientation was nowhere more clearly articulated than in the discussions of postwar Japan; without its overseas empire, the country would have to survive on its limited resources at home. Under the circumstances, Kirk, Ballantine, and others argued, a lenient economic policy would be the best way to ensure both domestic and external stability.

Robert Fearey, a Japan specialist in the State Department, offered a sensible and comprehensive analysis of the economic question. In a paper entitled, "The economic consequences for Japan of a possible loss of control over her present dependencies," he argued that the loss of overseas territories would in fact benefit postwar Japan. Under the existing empire, Taiwan and Korea were important suppliers of rice; South Sakhalin, of forest resources; the mandate islands, of bauxite; Manchuria, of soybeans; and China, of coal. However, Fearey pointed out, the best and most economical sources of supply were not necessarily within the Japanese coprosperity sphere. Japan had obtained these materials from other sources, and could do so again. In fact, Japan's almost complete dependence on the colonies and occupied territories had been "deliberately manufactured—built up by Japan in her efforts to create a self-sufficient economic bloc under her control." Even if the empire were destroyed, as long as the nation was permitted "access to world resources on a par with other nations," it would not need colonies for economic purposes. Even rice and soybeans would continue to be available to Japan, "whether the areas from whence they come remain under her control or not." Actually, without the burden of empire Japan would be in an improved position for economic development. In an insightful conclusion that accurately predicted the postwar scenario, Fearey stated, "Loss of political and monopoly control over any or all of her present dependencies would not seriously interfere with the normal, peacetime operation of the Japanese economy—provided, of course, opportunity to trade freely with those areas and the rest of the world is granted Japan. By inviting recourse to former, more economical sources of supply in non-dependent areas, that loss of control is in fact more likely to work to the advantage of than it is to the disadvantage of the nation."

Fearey noted that only a fraction of the overseas Japanese who would return and crowd the home islands after the war were engaged in productive endeavors such as agriculture and forestry. Most were in the public sector serving the occupation forces or in promotion, management, and the professions; they had not been colonists in the classical sense of the term. Their repatriation would undoubtedly cause hardship, but this should be understood in the larger context of the dissolution of an economically unsound imperial system. The overseas Japanese, not having deep roots in distant lands, would in time be absorbed into a more rational economic system in which the national well-being would depend on "normal, profitable trading relations with the rest of the world."[44]

Fearey's perception echoed the prevailing sentiment among officials concerned with peace terms. Inspired by the principle of reintegration, they wanted postwar Japanese society to contribute to and be solidified by an expanding network of trade relations with the rest of the world. For Japan, deprived of its overseas empire and short of indigenous resources, to make such a contribution, as Fearey was quick to note, the postwar world must overcome the restrictionism of the 1930s and accommodate mutilateral economic relationships. This was nothing less than a reaffirmation of the Atlantic Charter, and thus had implications beyond policy toward Japan; it aimed at generating similar changes in other countries' domestic and foreign policies to bring them closer to Wilsonian internationalism. In such a context the defeat of the Axis nations would not be enough unless accompanied by changes not only in the enemy countries but also in the rest of the world.

This was an ambitious vision, and its actualization was by no means assured. President Roosevelt and his military aides, concerned with prosecuting the war to its conclusion, did not necessarily share the vision. What is important, however, is that any vision of the world that went beyond military defeat of the enemy was bound to modify the unconditional surrender formula and thus work to Japan's benefit, for it implied the need for changes in all countries, not just in the defeated nations. Some Japanese already sensed the possibility of arguing that their objectives had been the same as those the United Nations were professing. That argument would have appeared far-fetched in 1943, but the course of events during the next two years steadily narrowed the conceptual gaps between Japanese and Americans so that even while engaged in fierce fighting, in nonmilitary affairs they were able to find common ground.

As a logical corollary to this question, State Department officials began a study of the occupation of postwar Japan. If Japan was to be reconstructed along more liberal, cooperative lines, it would be necessary to consider such questions as the areas to be occupied, the duration of the occupation, and the administrative mechanisms for carrying out policies. The security technical committee, at its May 26 meeting, generally accepted the view that all of Japan would have to be occupied for a time, but its members were divided on other questions. Colonel John Olive of the army called for the occupation of "industrial centers in Japan proper for several years after the war," and Cavendish W. Cannon of the State Department insisted that "administrative control" over the whole of Japan would have to continue until there was some assurance that Japanese liberals could check any resurgence of militarism. Grayson Kirk, on the other hand, thought such measures unrealistic because there would not likely be "sufficient trained personnel for the task" among occupation forces. It would be necessary, he said, to deal with some Japanese officials, especially at the local level. Durward V. Sandifer agreed, noting that because it would be unrealistic for the United Nations to administer Japan for more than a brief period of time, they might set up a system of supervision and inspection of Japanese disarmament, turning over other governmental functions to the Japanese.[45] Although no decision was made, the meeting revealed that the committee members were interested in considering the future of Japanese society. With the concurrent discussions on the status of the emperor and the Japanese economy after the war, it was inevitable that the question of occupation policy would lead to the wider issue of future United States-Japanese relations. That some concrete ideas were already being tossed about in the middle of 1943, albeit within the secret confines of government, indicates that Washington was making an effort to define aims and peace objectives, just when a small minority of officials in Tokyo were initiating similar endeavors.

American officials were also engaged in clarifying their objectives with respect to other Asian-Pacific countries and regions.
And again one can see a rather remarkable parallel between American and Japanese war aims. At the power level, to be sure, there
remained vast differences, most notably in the United States determination, since 1942, to deprive Japan of most or all of its overseas territories before the hostilities ceased. Japanese officials did not
yet contemplate that kind of ending. Even as they talked of refining
their war aims, they assumed that Taiwan, Korea, Manchuria, South
Sakhalin, and some of the mandate islands would remain part of
the empire after the war.

In particular, Japanese officials would not have shared the
view emerging in Washington in 1942 that a victorious United
States should establish more or less total control over Japan's Pacific mandates. Throughout 1943 this view continued to enjoy support. As Captain Pence of the navy summed it up, "The primary
responsibility in the Pacific would continue to belong to the United
States" after the war; the United States would retain the Japanese
mandate islands as well as bases in the Philippines. Ballantine,
George Blakeslee, and other members of the State Department's
postwar planning committees agreed with Pence that considerations
of self-determination need not be applied so rigidly as to exclude
American use of these islands as bases. They were even willing to
have United States forces occupy some islands south of the Equator
as military bases and as airfields for postwar commercial aviation
across the Pacific. President Roosevelt fully agreed and assumed
that the United States would establish a string of naval and air
bases in the Pacific after the war. With that in mind, he dispatched
Admiral Richard E. Byrd in September on an inspection tour of the
south Pacific to determine which bases the United States should
control.[46]

If publicized, such a definition of war aims would have given
the impression that the United States was taking an imperialistic
course in the war against Japan. Already in the beginning of 1943
the British embassy in Washington was reporting "a fairly clear
imperialist line" in American demands for postwar bases and commercial advantages.[47] Stated publicly, such demands would have
given the Japanese a propaganda advantage and made it very diffi-

cult for Japanese civilians to work for a compromise settlement, for it was in part against augmentation of American power in the western Pacific that the nation had gone to war. However, the picture was not so clear-cut. Although the Roosevelt administration supported the navy's demand for Pacific bases, it wanted to make this action compatible with the principles of the Atlantic Charter. The president did not approve of America acquiring the Japanese mandate islands outright. Instead, he wanted to find a way to retain the islands as American bases while exonerating the United States of any taint of imperialism. Predictably, he expressed an interest in placing the islands under an international trusteeship. As a trustee power the United States could use the islands to ensure security, without violating the Atlantic Charter, and to that extent would be contributing to the system of international cooperation and open administration.

The trusteeship idea, as noted earlier, had been entertained by both President Roosevelt and the State Department since early 1942, but the president had thought primarily in terms of a big-power scheme to administer enemy territories and less powerful lands, whereas the State Department had stressed the international cooperative aspect. The political problems subcommittee had, in fact, tried to envision various regional councils being established under the overall trusteeship framework. In the Pacific Ocean, the subcommittee considered north and south Pacific "regional supervisory councils," with authority delegated by an international organization. The United States would be a member of both councils but would share responsibilities with other countries. The councils would work for "promoting economic development" of each land under their jurisdiction, "while providing equal opportunity to all countries for investment and safeguarding native interests."[48] This clear reiteration of interwar internationalism was in conflict with the navy's determination to retain exclusive control over the security of much of the Pacific Ocean after the war. However, it appeared possible to combine the two viewpoints by having the navy control the Japanese mandates on behalf of an international trusteeship, which, in the words of Under Secretary Welles, would be "predicated upon the establishment of some United Nations authority superior to the trusteeship organization and the administering state."[49] Details still had to be worked out, but such a scheme would allow the

United States to profess its adherence to internationalism, not simply to an old-style punitive war, which was important for placating
anti-imperialist opinion within the country.

Ultimately it would also allow the Japanese leaders to justify
their surrender on the grounds that some of their ideals were being
implemented by the enemy. The Japanese, too, could claim to have
developed the idea of Asian regional development. Although they
had said little about the mandates, over which they were steadily
losing control, they had justified the war in the name of regional
welfare and progress, a concept not very different from those being
worked out within the State Department. Although the similarity
may have been purely coincidental at this point, officials in both
Tokyo and Washington were echoing the reform spirit of the 1920s
in their schemes for economic development, political stability, and
peace in the Asia-Pacific region.

Also with respect to the former European colonies under
Japanese occupation, American views were not diametrically opposed to Japanese conceptions. Since 1942 both sides had been
seeking a middle position betwen perpetuation of imperialistic
control (whether by Japan or by European powers) and immediate
autonomy for the native populations. This stand was confirmed
in Washington during 1943. A statement initially drafted within
the political problems subcommittee in August 1942 remained unchanged through March 1943: "As a general principle the peoples
of any Far Eastern country or territory under the domination of
European powers should be liberated after the war, and such possessions should be placed under an international trusteeship to assist
the peoples concerned to attain political maturity and to control
the raw materials of the area in the interest of all peoples."[50] The
dual emphasis on colonial reforms and international supervision
was incorporated into a memorandum submitted by Secretary Hull
to President Roosevelt on March 17. Entitled "Declaration by the
United Nations on National Independence," the document declared
it to be a policy of the United Nations that "opportunity to achieve
independence for those peoples who aspire for independence shall
be preserved, respected, and made more effective." But this sweeping
assertion was modified by other statements in the proposed declaration. Article I recognized that some colonial peoples were more
ready for independence than others and called on "all peoples that

aspire to independence to exert themselves in every feasible way to prepare and equip themselves for independence—socially, economically, and politically—to the end that they may . . . be able to create . . . efficient structures of stable self-government based on sound principles of social and political morality." Each metropolitan government was exhorted:

a. To give its colonial peoples protection, encouragement, moral support, and material aid and to make continuous efforts toward their political, economic, social, and educational advancement;

b. To make available to qualified persons among the colonial peoples to the fullest possible extent positions in the various branches of the local governmental organization;

c. To grant progressively to the colonial peoples such measure of self-government as they are capable of maintaining in the light of the various stages of their development toward independence;

d. To fix, at the earliest practicable moments, dates upon which the colonial peoples shall be accorded the status of full independence within a system of general security; and

e. To pursue policies under which the natural resources of colonial territories shall be developed, organized and marketed in the interest of the peoples concerned and of the world as a whole.

Article II called for the creation of an international trusteeship administration under the United Nations to prepare colonial peoples for eventual independence. The trusteeship administration was to "operate through regional councils composed of representatives of the nations having major interests in the respective regions."[51]

The proposed declaration was the United States government's most explicit statement on the colonial question during the war. In its recognition of gradualist reforms, global interdependence, international cooperation, and coupling of material well-being with political maturity, it was quintessentially Wilsonian. Statements by the Japanese government also stressed the responsibilities of developed countries to help other peoples achieve economic advancement and political stability, and both countries conceived of schemes for integrating a particular area of the globe and linking it with the rest of the world. The main difference between the Japanese and the American stands was that the United States was in a far stronger position to affect the Asia-Pacific region after the war. Moreover, it was already trying to coordinate policy with Great Britain, whereas Japanese policy was being formulated in isolation. American officials, in a sense, were doing what Japanese officials should have been doing, namely, designing specific arrangements for the future development of the region in accordance with the principle of coprosperity. But because the two sides were conceptually close, the Japanese toward the end of and after the war found it easier to persuade themselves that despite their military disasters, their policy of liberating Asia from imperialism was being achieved.

The Japanese were not willing to grant full sovereignty to the occupied territories, and the proposed United Nations declaration and other documents made it unequivocably clear that neither was the United States seeking immediate liberation of the European colonies in Asia. As a memorandum of the political problems subcommittee summarized its findings from March 1942 through July 1943, "The trusteeship plan should apply to only the present mandated territories and the Axis dependencies ... [The] United States, in supporting a trusteeship plan, would not seek to destroy any existing empire or to dictate to other countries concerning colonial administration."[52] During the summer the security technical committee endorsed that conclusion, arguing that future security required stabilizing the Dutch East Indies, maintaining Singapore as a naval base, and strengthening Australia and New Zealand. Indochina was more problematical. President Roosevelt had insisted that it be placed under an international trusteeship, but Grayson Kirk argued that "the existence of a strong France was of vital importance to the interest of the United States," and that France should therefore retain its authority in Indochina.[53] No definite decision was made, but virtually all American officials agreed that no matter what the ultimate status of Indochina, or indeed of any other colonial region, the whole of Asia and the Pacific ought to be brought together more closely, in terms both of general security and of welfare. Even those European countries that were to retain their colonies for a while were not expected to reinstitute protectionist policies and monopolistic arrangements.

Had the Japanese leaders known of the deliberations in Washington, they might have been struck by the similarity of their concerns. However, the Japanese were not yet prepared to promise self-government to Taiwan, Korea, Manchuria, and South Sakhalin, the core of the Japanese imperial domain. No Japanese leader could express, even rhetorically, readiness to give up these lands and expect to remain in power. Throughout 1943 the various committees of the State Department confirmed the guidelines they had established in 1942 that Japan should be deprived of territories it had acquired after the Sino-Japanese War of 1894–95. According to a political problems subcommittee memorandum of March 12, 1943, Japan might be permitted to retain the Kuriles, the Ryukyus, and the Bonins. South Sakhalin would be assigned to the Soviet Union, and Korea would be placed under trusteeship, pending independence. China would regain Manchuria and Taiwan.[54] Even more crucial than the disposition of these territories was the question of Asia's power relations after Japan was deprived of them. Would Japan be isolated indefinitely, or would one Asian power bloc be pitted against another so that Japan, even in defeat, might play a role as a balancer? Would the victorious powers aim at a fundamental transformation of the Asian power system, or would they restore some semblance of the interwar Asian order?

American officials in mid-1943 stressed cooperation among the countries that would be the major powers in postwar Asia: the United States, Great Britain, China, and the Soviet Union. Two aspects of this notion had become evident in 1942 and persisted throughout 1943. On one hand there was the idea that these four would act as a global police force after the war, and on the other there was the notion of economic and cultural, as well as political, cooperation. Both these strands of thought had proponents in 1943, but their debate became much more specific because of the progress of the war and developments in each country.

The best expression of the internationalist formulation was the "protocol of a proposed four-power security agreement," drafted by the State Department's security subcommittee in early May. The draft, proposed as part of the covenant of an international organization to be established after the war, was completed on August 11. It read that the four powers would declare:

> That their united action, pledged for the prosecution of the war, will be continued for the organization and maintenance of peace and security.
>
> That those of them at war with a common enemy will act together in all matters relating to the surrender and disarmament of that enemy, and to any occupation of enemy territory and of territory of their states held by that enemy . . .
>
> That for the purpose of maintaining international peace and security pending the re-establishment of law and order and the inauguration of a general system of security, they will consult and act jointly in behalf of the community of nations.[55]

This vision of four-power collaboration was clearly to be a step toward international cooperation, which alone would guarantee permanent world peace and security. In August Secretary Hull took this draft to Quebec, where the American and British heads of state met for another round of consultations.

The Quebec Conference, from August 11 to 24, was unique in that for the first time Roosevelt and Churchill were joined by Secretary of State Hull and Foreign Secretary Anthony Eden, who indicated their interest in discussing postwar issues as well as wartime strategy. Fortunately for Hull and his aides, the conferees agreed to base their discussion on the draft protocol and to invite Chinese and Russian officials to participate. Hull considered this a significant achievement, and in a major policy speech after his return to Washington he declared that including the Soviet Union and China in a cooperative mechanism for "a stable peace" was absolutely essential.[56] He was elated that even the British, despite their misgivings, agreed in principle to China's participation and that Stalin, though unable to come to Quebec, expressed readiness to meet with Roosevelt and Churchill in the near future. It appeared that the idea of four-power cooperation was fast taking hold. There was little doubt in Hull's mind or in the minds of those who helped him write his policy speech that cooperation would be along internationalist lines; the four powers would work together to create conditions "in which each nation will have enhanced opportunities to develop and progress in ways of its own choosing; in which there will be . . . improved facilities to attain . . . an increasing measure of political stability and economic, social and cultural welfare."

Hull's formulation deemphasized the purely tactical and expedient aspects of the wartime alliance, turning it into a more truly international mechanism. In that sense there was little in the idea to alarm or alienate those Japanese who were trying to define their own peace objectives.

However, there were also more power-oriented conceptions of the postwar world, tying the United States closer to one or more of the other three powers. Roosevelt continued to talk of the big four policemen as an extension of the wartime military alliance. Since he never doubted that the alliance was essential for victory in Asia as well as in Europe, it followed that they would continue to police the defeated nations and smaller countries to prevent future war. But he had not worked out a coherent plan to make the idea specific. In 1943 he continued to view future security in terms of balance of power, which sometimes meant a balance between one or two of the big four against the rest, rather than unity among the four to maintain global equilibrium. Other American officials were also concerned with this question, and they debated the most plausible ways to combine the power of the United States with that of other nations for postwar security. Unlike the internationalists, however, these officials could agree on very few concrete steps.

One such step was a secret protocol, signed by President Roosevelt and Prime Minister Churchill in Quebec, establishing an Anglo-American alliance in nuclear weaponry. The two leaders in effect established a binding joint agreement on the use of atomic weapons during and after the war when they pledged not to use them "against third parties without each other's consent" and not to communicate their technological information on atomic energy to third parties "except by mutual consent."[57] This was a far-reaching agreement, creating a framework for bilateral cooperation without any reference to the United Nations or to other countries. The two leaders may not have been fully aware of such implications or of the awesomeness of the new weapon. But they were binding their countries closer together in military technology in terms of their power relationship. There was little idealism in the arrangement. Rather, President Roosevelt seems to have viewed it as a desirable step for postwar security.

Robert Dallek has persuasively argued that in doing so the

president came close to accepting Churchill's view that they must reckon with the anticipated growth of Soviet power somehow and that atomic cooperation was one good way of dealing with the problem.[58] By the spring of 1943, if not earlier, Churchill had come to the conclusion that "the overwhelming preponderance of Russia remains . . . the dominant fact of the future." Only the Soviet Union would be in a position to apply force in Europe, "and that to a measureless and unlimited extent." But Britain alone could not "undertake to police Europe, and both our finances and systems of recruitment would collapse under the weight of such a task." Moreover, he doubted "where there will be any American troops in Europe four years after the 'Cease Firing.' "[59] Instead of an American presence in Europe, Churchill thought Britain should have nuclear weapons, and the surest way to develop them was through sharing information with the Americans. Roosevelt endorsed such views, although his subsequent policy decisions and enunciations revealed that Soviet power was not Roosevelt's only concern, nor was cooperation with Britain the only method he considered. Still, the signing of the Quebec protocol had been preceded by months of deliberation in the president's inner circles; at the very least this crucial step indicated that the vaunted four-power collaboration was being challenged by a scheme for bilateral cooperation in power terms.

Britain's main concern at this time, however, was with the growth of Soviet power in Europe and the Middle East, not in Asia or the Pacific, which meant that Britain's bilateral relationship with America did not automatically extend to those areas. Churchill's main interest was to build up "a strong France" and to establish a community of Britain, France, and other European countries as "a self-governing body, capable of managing her own affairs." Only a concerted effort by the European countries could maintain peace and security in postwar Europe, both domestically and vis-à-vis the Soviet Union. In the Middle East, Iran was a primary area of British-Soviet tensions, if not confrontation, in 1943. The two countries had occupied the country since 1941 and both had put pressure on the Iranian government for additional oil concessions. This was viewed as a sparring prelude to what would happen after the war. As Charles E. Bohlen, the State Department's Soviet expert, reported to the security technical committee in late April, after the war "Russia would insist on a sphere of influence in the north. The Soviet Union attaches the greatest importance to this area for security reasons . . . [It] would want a special position in the north and full participation in any foreign influence over the central government." Britain, on its part, would wish to preserve its own special interests in Iran and oppose extension of Soviet influence. The United States, Bohlen said, might have to either side with one of these two powers against the other or undertake a mediatory role so that they would not collide. Or else it would have to push for their acceptance of more internationalist policies in Iran.[60]

In Asia and the Pacific, on the other hand, bilateral Anglo-American military collaboration after the war was not considered a strong possibility, let alone a definite policy. Roosevelt's and Churchill's ideas about joint action to prevent Soviet expansion were limited to Europe, the Middle East, and atomic weapons. In the Asia-Pacific region neither power was overly concerned with the growth of Soviet power, even though they assumed that Russia would enter the war sooner or later and that it would emerge as a major power in the area after the war. Because they hoped that the first assumption would prove accurate, there was little to be done about the second possibility but to accept it.

This did not mean that there was a strong likelihood of U.S.-Soviet cooperation after the war. It was quite clear in 1943 that even against Japan their collaboration was going to be limited. Stalin persisted in rejecting, politely but firmly, Roosevelt's offer to place American air force units in eastern Siberia, with the condition that Americans be allowed to survey Soviet air force facilities in the region. Stalin told Roosevelt, "It would seem obvious that Russian military objects can be inspected only by Russian inspectors, just as American military objects can be inspected only by American inspectors. In this respect [there] must be no misunderstanding."[61] Such remarks, along with general impressions of Soviet strategy, led the United States to the view that, as the joint chiefs put it, regardless of American wishes, Russia "will make her decision in the light of her own interests and will intervene only when she reckons that Japan can be defeated at a small cost to her."

But the joint chiefs believed that Russia did indeed have strong interests in Northeast Asia. As they pointed out, "There exists between Russia and Japan a basic conflict of interest. Japan cannot enjoy complete strategic security without gaining control of the eastern region of Siberia. Russia is determined to hold that region, the strategic security of which requires the ultimate expulsion of Japan from the mainland of Asia and from southern Sakhalin."[62] It was assumed that the United States could do little to influence Russian thinking, although at least one State Department official expressed misgivings about the transfer of South Sakhalin to Russia, fearing that it would create Japanese resentment and thus perpetuate instability in the region.[63] American military and civilian officials, however, were virtually unanimous in sensing the hopelessness of influencing Soviet behavior. They could readily see that Japan and the Soviet Union had confronted each other in Northeast Asia for several decades and that Japan's defeat would necessarily mean an extension of Russian power. As long as their thinking was in the framework of power politics, there was not much they could add to such rudimentary analysis. This realization led Secretary Hull and others in the State Department to espouse an idea of internationalism in which Russia would emerge as a responsible and cooperative member of the international community rather than just a great military power. Even that group, however, had difficulty envisaging Russia's role in Asia. Their memoranda and study papers in 1943 indicate that they were able to view the Soviet factor in postwar Asia only in conventional terms.

Stanley Hornbeck wrote in a memorandum for Assistant Secretary of State A. A. Berle in February, "The powers that can help or can hinder us most in connection with what we believe in and what we will want to do in regard to the Far East are Japan, the Soviet Union, China, and Great Britain. Query: What of those powers is capable of giving in greatest degree the kind of cooperation and assistance which we will need and desire? Answer: China." Anything that would increase China's power and status should be encouraged.[64] This memo is interesting for a number of reasons. First of all, it shows that even an internationalist like Hornbeck tended to view postwar Asia in the framework of balance of power. He was in effect advocating an entente between the United States and a strengthened China as a check on the other two. Second, the memo reveals that he was pessimistic about cooperation between Russia and America in postwar Asia. Third, assuming that Soviet power was on the increase, Hornbeck sought to counter it by means of cooperation between the United States and China. In this sense, he was saying what President Roosevelt later, in May, told Foreign Secretary Eden, that "China, in any serious conflict of policy with Russia, would undoubtedly line up our side."[65] It is not clear what sort of "conflict of policy" Roosevelt had in mind, and it is doubtful that he was thinking of a major military confrontation between America and Russia in Asia. Rather, he was expressing the generally shared view that the Soviet Union would emerge as a major military power and that in the event of difficulties, the United States should be prepared to count on the support of the Chinese.

That such a strategy was not worked out consistently even in a preliminary fashion at this time indicates lack of concern with the implications of Soviet power. Neither Roosevelt nor the State Department, nor even the joint chiefs, pushed the idea of U.S.-Chinese cooperation vis-à-vis Russia with any vigor or consistency. They did not conduct American policy toward China in a way that would in fact ensure such cooperation against the possible danger of Soviet power in postwar Asia. Awareness of the power problem did not induce them to work out a specific plan of approach; it seemed sufficient to continue the wartime alliance with Moscow and defeat the Axis powers as expeditiously as possible. Instead of trying to restrict the growth of Russia's power or to establish a solid foundation for bilateral cooperation, the United States gave the Soviets a de facto free hand in Northeast Asia.

For that reason the Japanese later found it difficult to divide Russia from the Anglo-American powers or to ingratiate themselves with the Russians in the hope of obtaining special understanding. At the same time, lack of a specific American design for Northeast Asia meant that the Japanese wartime strategy as well as plans for peace had to deal primarily with American power in the Pacific. This simplified matters in that they did not have to worry about the implications for the Asian continent of a possible peace with the United States. There is little doubt that this situation in the end facilitated Japanese efforts to end the war.

ONE FUNDAMENTAL reason why the United States failed to envisage a specific plan for cooperation with China was the continued difficulty of defining that cooperation. That difficulty, in part a product of unstable Chinese domestic conditions, never abated during 1943, despite the fact that the year opened auspiciously as the Americans and British signed a new treaty with Chungking, abrogating extra-territoriality and other privileges they had enjoyed in China. The announcement was followed by Madame Chiang Kai-shek's visit to the United States, which was an immense success in that it endeared her and through her the Chinese people to the Americans, reinforcing the vaguely held sentiment that the two peoples shared certain ideals and historic ties of friendship. President Roosevelt gave this sentiment official endorsement by declaring that the Chinese "have been, in thought and in objective, closer to us Americans than almost any other peoples in the world—the same great ideals. China in the last—less than half a century has become one of the great democracies of the world."[66] The obvious implication was that the Chinese-American alliance was far more than a marriage of convenience but was grounded on shared values and political outlooks. Thus their cooperation would persist throughout and after the war in building a more peaceful world. Such an expression of faith in China may have perpetuated popular notions about that country, and indeed Roosevelt may have intended to do just that to rationalize giving aid to Chiang Kai-shek. He may also have wanted to accustom the American people to the idea of postwar involvement in world affairs; the two countries, he may have reasoned, could continue to work together after the war, and the United States would be justified in sharing some of its responsibilities as a world power.

Whatever the utility of these domestic strategies, the evidence is undeniable that privately Roosevelt was baffled by the situation in China. He was concerned with it apparently chronic and worsening instability, which his aides attributed to Chiang's weak and inefficient leadership. Despite the public rhetoric of China being a great democracy, there was an obvious asymmetry in U.S.-Chinese relations, and it was not easy to specify how the two countries would work together after the war. In fact, even the nature of their wartime cooperation was being questioned by American officials. The joint intelligence committee noted in January that "China's contribution to the Allied war effort . . . at the present time . . . is perhaps greater on the negative, defensive and political, than on the positive, offensive and actual side."[67] The Chinese forces contained the Japanese, caused a drain on Japanese aircraft and shipping, and prevented

Japan from consolidating and developing its enlarged empire. As long as China remained in the war, it contributed indirectly to the Allied strategy in the Pacific by effectively minimizing the chances for Japanese operations and by severing connections between Japanese forces in China and those in the southern Pacific. In this sense, China's role complemented American efforts in the south seas. But this was not exactly full-scale cooperation with the United States, and some officials in Washington felt that China should be asked to engage in a more offensive action against Japanese forces on the continent.

In early 1943 the idea of using China for an air offensive emerged as a possibility in United States strategy. The intelligence staff of the Chief of Staff headquarters in Washington advocated early launching of a ten-day spectacular offensive, involving heavy air bombardment of Japan proper from bases in China with simultaneous attacks upon the Japanese-occupied western Aleutians and Wake Island.[68] The plan was rejected as premature, but it indicated an interest in making greater use of China as a cobelligerent in the war against Japan. President Roosevelt, who shared this interest, decided in March to organize a 500-plane air force in China under the command of General Claire Chennault and to urge Chiang Kai-shek to prepare ground facilities for launching air attacks. Although General Marshall, Stilwell, and other army leaders were skeptical of this emphasis on air power, Roosevelt reasoned that it was the most effective and dramatic way to demonstrate strategic cooperation between the two countries.

In endorsing some such dramatic action, Roosevelt was aware that he was trying to ensure Chiang's political survival and contribute to domestic stability in wartime China. He told Marshall in May that "politically he must support Chiang . . . [In] the state of Chinese morale the air program was therefore of great importance."[69] However, he may not have clearly understood the implications of endorsing a policy that pitted Chiang and Chennault against Stilwell and Marshall. By 1943 Chennault and the air force officers stationed in China were closely tied to the political interests of Chiang Kai-shek and his Kuomintang supporters, so that any augmentation of air power by the United States could be seen as a move to enhance Chiang's authority. But President Roosevelt saw no alternative to supporting Chiang, for otherwise there would be chaos and anarchy in China, which would be disastrous for the war effort and also undesirable from the point of view of postwar cooperation. Anarchy in China, he told Eden, would be "so grave a misfortune that Chiang Kai-shek must be given the fullest support."[70]

Beyond the clearly stated policy of supporting Chiang, Roosevelt's conception of American-Chinese cooperation was still rather vague. He had the idea, as he stated to Eden, that "we should probably see in China, in the next 50 years, a development similar to that of Japan in the later years of the 19th century." Japan was at that time in the process of strengthening and unification and was dependent on the United States and other Western countries, but later it became a menace to them. That should not be allowed to happen in China, Roosevelt warned. The West must somehow try to anticipate China's transformation and keep it from becoming an antagonistic force.[71] But how could such a future be ensured? What specifically should the United States do to make sure that a stronger and more advanced China would work with, not against, the United States and Europe? Roosevelt did not spell out an answer. Other officials in Washington were willing to try, and at a meeting of the political problems subcommittee in the State Department on March 13, the participants expressed divergent viewpoints about the future of U.S.-Chinese relations. Senator Elbert Thomas, representing one extreme, seriously questioned whether a militarily strong China was desirable from the American point of view. He evoked an old fear by saying, "Genghis Khan got into Europe, and we can loose in Asia a force so great that the world will be deluged, and there will be no way to prevent it." The force he was referring to was the nationalism that Chinese victory would give its 400 million people. Such nationalism, he asserted, "will not be healthy to the world if we allow [it] to take form." The thinly disguised fear of racial conflict was echoed by Representative Charles A. Eaton, who expressed the fear that the Oriental people wanted the end of Western domination of Asia and that "eventually the United States might be pushed off the map too." There might develop "racial war between the yellow men and the white men in the future—we may be liquidated." Under Secretary of State Welles, though not as extreme as Thomas or Eaton, admitted that "the trend in the Far East is the development of an Asia for the Asiatics."

The questions, in such a situation, were "what is to the interest of the United States" and "what this country can do to make China a stabilizing, peaceful factor rather than a force of future danger." The questions were precisely put, exactly as Roosevelt himself had phrased them. But the discussion at this and other meetings within the State Department indicated that there were no easy solutions.[72]

Some officials were willing to accept the fact of Chinese nationalism and pan-Asianism and to try to co-opt these forces in the interest of American security and Asian stability. Hornbeck represented this approach. He believed that the only way to keep the Chinese friendly toward the United State was to treat them as a people worthy of trust and respect. In a March memorandum he, along with Maxwell Hamilton, pointed out that China was not represented on any of the more than twenty important wartime United Nations organizations, such as the Combined Chiefs of Staff, the Munitions Assignments Board, the Combined Food Board, and the Combined Raw Materials Board. Although China was a member of the Pacific War Council along with the United States, Australia, Canada, the Netherlands, New Zealand, the Philippines, and Great Britain, that body was little more than a forum for informal exchanges of views and information. Hornbeck and Hamilton wanted to create new boards in which the United States and China, as well as some other countries, would actively participate to ensure cooperation in military operations, procurement of goods, and intelligence and propaganda activities. Such a step would "go far to advance the United Nations cause in the eyes of all Oriental and colored peoples and might placate China's feeling that she is being 'left out of' decisions affecting prosecution of the war." Moreover, associating China more closely and organizationally with the Anglo-American powers would have political significance for postwar Asia. Active Chinese participation in Allied strategic, economic, and intelligence planning would bring about "the development of conditions conducive to stability and orderly evolution in the Pacific area."[73] Unless these steps were taken, Hornbeck and Hamilton warned, the Chinese would ultimately turn their nationalism and military power against the United States.

Even this modest degree of cooperation, however, was difficult to realize. For strategic reasons United States officials were reluctant to have their plans encumbered by close consultation with the

Chinese, but apart from that there persisted the view that bilateral collaboration would be detrimental to the framework of cooperation between the United States and Great Britain. America's espousal of China would imply a challenge to British colonial domination of Asia, which the Chinese clearly resented. To some at the March 13 meeting in the State Department, it was not at all clear that the United States should risk undermining the familiar relationship with Britain for the sake of a more uncertain scheme for befriending the Chinese. Representative Eaton asserted that "control by the English-speaking powers" should continue to be the mechanism for promoting security and stability in Asia. John V. A. MacMurray, a veteran diplomat, agreed, saying, "It is more valuable for the peace of the world that we should maintain our relations with the British than that we should jeopardize them and inevitably destroy the possibility of confidence on both sides by participating in the breaking up of the British Empire." United States policy throughout 1943 indicated that there was no intention of breaking up the British empire or of forsaking the British alliance for a new partnership with China.

At the May 7 meeting of the security technical committee, referred to earlier, Grayson Kirk noted that "of the Great Powers none was exclusively a Pacific power except China, and to a certain extent the United States." The implication was that these two countries would have to work together for peace and security in postwar Asia. But again other conferees objected to this expression of the equation, pointing out, among other things, that Australia, New Zealand, and Britain could not be ignored, that "containment" of China, in the words of Amry Vandenbosch, might become the key postwar issue because of the millions of Chinese throughout Southeast Asia, that Japanese help might be solicited by the British against the Russians, as Cavendish Cannon said, and that what the United States needed most, according to John Masland, was "the restoration of the Japanese market for its goods."[74]

As these discussions indicate, any mention of future U.S.-Chinese relations tended to raise questions about the whole Asia-Pacific region and to provoke debate about other countries. American officials simply were not ready to agree on a firm policy toward China. Compared with the general consensus on the treatment of Japan or the immediate future of the British empire, the idea of

U.S.-Chinese relations was quite unspecific. Even President Roosevelt's idea that the United States should give all its support to Chiang Kai-shek to prevent Chinese domestic instability began to be challenged inside the government. Roosevelt, with Hornbeck's concurrence, had adopted that policy to check chaos and anarchy in China. An increasing number of reports from American officials in China, however, cast some doubt on the advisability of singling out Chiang for support. Their doubt resulted from a number of factors, including the apparently growing opposition by Chinese intellectuals to Kuomintang rule. But most important were indications of continuing rift between the Nationalists and the Communists. As summarized by Augustus S. Chase of the Far Eastern division of the State Department in June, "Information received by the Department indicates that the differences between the Chinese Communists and the Chinese National Government at Chungking are probably of too fundamental a nature to be susceptible of adjustment by amicable negotiation."[75] Although Communist leaders Chou En-lai and Lin Piao were in Chungking, trying to work out a compromise between the two groups, their negotiations were getting nowhere, with each side holding what the other side considered an untenable position regarding the Communists' military and political autonomy. These were internal matters, but they raised questions of Chinese stability, on which the future of U.S.-Chinese relations would depend. Moreover, it was widely believed, in Washington as well as Chungking, that the Soviet Union held a key to the strength of the Chinese Communists and that it would be difficult therefore to separate the issue of American support of Chiang from Soviet policy toward the Chinese factions.

John Paton Davies, second secretary of the American embassy in Chungking, wrote perhaps the earliest systematic exposition of these matters when he was temporarily back in Washington in mid-1943. After outlining the history of the two parties, Davies predicted that their rift would continue until the central government tried to liquidate the Communists by force, precipitating "a civil war from which one of the two contending factions will emerge dominant." The Nationalists' attack would "in all probability force the Communists into the willing arms of the Russians." In that event, the pro-Russian Communists would gain influence. "The present trend of the Chinese Communists toward more or less democratic nationalism . . . would thereby be reversed and they could be expected to retrogress to the position of a Russian satellite." With such an alliance the Communists would probably defeat the Nationalists "and eventually take over the control of most if not all of China." A "Russo-Chinese bloc" would come into existence, undermining Asian and world stability. Chiang Kai-shek, faced with such dire consequences, could be expected to "involve us in active support of the Central Government," and the United States would be "entangled not only in a civil war in China but also drawn into conflict with the Soviet Union." This would be the precise opposite of the stated American policy of ensuring Chinese domestic order and U.S.-Chinese cooperation in postwar Asia. What should the United States do to prevent these events from happening? Davies was reluctant to offer specific suggestions, but he did insist that the United States place a military observer's mission and a consulate general within the Communist region to obtain more accurate information about the situation.[76]

Nothing immediately came of that suggestion or of Davies's general observations. The United States government continued to deal with the Chungking regime as the sole government of China and Chiang Kai-shek as a leader worthy of American support. Nevertheless, it was important that the State Department took note of the seriousness of Chinese internal conditions just when Roosevelt was reaffirming his support of Chiang. Officials were beginning to believe that such a policy, instead of contributing to Chinese stability, might actually precipitate a crisis, further enhancing the danger of civil war in China. Although officials in Washington shied away from squarely confronting the issue at this time, their awareness of these difficulties increasingly stood in the way of developing a specific policy for American-Chinese relations. This was another instance in which United States policy was no more precisely defined or successfully executed than Japan's; starting from opposite ends of the spectrum, Tokyo and Washington were in a sense converging on an impasse in China.

LOOKING AT THE positions of the United States and Japan in 1943, one notices rather remarkable parallels in official thinking about war aims and peace objectives. Although their wartime rhetoric and the fierce fighting in the Pacific created a picture of two diametrically opposed systems of power and culture struggling for survival against each other, in actuality much in their strategies and plans reflected similar assumptions about Asia and the Pacific. American officials and a small but increasingly articulate number of Japanese were holding to the framework of 1920s internationalism, with its emphasis on regional stability, economic development, and internal order as prerequisites to peace. That meant a reformist scheme for developing the colonial areas as well as an agenda for China's political and economic maturation. The Soviet Union was viewed as a power factor, part of the future framework of Asian politics defined in power terms. That definition, to which American strategists were becoming more and more receptive, was not very different from the Japanese view. Thus both in internationalist and power conceptions, American and Japanese thinking was coming closer. To be sure, this was in part a result of Japan's military reverses, which forced its leaders to reevaluate their position and to revert to some ideas they had shared with Americans before the war. More important, this convergence derived from the fact that the Japanese-American war remained primarily a power conflict; in economic, cultural, and ideological terms there was much less conflict than both sides assumed.

JAPANESE-AMERICAN RAPPROCHEMENT

4

ON SEPTEMBER 27, 1943, Hugh Borton, a historian working for the State Department, wrote a sixteen-page memorandum for the territorial problems subcommittee of the State Department. At that time this committee and others that had been created to plan for the postwar world were being reorganized and would emerge as new committees at the beginning of 1944. In the meantime, a number of "country and area committees" were being set up within the State Department to enable area specialists to offer their expertise to postwar planning. Borton was a member of the Far Eastern area committee, launched in October under the nominal chairmanship of Stanley Hornbeck but the actual leadership of George Blakeslee. Blakeslee and Borton worked closely together, and this teamwork created greater coherence in State Department thinking about Japan than there might otherwise have been. Borton's memo, written at this juncture, was thus of more than passing interest; Blakeslee supported the ideas it contained, which provided a framework for long-range planning for U.S.-Japanese relations.

Borton argued first that "[if] the terms of surrender and the subsequent agreements and treaties provide for the impoverishment of Japan and its reduction to economic impotency, permanent peace in the Pacific will be seriously threatened. Such a policy will only create an economic vacuum in the north Pacific, where the desire for special economic privileges by outside powers may make Japan the prey of powerful neighbors." He obviously had in mind Russia and China, viewing them as disruptive rather than stabilizing factors

[149]

in postwar Asia. Peace and stability in postwar Asia, Borton believed, depended on Japan, which should be given a chance "to maintain a standard of living required for a stable society and to develop a healthy and peaceful political structure."[1] In a memorandum written two days later, Blakeslee agreed. "Economic and financial conditions in the postwar period," he said, "so far as they may be controlled by the United Nations, should ultimately permit Japan, within the framework of the restrictions necessary for international security, to share in the development of a world economy on a non-discriminatory basis, looking toward a progressively higher standard of living."[2]

These two men were trying to establish a liberal policy toward defeated Japan, designed to reintegrate it into the world community of economic interdependence. This kind of clearly Wilsonian thinking had been partly submerged under the pressing needs of the war and the growing influence of power-political thinking at the highest levels of the United States government. But Borton's and Blakeslee's memoranda were no longer an isolated cry in darkness. Their writing coincided with the State Department's preparation for a conference of foreign ministers in Moscow, to be held during October 19–30, 1943. Secretary of State Hull was to submit a paper on international economic cooperation after the war, expressing a commitment to an open international economic system based on principles such as "elimination of arrangements, public or private, to restrict production and trade," "interchangeability of currencies," "promotion of the development of resources and industries wherever international assistance is necessary for this purpose," and "improvement of facilities for shipping, air traffic and other means of transportation."[3] This explicit reiteration of economic internationalism indicated the State Department's judgment that the time was ripe for presenting these principles formally at an international conference.

The Borton-Blakeslee formulation, then, fitted into the State Department's emerging self-consciousness as a spokesman for a liberal postwar order, grounded on a negation of the particularistic economic policies of the 1930s when nations responded to domestic needs and were unconcerned with world order. The State Department considered it imperative to resume the effort to construct a more stable international economic system so that countries would have no need or justification for reverting to those policies. Even enemy nations should be reintegrated into the scheme by orienting themselves away from nationalism and imperialism toward a commitment to internationalism. However, such an orientation must be derived from stable domestic conditions, so the United Nations must ensure, in the defeated nations, the restoration of those leaders who shared internationalist views and had a stake in an open economic policy. These leaders would be the force for domestic stability and world development. Conversely, as Blakeslee noted, a more open international environment would enable such leaders to remain in power and check the resurgence of militaristic and reactionary forces.

What leaders in postwar Japan could be expected to act according to such a scenario? In one of the earliest papers on the subject, Borton noted on October 6 that there was evidence "to warrant a hope that sufficient moderate or liberal elements in Japan may exist to operate a reformed government, providing a situation will be established which will be conducive to the development of liberalism . . . and will make feasible the inauguration of effective checks on the power of the military." As possible candidates for leadership, Borton mentioned Matsudaira Tsuneo, Kido Kōichi, Wakatsuki Reijirō, and Konoe Fumimaro, all prewar leaders who had not been identified with the military. Moreover, these men were close to the throne, either because they had been prime ministers and thus were *jūshin* (senior statesmen) with access to the emperor or because they worked in offices in the Imperial Palace. By naming such leaders, Borton revealed that he did not consider the emperor and the emperor system guilty in themselves of militaristic aggression and dictatorship; on the contrary, he believed they had been manipulated and subverted to serve the interests of reactionary and imperialistic forces. For this reason, he argued, the emperor system could again become a positive factor for demilitarization and postwar reconstruction. As he wrote, "The institution of the Emperor is likely to be one of the more stable elements of postwar Japan. As such, it may be a valuable factor in the establishment of a stable and moderate postwar government."[4]

This remarkably coherent statement did not go unchallenged. Borton's stress on reintegrating a stable Japan into a liberal world after the war, although reflecting State Department thinking on economic internationalism, was met with Hornbeck's retort that he did not think "an orderly and stable Japan" should be America's major objective after the war; "it will be possible for us," he remarked, "to get along without Japan in the postwar world."[5] Hornbeck's negative view of Japan reflected his continued emphasis on China as the key to postwar Asian peace and American interests. In London in October he reiterated his favorite theme to Prime Minister Churchill. "The democratic powers [must] retain China as an asset both in the war effort and in the post war effort rather than take chances on having a huge block of oriental peoples, including China and India, as a liability in connection with the problem of establishing and maintaining conditions of peace and security." A China that was tied "on the basis of moral considerations" to the United States and Britain would do more for a liberated and peaceful Asia than a reconstructed Japan. Also Hornbeck was skeptical that Japan could be reformed and liberalized as readily as Borton seemed to assume. A stable Japan, far from being a force for democracy and peace, might simply perpetuate aggressive national traits. "As Japan did not have a complete revolution in the 1860s," Hornbeck insisted, "and hence many aspects of feudalism still exist, it would probably be to our advantage to have a revolution within Japan." Although it might lead to domestic turmoil, it would eventually produce reform.[6]

In the late fall of 1943, Borton rather than Hornbeck represented the majority view among civilian officials. It is true that the idea of China as a major factor in world politics was officially endorsed at the Moscow foreign ministers' conference, which issued a four-power declaration almost identical to that presented at the Quebec Conference. As noted earlier, that declaration enunciated the principle of cooperation among the four great powers after the war and supported the establishment of an international organization to preserve the peace. But such a declaration did not obliterate all the complex questions about cooperation with China that American officials had grappled with, not too successfully, throughout 1943. If anything, formal acceptance of the idea of China as a full partner sparked debate within the State Department about Chinese government. Obviously, the United States needed a strong and efficient government in China that it could work with for peace as well as for war. Roosevelt did not waver from his support of Chiang Kai-shek—as indicated by his invitation to Chiang to meet with him in Cairo in late November—but the realities of Chinese domestic politics soon intruded upon the formation of United States policy, creating a serious rift among officials. In contrast, a moderate policy toward Japan fitted nicely into the plan for economic internationalism presented at Moscow. Hornbeck's thinking, Borton candidly pointed out, was "in opposition to that upon which my memoranda on Japan are based." Within the Far Eastern area committee, Borton's thinking was generally accepted, as indicated by a statement by F. S. Williams of the Far Eastern division that the United States must try to fit "Japan into the most beneficial place in the family of nations."[7] Such a view signaled the possibility of rapprochement across the Pacific.

On the surface, the Japanese appeared as adamant as ever in their opposition to Western interests and influence in Asia. The Great East Asia Conference in Tokyo in early November, mentioned in chapter three, demonstrated their determination to prosecute the war to the bitter end and establish a new Asian order. The self-conscious enunciation of pan-Asianism was in sharp contrast to various declarations by the United Nations at that time— for instance, the one by the foreign ministers in Moscow that talked of international, not Asian or Western, cooperation and indicated the solidarity of the United States, Britain, the Soviet Union, and China in working for peace as well as for military victory. Nevertheless, we have seen that the Great East Asia Conference was an attempt to clarify Japan's war aims and prepare for an eventual termination of hostilities. Although the conferees in Tokyo called for an Asia free of Western domination, their visions of economic development, political maturation, cultural interchange, and racial equality were not necessarily anti-Western. Indeed, they paralleled State Department thinking, as exemplified by Secretary Hull's statement at the Quebec Conference. To the extent that Japanese officials took these ideas seriously as a basis for accommodation with the Anglo-American powers, they were signaling a willingness to return to the shared framework of the 1920s, rather than a determination to destroy that framework for a drastically altered future.

In reference to China, too, the gap between the United States and Japan was narrowing, although not necessarily intentionally. The Japanese government and the supreme command had adopted a new approach, emphasizing political moves to Chungking so as to arrive at a settlement with the Nationalists and detach them from their Anglo-American alliance. In return the Japanese had expressed their readiness to withdraw all forces from China and to enter into a relationship of full equality. That such maneuvers made not the slightest impression on Chiang Kai-shek was demonstrated when he flew to Cairo in late November to the embrace of Roosevelt and Churchill. The trip, only a few weeks after Wang Ching-wei's journey to Tokyo to attend the East Asia Conference, clearly revealed Chungking's choice to stay with the wartime Allies and their readiness to consider Chiang and, through him, the Chinese nation as a partner in the war. As if to commemorate the liaison, American planes based in China bombarded Taiwan in late November. The Japanese-American war was steadily coming closer to the Japanese homeland.

The Cairo Conference, from November 22 to 26 and December 4 to 6, readily reached agreement on the disposition of Japanese territories. The three leaders declared that "Japan shall be stripped of all the islands in the Pacific which she has seized or occupied since the beginning of the First World War in 1914, and that all the territories Japan has stolen from the Chinese, such as Manchuria, Formosa, and the Pescadores, shall be restored to the Republic of China. Japan will also be expelled from all other territories which she has taken by violence and greed." This was a rather open-ended declaration, but the implication was obvious. After defeat the Japanese would be virtually confined to their home islands. Although the declaration said nothing about Sakhalin and the Kuriles, Roosevelt later claimed that Chiang Kai-shek agreed to their retrocession to Russia. (At Cairo the president also talked of giving the Ryukyus and Hong Kong to China.) As for Korea, the three powers declared that "in due course Korea shall become free and independent."

These territorial issues had long been discussed within the State Department's numerous advisory bodies, and the Cairo declaration merely put an official stamp of approval on their plans. The British and Chinese were consulted only at the last moment, but they did not object to the principle of reducing Japan to its nineteenth-century possessions.[8] For all practical purposes, the matter was sealed and would not be subject to negotiation when

Japan sued for peace. Roosevelt justified this decision long before the termination of hostilities, saying in his report to the American people that in the First World War the allies had made a mistake in opening territorial issues for debate at the peace conference. "The result was a peace which was not a peace," he asserted. "That was a mistake which we are not repeating in this war."[9] No one took exception to the idea, least of all Chiang Kai-shek, who had the satisfaction not only of recognition as a world leader but also of enhanced prestige domestically, because he could assure his people of what victory would bring to the country.

And yet Japanese intelligence analyses were not totally inaccurate when they surmised, on the basis of their reports of the Cairo Conference, that the meeting was an attempt by Britain and the United States to keep the Nationalists on their side. There must have been a deep rift between China and the Allies, it was pointed out, or there would have been no need for a conference.[10] Although wishful thinking undoubtedly played a part in such an analysis, the Japanese were correct in guessing that Roosevelt and Churchill were giving Chiang Kai-shek anything but full and substantial cooperation. At Cairo, for instance, the three leaders had agreed on a major counteroffensive in Burma, with Anglo-American and Chinese forces led by Stilwell attacking Japanese forces in northern Burma and a cross-Bengal assault by the newly established Southeast Asia Command under Lord Louis Mountbatten. However, the plan was canceled as a result of the talks at Teheran, which lasted from November 28 to December 1. At Teheran Stalin formally promised Roosevelt and Churchill that Russia would enter the war against Japan after Germany was defeated. Given the prospect of Soviet participation, the Pacific theater, rather than the China mainland or Southeast Asia, emerged as the principal area of Allied military operations. Coupled with Churchill's strenuous opposition to a large-scale Burma campaign before the cross-Channel invasion of France, Russia's promise of participation persuaded Roosevelt to postpone the counteroffensive agreed upon at Cairo. He informed Chiang, who had returned to Chungking, of the decision and requested that in the meantime the Chinese invade northern Burma without a simultaneous amphibious campaign in the south.[11]

This proved to be a key turning point in the Roosevelt-Chiang relationship. The euphoria of Cairo was short-lived. When Chiang received Roosevelt's message, he did not conceal his disappointment, declaring that the Chinese were being asked to commit suicide in northern Burma. If Anglo-American forces had to be concentrated in Europe, he asserted, he should receive more equipment, arms, and other goods from the Allies. More specifically, he requested a new loan of one billion dollars from the Allies.[12] Without intending to do so, he thereby compelled American officials to make an intensive examination of China policy.

When Ambassador Gauss was told of Chiang's request for the billion-dollar loan, he sent a lengthy telegram to Washington, strongly objecting to granting the request. First of all, he said, Chungking had dollar reserves of over $300 million, which was more than adequate for purchases from abroad in the near future. Moreover, the bulk of such purchases would be military supplies that could be financed under the lend-lease agreement. Second, there was no longer any political justification for such a loan. "[With] the military action of the United Nations promising eventual complete victory and restoration to China of all lost territory, there is no reason to fear that China might seek a separate peace." The Moscow and Cairo conferences had clearly indicated the Allies' willingness to consider China a major partner and a postwar power, and there was no need to give the Chinese additional assurances. Third, past American loans to China with no strings attached had failed to induce the Chinese to undertake significant reforms. Gauss had found that "in discussions for the formulation of plans for a new and powerful China the tendency is distinctly toward a closed economy designed solely for Chinese benefit and definitely away from those liberal principles for mutually beneficial world economy" that the United States stood for, as demonstrated at the Quebec Conference. An American loan would only encourage the Chinese to perpetuate their particularistic economic system. For all these reasons, Gauss said, the United States must stop meeting Chinese requests automatically but insist on bilateral obligations. The Chungking regime had been exploiting the Americans' goodwill by fixing an unreasonable exchange ratio between the dollar and the yuan, thus raising the costs of goods and services to Americans in China out of all proportion to their actual costs. Additional loans should be held up, pending negotiation for protection of American interests in China.[13]

This was the clearest expression of the United States embassy's criticism of the Chinese leadership during the war. The formal endorsement at Moscow and Cairo of the idea of China as a major power revealed a serious gap between such a status and the actual performance of its leaders. To the extent that American officials and the public had equated China with Chiang Kai-shek, such criticism was bound to raise serious questions about the wisdom of supporting him as the sole regime. Even as staunch a supporter of the Nationalists as Secretary of the Treasury Morgenthau was driven to ask, out of desperation over the billion-dollar request, how long "the Kuomintang group or any other group [would] stand for this grafting family at the head of the Government?"[14] President Roosevelt was also concerned with Chiang's leadership. "How long do you think Chiang can last?" he was reported to have asked Stilwell at Cairo in December. Told that the situation was getting quite serious, the president remarked, "Well, then we should look for some other man or group of men, to carry on."[15]

A less impressionistic but equally candid assessment of the Chinese leadership was made by John P. Davies. The ideas he had expressed in June were confirmed by what he took to be the Nationalists' continued failure to prosecute the war vigorously. Now more than ever, he thought, it would be necessary for the United States to broaden its contact with other forces in China, especially the Communists. At Cairo Davies and Roosevelt briefly discussed the Chinese internal situation. On his way back to Chungking, in a memorandum to presidential advisor Harry Hopkins, Davies painted an even more dramatic picture than before. "Because [the] Kuomintang Government has no popular base," he said, "because the centrifugal forces in China are growing under prolonged economic strain and because the Soviet Union may join the war against Japan and enter Manchuria and North China, the Generalissimo faces next year the gravest crisis of his career." Now that Soviet entry into the Japanese war and, consequently, into China appeared genuinely likely, Davies repeated his plea against committing the United States to the support of a corrupt regime. "We should wish," he declared, "to avoid finding ourselves at the close of the war backing a coalition of Chiang's Kuomintang and the degenerate puppets against a democratic coalition commanding Russian sympathy." He stopped short of advocating abandonment of Chiang and support of the Communists, but he implied as much when he called for "readiness to support a strong new coalition offering cooperation mutually more beneficial to China and the United States." Such a course of action would ensure the emergence of "a strong and independent China" that was not tied to the Soviet Union against the United States.[16] Although this memorandum was not written in response to Chiang's request for a loan, Davies clearly was opposed to granting the request, for it would only solidify ties between Washington and Chungking, making the latter more than ever dependent on the former, a relationship the United States would find it increasingly difficult to extricate itself from. The result would be to drive the anti-Chiang forces to the Russians.

Interestingly enough, Hornbeck, a staunch supporter of the Nationalist regime, countered this argument by also introducing the Soviet factor into the equation. As he wrote in a memorandum at the end of December, it was important to consider the political ramifications of the loan issue; "the United States and China are natural and actual friends and allies . . . [In] regard to establishing conditions of security and welfare in and around the Pacific Ocean, the United States and China have a primacy of common interest." Hornbeck was particularly concerned that China might become so alienated from the United States that it might "move into a position of reliance upon the Soviet Union or acceptance of the Japanese thesis that oriental peoples must combine in opposition to the influence of occidental peoples."[17] Whereas Davies was worried that the Chinese Communists would turn to the Russians if the United States dealt exclusively with Chungking, Hornbeck argued the opposite, that the Nationalists might approach the Soviet Union if they were refused American assistance.

The importance of the Soviet factor in the developing debate was obvious. In any event, few State and Treasury Department officials shared Hornbeck's premonitions and recommended refusing Chiang's request for a billion-dollar loan. Instead, only a small-scale shipment of gold was promised to help Chungking's current transactions, and that was to be followed by negotiations for a revised exchange rate. The question of exchange rates was considered so serious that officials in the War Department was even willing to consider pulling the United States army out of China unless a satisfactory settlement was arrived at.[18]

Hornbeck's other point, that the Chinese (that is, the Nationalists) might be enticed to join the Japanese in a pan-Asianist move if they were not given support and recognition, echoed the alarm that had been sounded from time to time within and outside the government in Washington. The fear of pan-Asianism may have appeared justified when Chiang Kai-shek declared, in a New Year's message for the Chinese people, that the anticipated victory over Japan would not only restore lost lands to the nation but also give hope to "all the oppressed and maltreated Asiatic peoples both in the Pacific and Asia mainland." At the same time he scarcely concealed his bitterness toward Roosevelt and Churchill for having reneged on the Burma operation. "I have nothing to say," he cabled Roosevelt, "if the [Combined Chiefs of Staff] wants to divert all available materials for an assault on Germany, because I have not been consulted." When informed of America's rejection of the loan request, he retorted that the response was "to my mind, not [that] of one Allied nation to another."[19]

Obviously, official relations between Washington and Chungking were entering a period of greater uncertainty. Just when Chiang Kai-shek seemed to be enjoying unprecedented personal prestige at home and throughout the world, questions were being raised about his leadership and about U.S.-Chinese relations. China's pretensions as a great power under Chiang were being undermined by the prospect of Russian entry into the war, which could affect Chinese domestic politics as well as foreign relations. The Soviet Union, Chiang was convinced, would back up his Communist foes, and he would need American help to check Russian intervention. But further United States involvement in China might result in pressure on Chungking to undertake reform measures. In other words, China might have to sustain its status as a major power under the Kuomintang through a relationship of dependence on the United States. Chiang's China might become no more independent than Wang Ching-wei's China. Thus, while the Japanese were making further concessions to Chinese rights and hinting at the possibility of an eventual withdrawal of its forces, the United States was moving in from the opposite direction, making additional demands on the Chinese government and threatening to withdraw its forces from the China theater. Although these developments did not spell a Japanese-American convergence on the China question, they indicated an interesting, although unintended, reversal of roles in the two countries' respective approaches to China. Japan was lessening its pressures while the United States was becoming more deeply involved in Chinese political affairs. At the same time, neither Japan's nor America's commitment to their professed goals in China was unambiguous. Much depended on the course of fighting away from the Asian continent, and, more important, on the timing and intensity of Soviet participation in the war.

Regarding the Russians, as well, Japanese and American thinking showed similar developments. At the time of the Teheran Conference, Japanese and Russian officials were negotiating for settlement of the North Sakhalin question. Japan was willing to restore to the Soviet Union its concessions there in return for indemnity payments and for a mutual reaffirmation of the neutrality treaty. But the Russians, fully aware that the Japanese were willing to pay a high price to prevent Soviet entry into the war, refused those terms. Japan ended up agreeing to restore North Sakhalin rights unconditionally, and Russia did nothing to reaffirm the neutrality pact. The Japanese government consoled itself by believing that at least for the time being the Soviets would abide by the treaty. In any event there was growing recognition in Japan, and readiness to accept the prospect, that the Soviet Union would emerge as a major power regardless of the outcome of the Japanese-American war. The more the Japanese wanted Russian neutrality, the more willing they would be to make concessions.

American officials were also viewing postwar Russia as a principal factor in Asia because of the emerging wartime alliance against Japan. As the joint chiefs of staff noted at this time, "We are agreed that every effort should be exerted to bring the U.S.S.R. into the war against Japan at the earliest practicable date, and that plans should be prepared in that event." Such plans included deploying Russian forces in the Kuriles and Sakhalin as well as the Soviet Far East to blockade and bombard Japan, while United States forces advanced across the Pacific.[20] Moreover, although the transfer of specific Japanese territories to Russia was not discussed at Teheran, the United States government had long endorsed the retrocession of South Sakhalin to the Soviet Union. In addition, Roosevelt expressed his willingness to turn Dairen into a free port under international guarantee to give the Russians an ice-free outlet in the east. The Japanese would have vehemently opposed giving up South Sakhalin or the Kuriles at this time, but at Teheran nothing was said officially about these lands. What stood out for both Japan and the United States was the increasing weight of the Soviets in world affairs, in Asia as well as in Europe. In that sense, the Japanese and the American positions were coming closer.

The conferences at Cairo and Teheran touched on the future of Korea and Indochina, and here the position adopted by the Allies, vague as it was, would have been unacceptable to the Japanese. The Cairo declaration stated that the United States, Britain, and China, "mindful of the enslavement of the people of Korea, are determined that in due course Korea shall become free and independent." This was a concession to pressures by Korean nationalist groups and their supporters in China, the United States, and elsewhere, as well as a response to the Soviet Union, which had called for Korean independence. But the declaration did not promise immediate independence, for fear of precipitating a struggle among Koreans overseas who might vie with one another for recognition as the true representative of the Korean people. Moreover, Allied officials were skeptical of the Koreans' ability to govern themselves, since they had been denied autonomy and self-expression under the long Japanese rule. Under the circumstances, it seemed best to placate Korean nationalism by supporting future independence but without recognizing any particular faction as the provisional government of a free Korea. In the meantime, some sort of international supervision might be instituted, for instance a trusteeship by the United States, the Soviet Union, and China, as the State Department's various advisory groups were suggesting. However, Korean trusteeship was not mentioned in the Cairo declaration, and therefore the future of the Japanese colony remained ill defined. Nevertheless, the Allies' gesture was more than the Japanese were offering the Korean people in 1943—which essentially consisted of exploiting them as laborers to supplement the depleted work force at home, and more fully integrating them into the Japanese economy and polity. This policy of denationalizing the Koreans was in obvious contrast to the Allies' endorsement in principle of Korean nationalism.[21]

The future status of Indochina was not mentioned in the formal communiqués after the conferences, but President Roosevelt discussed the matter briefly with Chiang Kai-shek in Cairo and with Stalin at Teheran. He reiterated the idea, first expressed in the spring of 1942, that the French colony should not be restored to France but be placed under an international trusteeship. This view was contrary to the thinking within the State Department which, as seen earlier, had stressed solidarity with the European powers, including France. But Roosevelt continued to think trusteeship for Indochina would be a good idea, for China would be one of the trustees, which would help make it a major power in postwar Asia. At one point he asked Chiang bluntly if "he wanted Indo-China," whereupon the latter reportedly replied, "Under no circumstances!"[22] Chiang was favorable to the idea of a trusteeship, as was Stalin. But neither Stalin nor Churchill shared Roosevelt's idea of China as a great power, and for this and other reasons nothing definite emerged about the future status of Indochina. The president did not give up the trusteeship concept easily; after returning to Washington he declared that he wanted "some United Nations trusteeship to govern those people . . . somewhat after the manner of developments in the Philippines."[23] These expressions of hope, though vague, for eventual self-government for Indochina were in sharp contrast to Japan's singular silence regarding the French colony. The Japanese had begun to sympathize with the anticolonial aspirations of most other peoples in Asia and to put into effect some limited autonomy measures for Burma, the Philippines, and the East Indies. But they had not considered any change in the arrangements in Indochina, where Japanese military authorities worked through the French colonial establishment. Only later, in 1944, did the Japanese government initiate policy discussions on the future of Indochina.

Thus there were obviously areas where the positions of Japan and of the Anglo-American powers remained far apart. It should be noted in this connection, however, that Japanese officials on the whole accurately assessed the significance of the conferences at Cairo and Teheran and their combined impact on Japan. The liaison conference members agreed, as early as December 4, 1943, that the Teheran Conference demonstrated the solidarity of the United States, Britain, and Russia. These powers, the Japanese assumed, must have agreed on a speedy opening of the second front in Europe to end the war as quickly as possible. The Cairo Conference, on the other hand, was notable because of the exclusion of Stalin, according to the Japanese analysis. This must have meant that the Soviet Union was not quite ready to precipitate a crisis with Japan, that the Anglo-American nations and the Soviet Union had not yet fully exchanged views regarding Japan, and that Roosevelt and Churchill were trying to keep Chiang Kai-shek on the anti-Axis side in the meantime. The overall effect of the meetings, the liaison conference agreed, was to make the European situation extremely critical. Germany might collapse under the weight of the United Nations' winter offensive, the opening of the second front, and possibly peace feelers designed to take advantage of the German people's war weariness.[24]

This was a fairly accurate assessment of the world situation. For Tokyo's leaders the war's outlook was becoming grimmer. Predictably, they responded to the situation with a propaganda campaign of their own. If defeated, they pointed out, Japan would be lorded over by greedy Western imperialists. Surely the Japanese would fight to the end rather than submit to such humiliation. On December 8, the second anniversary of the beginning of the war, Prime Minister Tōjō made a radio broadcast denouncing the Cairo Conference as demonstrating that the American, British, and Chinese leaders had reaffirmed their pursuit of self-interest and exploitation of other peoples. They were, Tōjō said, trying to reduce Japan to the status of a third-rate nation and replace it with Chiang Kai-shek's China, thus dividing Asians against one another. The fact that Roosevelt and Churchill had said nothing about the future of Asia revealed their deep-rooted disagreement on the colonial question. Only by clearly indicating how they intended to deal with that question in the event of victory would the Western nations be true to "the rationalism of what they call true democracy." As it was, all their ideals—justice, humanism, morality, and equal opportunity—were empty slogans. Under their rule, Asia's one billion people would continue to suffer oppression. The Teheran Conference, Tōjō asserted, revealed that disagreement between Britain and Russia persisted on the European boundary question and showed the Anglo-American powers' naked ambition for world domination. The two conferences demonstrated once again that Japan's enemy had no other war aims than exploitation of other peoples, which was in sharp contrast to Japan's dedication to "the principles of friendly relations with all nations, abolition of racial inequality, promotion of broad cultural exchange, the development of natural resources, and the progress of the entire world."[25]

Despite the effort to depict the two camps as pursuing diametrically opposite ends, Tōjō's enumeration of Japan's alleged war aims in reality echoed the three-power declaration at the end of the Teheran Conference: "We recognize fully the supreme responsibility resting upon us and all the United Nations to make a peace which will command the goodwill of the overwhelming mass of the people of the world and banish the scourge and terror of war for many generations . . . We shall seek the cooperation and active participation of all nations, large and small, whose peoples in heart and mind are dedicated . . . to the elimination of tyranny and slavery, oppression and intolerance." No wonder that the diarist Kiyosawa Kiyoshi thought the declaration read like that issued at the end of the Great East Asia Conference. Other Japanese stressed that while the Allies professed high-sounding ideals, these had not been realized. As an *Asahi* editorial noted, the liberal democratic principles enunciated in the Atlantic Charter had not been implemented, and as a result the enemy was no longer certain what the war was all about, whereas the Japanese knew they were fighting for Asian liberation, autonomy, and independence. It was by holding on to these objectives, the editorial continued, that the nation could overcome possible military reversals and win an ultimate victory.[26]

Such thinking provides evidence for the continued importance of war aims. By stressing idealistic goals and saying that the Japanese were being more true to them than their adversaries, they were paving the way psychologically for acceptance of defeat. However misguided or unrealistic, the perception enabled Japan's leaders to separate the physical from the moral aspect of the war so that in time they could claim a moral victory in the midst of military defeat. There was a large element of self-delusion in such thinking, but the Japanese were not entirely wrong in their criticism of the Allies' alleged failure to actualize their ideals, for they failed at Cairo and Teheran to clarify the future of their colonies in Asia. The failure provided ammunition to those who argued that Japan was a truer champion of Asian reconstruction than either China,

Russia, or the Anglo-American powers. The truth was, of course, that Japan itself was not advocating an immediate liberation of all colonies. The bulk of Chinese, Indians, and others saw nothing but hypocrisy in the Japanese rhetoric of Asian freedom. But the crucial point was not so much the sterile rhetoric as the belief that "political, diplomatic, and ideological warfare" was becoming of crucial importance, as *Asahi* asserted.[27] Consciously or unconsciously, the Japanese were beginning to persuade themselves that the physical outcome of the fighting was less important than the future of Asia and the Pacific—and, indeed, the future of their own country.

It was but a step from such a view to the belief that the war should be terminated now that Japan had demonstrated the nobility of its war aims. At least such a belief induced a handful of influential Japanese to begin secret moves aimed at bringing about a political end to the hostilities before the country was militarily destroyed. According to the postwar testimonies of Foreign Minister Shigemitsu, his predecessor Tōgō, and others, they decided to take the initiative at the end of 1943. Shigemitsu writes that he kept in close touch with Kido to exchange ideas about the best ways of restoring peace. Realizing the need for a core of politically influential men, Shigemitsu proposed that a conference of *jūshin* be held periodically at the Imperial Palace to function as an effective force for peace against the still bellicose military leadership. But it was considered best not to act too rashly and to make plans for peace in secret, looking ahead to Germany's defeat, which would release Japan from the obligations of the Axis pact.[28] Around this time Count Kabayama Aisuke told Kido of a meeting he had had with a group of students who had been repatriated from the United States. They reported that Americans were interested in peace talks and suggested that Japan, too, start thinking about diplomatic steps to bring the war to an end. Kido was impressed, and his diary recorded more meetings of this sort.[29] Former Foreign Minister Tōgō was no less active. According to his memoirs, he contacted several Japanese statesmen toward the end of 1943 to make the point that time was running out on Japan and that they should consider replacing Prime Minister Tōjō in order to prepare for peace. But at this time, Tōgō writes, none of the men he talked with—former prime ministers Konoe Fumimaro and Okada Keisuke, Count

Makino Nobuaki, and Marquis Matsudaira Tsuneo—was ready to strike, either because they did not think the time was opportune or because they felt powerless to challenge the army.[30]

IT IS INTERESTING that the men who began these discussions, however informally or reluctantly, included some of those on the list cited by Hugh Borton as possible candidates for leading Japan back to a more liberal course. Both Borton on one side and Shigemitsu and Tōgō on the other were aware that the best hope for ending the war and dealing a blow to militaristic excesses lay in the former prime ministers and court officials who had easy access to the Imperial Palace. The men around the emperor were considered a potential force for peace and reform, to put an end to the unhappy period of militaristic and authoritarian rule in Japan. Around the time of the Cairo and Teheran conferences, American officials were engaged in another round of intensive discussions about the future of the emperor system in Japan, and men like Ballantine had already expressed the opinion that the emperor could be a force for moderation and reform in a defeated Japan. At that time the question of the emperor had arisen in connection with the issue of war criminals, but several months later the matter assumed importance in the context of a possible termination of hostilities.

At the time of the Cairo Conference, George Kerr, a naval officer with the military intelligence section of the Joint Chiefs, wrote a memorandum suggesting that the Japanese might offer to open peace negotiations before the Americans carried an assault to Japan proper, which could completely destroy the country. The Japanese might justify such a step by rationalizing that it was only a "stage in the evolution of Japan's manifest destiny." They might reason that by losing the war they were laying the groundwork for a continuous struggle in which they could "count upon the awakened race consciousness of the Orient . . . If the Japanese can make their forced withdrawal seem to be a further invasion of Asia by imperial white powers, they can leave behind them the foundation for another effort some time in the future." Moreover, Kerr argued, the Japanese, seeing an essential antagonism between the Anglo-American powers on the one hand and China and Russia on the other, might assume that the former powers would want to "maintain a reasonably strong Japanese nation in the extreme northeast as a counter-balance of power vis-à-vis Russia and China." In other words, the Japanese might try for a peace short of complete destruction by taking advantage of a potential rift among their enemies. Finally, by losing "a new and as yet unprofitable empire" and accepting the Allies' dictates for economic policy, the Japanese might reason that "they would be accepting a tremendous benefit, for without foreign aid the Japanese economy can scarcely hope to avoid a complete post-war breakdown, win or lose, and that the nations of the world are being forced into closer economic cooperation."[31] Kerr recommended that the United States should respond favorably to any Japanese peace feelers. The United States, he asserted, would thereby gain its objective of ejecting Japan from its conquered territories; further destruction of Japan would have no particular value. If Japan were invaded, the Japanese could be expected to resist to the last man, and no government that could negotiate for peace would be functioning.

Kerr's argument favored driving Japanese forces out of their conquered territories without destroying the country's political and economic institutions. The reintegrationist thinking underlying his memorandum also raised the question of preserving existing institutions, and it was here that the issue of the emperor became relevant. Alger Hiss, Hornbeck's assistant, was impressed with Kerr's analysis but disagreed with its conclusions. Hiss insisted on "the importance to our national interests of Japan's being *thoroughly* defeated in the sense that . . . her entire national psychology be radically modified." In particular, he stressed the importance of undertaking "careful evaluation of the real significance of the Imperial concept in Japanese psychology and in the Japanese way of life."[32] Kerr and Hiss shared a perception of "Japanese psychology," but whereas the former sought to shorten the war by taking advantage of this psychology, the latter insisted on "radically modifying" it to eradicate the chances of future wars. The Office of War Information, headed by Elmer Davis, was also interested in Japanese psychology, especially as it related to Japanese soldiers' alleged reluctance to surrender. An OWI memo of December 3 noted that "The Japanese refusal to surrender is not a result of a basic difference in psychology but of a program of careful indoctrination," which included subordination to the imperial symbol and acceptance of the mythologies about the emperor; in any event, what was important was that it would not be necessary to destroy the imperial institution to bring about Japanese surrender. Indeed, such destruction might even strengthen their resistance.[33]

The question of the emperor system was taken up at the last meeting of the territorial subcommittee of the Advisory Committee on Postwar Foreign Policy, held on December 17. (This was the only subcommittee in the political fields that continued to meet after August.) Borton, Williams, and other Japan specialists argued that "the only way in which the surrender would be valid for the Japanese people would be over the signature of the emperor." Therefore, the emperor must be preserved at least until the Japanese surrender. Hamilton Fish Armstrong, echoing the misgivings felt by others that the United States might appear to be exonerating the emperor from the crimes of war and militarism too easily, asked "whether, at some time before Pearl Harbor, the emperor could have used his authority to alter the course of events." Hornbeck replied that the emperor could not have done anything about it, whereupon Armstrong concluded that "the emperor was nothing more than an impotent and dangerous symbol, and he [Armstrong] could see no reason for trying to preserve or use him during the peace negotiations or after the war." Borton, Ballantine, and others, however, insisted that the emperor still had a certain intangible hold upon the Japanese people and that the only way to destroy his prestige was to have him recognize the fact of military defeat. The Japanese, these specialists asserted, were "relatively easy to influence . . . they had already gone through kaleidoscopic changes in the past." Regarding the question of whether the United Nations should "drop bombs on the head of the emperor," they replied that "Japanese morale would be greatly strengthened by a direct attempt to injure the emperor."[34] Nothing specific was decided at this meeting on the emperor question, but the drift of this and other discussions indicated that Japanese and American officials might be, at least partially, coming to terms in groping for the best ways to end the war.

SUCH PRIVATE thoughts of various leaders in Tokyo and Washington were expressed more candidly and with greater specificity in 1944. "The coming year will be Japan's year of disaster," recorded Yabe Teiji, a political science professor at the Tokyo Imperial University and a detailed chronicler of those days, in his diary entry for December 31, 1943.[35] "An important year has arrived. The time has come that will determine history," wrote Kiyosawa Kiyoshi on January 1, 1944.[36]

Five days later, Kido Kōichi penned some private thoughts, summing up his discussions with others who shared his concern. Japan's fate, he wrote, depended on the course of the war in Europe. If Germany should collapse completely by the end of the year, "our nation's very existence will be put in an extremely dangerous situation." If Germany surrendered unconditionally, the enemy would certainly launch a political offensive, looking to the emergence of a Japanese Badoglio, thereby throwing domestic politics into utter chaos. The Japanese must decide on the specific steps to be taken in case of a German surrender. First of all, Kido wrote, Tōjō's cabinet would have to be replaced by one that would end the hostilities and would reflect the wishes of the *jūshin*, who would have to prepare a plan for peace. Echoing the views of Shigemitsu, Tōgō, and others, Kido argued that the peace should enable the Japanese to say in good conscience that, even though they had lost the war, their initial objectives had been achieved. This would be possible if the peace embodied the principle of an Asian-Pacific regional community to replace the conflict and divisiveness within the region that had created conditions for the war.

In the new scheme Japan, China, the United States, Great Britain, and the Soviet Union should constitute a Pacific council to deal with the area's problems and to administer the demilitarized territories and islands that had been occupied by Japan. All other countries except for Manchukuo should become neutral like Switzerland. (Kido was unspecific about the future of Manchuria.) Throughout Asia and the Pacific, economic development and prosperity should be fostered on the principles of "freedom, reciprocity, and equal opportunity." If these ideas were accepted by all parties, the Japanese would be able to say that they had successfully breached the "ABCD encirclement," that is, the isolation and ostracization of Japan by America, Britain, China, and the Dutch East Indies, on which Japan had blamed the outbreak of the Pacific war. Because the Pearl Harbor attack had been an inevitable response to that encirclement, Kido argued, only a bold scheme that kept Japan from being isolated would ensure stable peace. If that scheme were the basis for peace, the Japanese could admit their military weakness, put an end to the war, and concentrate on recovery and strengthening for another century. Finally, Kido wrote that the best way to bring about such a peace would be to seek mediation through the Soviet Union, thus preventing Soviet entry into the war, which would only prolong it. Moreover, Soviet mediation might lead eventually to a close union among Japan, China, and Russia, undermining the hold of the Anglo-American powers in the region. Such an outcome, too, would be evidence that Japan's pan-Asianist crusade had not been totally in vain.[37]

Vague and often contradictory as their ideas were, men like Shigemitsu and Kido were trying to formulate realistic approaches to terminating the hostilities. It is clear that they were hoping to salvage the war from a complete disaster by devising a formula for a symbolic "victory." Conclusion of the war short of unconditional surrender, a peace that recognized the legitimacy of some of Japan's aspirations and achievements in Asia, a postwar settlement that defined Japan's place not as a vanquished and humiliated nation but as a country that had met a temporary setback because of inadequate resources, inept leadership, and infatuation with military power—these were the objectives they sought. In order to attain them, these men recognized that both intensive diplomatic efforts and changes in domestic leadership were needed. It is noteworthy that Kido's only specific agenda was the replacement of the Tōjō cabinet with one more in line with his ideas and strategies.

There was a striking parallel between Kido's views and those being developed by some officials across the Pacific. Kerr's memorandum, for instance, anticipated precisely the same logic, that the Japanese would welcome an early peace as more beneficial to the nation than their "new and as yet unprofitable empire" and that they would justify the conclusion of the war as a temporary setback as "but one stage in the evolution of Japan's manifest destiny." Just as Kido talked of the need to end the war in order to concentrate on "true internal strengthening for another century," Kerr noted that the Japanese saw themselves in a long-range perspective and would seek a successful culmination of their efforts in a hundred years. More important, Kido's vision of postwar regional cooperation contained several principles that had by then been accepted as axiomatic by State Department officials—economic development, equal opportunity, and reciprocity. Kido's concept of five-power cooperation was similar, if not identical, to America's view of Japan reentering "the family of nations" and to the idea of cooperation among all major powers.

There were, of course, significant differences between Kido's and the American officials' conceptions of the peace. If the Japanese government had submitted Kido's outlines as conditions for ending the war, the United States would certainly have taken exception to his silence on Manchuria, which implied that Manchukuo would continue to exist as an independent country. Moreover, Kido's scheme for a five-power administration of the demilitarized Pacific islands would have been unacceptable to President Roosevelt and his naval aides, who were planning to use some of them as American military bases after the war. Public opinion in America would have strenuously opposed a peace that left Japan as one of the five major regional powers.

Nevertheless, the Kido memorandum shows that at the least, this sort of vision might have served as a point of departure for negotiating a truce. Many in both countries might have preferred such a development to continuing their fighting for many more months. In retrospect, what is most striking about the memorandum is that it rather accurately anticipated the thinking and actions of Japan's leaders during the remainder of the war. They did not diverge significantly from Kido's framework, and their agenda for action followed his suggestions.

Asking the Soviet Union to act as mediator was, and remained, the least justifiable point in the whole scheme. Unlike the rest of Kido's conception, it was not oriented toward reintegrationism. The stress on Soviet initiatives instead assumed that Russia could be detached from the Anglo-American powers—Kido in fact referred to the Soviet Union as "Asiatic"—and pitted, along with China and Japan, against the United States and Great Britain. Here again Kerr may have been right in suggesting that the Japanese would try to turn the four powers against one another and to make it appear that their pan-Asianist campaign had successfully diminished Anglo-Saxon power in the East. But the fact remains that such moves ran counter to the overall objective, as Kido stated it, of regaining security and stability through five-power cooperation in Asia and the Pacific. He may have felt that approaching the Soviet Union first would placate, if not silence, those in Japan who would vehemently object to restoration of friendly relations with the United States and Great Britain. Whatever the reason, the internal contradiction in the idea of working for peace with the Anglo-American countries by moving closer to Russia and China remained a serious obstacle to Japanese efforts for a speedy termination of the war.

The fruitlessness of the tactic was clearly revealed in early 1944 when Japan and Russia resumed negotiations on the North Sakhalin question. Prime Minister Tōjō noted on February 2 that it was absolutely essential "to maintain quiet and stability" in the north, and Foreign Minister Shigemitsu expressed the hope that the North Sakhalin talks would pave the way for negotiations of other issues between the two countries (such as the fishery and the Manchukuo-Russia border disputes), and for reconfirmation of the neutrality treaty. By then, of course, Stalin had expressed to the Allies his country's determination to enter the Asian war, and he must have been confident that the Soviet Union would regain the whole of Sakhalin as a result. Japan's offer to restore oil, coal, and other concessions in North Sakhalin in full to Russia, therefore, was not something the Soviet government would feel grateful for. The Russians did agree to a five-year extension of the fishery convention with Japan, but when the latter proposed a new treaty of commerce, or at least an agreement for exchange of goods— Japan's sugar, tea, salt, tin, and rubber for Russia's copper, manganese, and other minerals—they showed not the slightest interest. Nothing came of the proposal, and the upshot was that Japan gave up all its concessions and installations in North Sakhalin in return for a payment of five million rubles, but without obtaining any further expression of Soviet goodwill.[38]

The Kido memorandum referred to the possibility of establishing close ties between Japan and China. In justifying the talks with the Soviet Union on the Sakhalin issue, Shigemitsu remarked that they might have favorable repercussions in China, especially among the Communists, who might soften their hostility to Japan. To ensure Soviet neutrality and, if at all possible, amity, the Japanese now considered it necessary to end the extreme antagonism between Japanese forces and the Chinese Communist movement. This emphasis on the Communists reflected Japan's sense of desperation that none of its policies and approaches in China had worked.

The new China policy enunciated in late 1943, proposing sweeping changes in Japan's position on the continent, had not even been tried, but Tokyo's leaders judged that the Nanking regime under Wang Ching-wei, which was visibly losing morale, was almost beyond redemption, with Wang himself ill and unable to conduct governmental affairs. The Chungking regime appeared more vulnerable than ever to attacks by Communists and other dissidents. For these reasons Japanese strategy toward China during the first half of 1944 was to isolate the Kuomintang leadership by various means, including launching a massive military campaign to destroy the airfields under Nationalist control that United States forces had begun to utilize. The campaign, called the *Ichigō* (number one) operation, was formally adopted on January 24. It called for the destruction of "the enemy air forces' principal bases in southwestern China" by means of assaults from north and south China in late spring and summer. Lands along the major railway arteries from Peking to Hankow and to Canton would be seized, and Nationalist strongholds would be demolished. Concurrently, Japanese forces in China would tone down their anti-Communist slogans, instead referring to the Communists as "the Yenan regime." Communist guerrillas who were to be destroyed would be called "bandits," and the Japanese army would stop describing such campaigns as anti-Communist extermination operations. Other factions, including warlords and those under Chungking's only nominal control, would be dealt with skillfully so as to alienate them from the Nationalist leaders. In order to tie all these tactical moves together, the Japanese government on July 3 asserted that the military operation in China was aimed at the destruction of Anglo-American ambitions, not against the Chinese people or even the Chinese soldiers. The people were invited to reject cooperation with America and Britain and to cooperate with Japan in a new relationship of permanent friendship based on the principle of independence.[39]

In contrast to the fruitless maneuvering toward Russia, there was some success in China, at least on the battlefield; Japanese forces were able to capture several key bases in China by July, including the airfields at Changsha and Hengyang. Much of north and central China fell to them, as guerrillas retreated and Nationalist armies in direct contact with the Japanese collapsed. However, such reverses would have induced the Chinese to reconsider their resistance to Japan only if they had been persuaded that the determination of America, Britain, and Russia to punish Japan was also weakening. That, of course, was not the case. Precisely when the Japanese were concentrating on Russia and China, their "absolute defense perimeter" in the Pacific Ocean was being breached by the American offensive. First the Marshall Islands fell at the beginning of 1944, followed by landings on Truk, Saipan, and other islands inside the perimeter. It appeared only a matter of time until the United States would control the western Pacific, leading to the blockading and bombing of Japan proper. To cope with these developments, Japan's leaders recognized that air power must have top priority. In 1944, however, only 28,000 new aircraft were produced, and it was estimated that at least 52,000 would be needed to defend what was left of the empire as well as the home islands.[40]

It was against this background that another part of Kido's agenda was steadily being prepared for: a change in Japan's political leadership to remove the obstacles to terminating the war. Tōjō's leadership would have come into question under any circumstances because of the frustrations of the war, but he compounded his own vulnerability when he named himself army chief of staff in February. The idea, obviously, was to concentrate in his hands authority over strategic and operational decisions, in addition to governmental and economic affairs. That step inevitably meant that military reverses would be blamed on him. The loss of the Marianas, especially Saipan (in July), was catastrophic not only because the island lay clearly within the defense perimeter but also because the enemy would now be able to fly bombing missions to Japan from the Pacific Ocean, not just from China.

Although the first air raids by the new B-29 bombers did not happen until November, Japanese leaders did not conceal their concern that the war was entering its final stages. Maneuvers to remove Tōjō from office became bolder and more open. The group of Kido, Shigemitsu, Tōgō, and a few others who were sworn to secrecy were joined after June by many others, even including the military. Within both the army and the navy, staff officers were admitting that the war had been irreparably lost, and that preparations should begin to bring it to conclusion. Some officers conferred with one another and with civilian leaders, such as Konoe and Kido, and agreed that the most urgent need was to organize a coalition of anti-Tōjō generals, admirals, and civilians to force his resignation. Lieutenant General Sakai Kōji of the General Staff told Konoe in late June that the General Staff wanted the cabinet replaced and guidelines set up for a peace negotiation. Prince Konoe, on whom some American officials were pinning hope for persuading Japan to end the war, also believed it was necessary to remove Tōjō as prime minister. The new cabinet should be headed preferably by an imperial prince who would immediately declare an end to hostilities. However, Konoe thought such a sudden end of the war might cause a strong and sensational reaction among the military and the people, so it might be prudent to first organize an interim regime headed by a die-hard, pro-war leader. The interim government could mobilize the fleet for one last struggle against the enemy, to demonstrate that it was doing all it could to prosecute the war, and then, as soon as defeat became apparent, offer to end all hostilities.[41]

Marquis Kido, in the meantime, was meeting with civilian leaders such as Foreign Minister Shigemitsu, Prince Takamatsu (a younger brother of the emperor), and several *jūshin*. They feared that prolongation of the deteriorating war would not only cause further disaster to the homeland but would create domestic turmoil and even a revolutionary situation, undermining the social fabric and the emperor system. To prevent such a calamity, the time seemed at hand for replacing the Tōjō ministry. The cabinet was becoming so unpopular that a small-scale reshuffling of its personnel did not appear sufficient. Rather, the government would have to be drastically reorganized and Tōjō persuaded to resign immediately. If he refused, he might have to be forced out of office through a coup, but Kido and others considered this unwise because it would implicate those close to the throne, and even the emperor himself, in political machinations. No matter what happened, these men were determined to protect the imperial institution. That, they were convinced, was the best guarantee of future national unity even if Japan should meet with military defeat.[42]

Tōjō was well aware of these moves and tried to prolong his political life by resigning as chief of staff and by changing some personnel in the cabinet. But Kido and others, sensing Tōjō's desperate situation, stood adamant. On July 18, when the supreme headquarters announced the fall of Saipan, Kiyosawa noted in his diary that it was rather unusual for the military to admit a defeat candidly. Tōjō himself expressed his regrets over the disaster and moments later resigned as prime minister.[43]

This was not to be the end of the Japanese-American war, although a handful of people insisted that the country should take advantage of Tōjō's resignation and immediately prepare for peace. Men like Hosokawa Morisada, Konoe's son-in-law and private secretary, called for the formation of "a cabinet willing to accept an unconditional surrender, insisting only on the retention of the emperor system."[44] But most of the senior statesmen felt this was moving a bit too fast. They sensed the need for an interim cabinet to continue the war a little longer; when it failed to improve the military situation, they would decide on a peace cabinet.

In retrospect, it is obvious that by such hesitation and indecisiveness the Japanese leaders prolonged the war by one year. But they were preoccupied with placating military and civilian fanatics and ensuring domestic stability in the event of a surrender, and they judged that too abrupt a halt in fighting, followed by a humiliating defeat, would not serve their purpose. The outlines of their thoughts are evident in the record of a five-hour meeting of the *jūshin*, held in the Palace, on the day of Tōjō's resignation. None of them was willing to advocate an immediate cessation of hostilities. They all knew the war would have to be terminated sooner or later but felt that conditions were not yet ripe for establishing a peace cabinet. Only former prime minister Hirota Kōki advocated a new cabinet headed by an imperial prince, presumably to end the war. The others present felt this should be reserved as a last resort and that in the meantime an interim government headed by a military person should make one last attempt to improve the military situation. That would make it easier for the armed forces and the people to accept a cease-fire as something other than a humiliating surrender. Prince Konoe echoed the sentiment of the *jūshin* when he said that he feared "a leftist revolution more than defeat in the war, since we can preserve and maintain the imperial household and the emperor system after defeat, but not after a revolution." He was deeply concerned by the spread of radicalism among the ranks of the armed forces and within the bureaucracy. He repeated his argument that the best way to prevent domestic turmoil was to appoint an army general as the new prime minister. Yonai Mitsumasa, Hiranuma Kiichirō, Wakatsuki Reijirō, and other former prime ministers agreed, and they proceeded to discuss possible candidates. Several army generals were mentioned, and the conferees narrowed them down to three: Generals Terauchi Juichi, their first choice, commander in chief of the expeditionary force in Southeast Asia; Koiso Kuniaki, governor general of Korea; and Hata Shunroku, who commanded the expeditionary force in China. Some other full generals were considered less desirable from the point of view of army discipline; they were less in touch with the field officers and rank-and-file soldiers, and therefore the appointment of one of them as prime minister might create difficulties within the army and encourage leftist movements.[45]

After the meeting of the *jūshin*, Kido went to the emperor to obtain his approval of the proposed nominees. The emperor consulted Tōjō, who strongly opposed Terauchi's appointment, saying that he was still needed in Southeast Asia and that his withdrawal to Tokyo would adversely affect morale, giving the armed forces the impression that politics took precedence over military command. The emperor then named Koiso. At the same time, on the insistence of Konoe, Hirota, and others that the next cabinet be a united national government, the emperor summoned retired Admiral Yonai to the Palace along with Koiso and commanded them to organize a new cabinet. The new Koiso-Yonai cabinet was inaugurated on July 22.[46]

As they launched their regime, Koiso and Yonai were exhorted by the emperor to "observe the articles of the constitution" and to "avoid provoking the Soviet Union as the nation carried on the war." Koiso took this cryptic command to mean that the emperor wanted the government to carry on the war as effectively as possible and then at some point to prepare the groundwork for peace. Although, as governor general of Korea, he had been out of touch with strategic and operational decisions made in Tokyo, he had already come to the view that the war should be ended before the country was totally devastated. He thought that Japan should have offered to negotiate a truce when Guadalcanal was lost. The fall of Saipan had impressed him as the decisive event of the war, a point of no return. He had even telegraphed Tōjō that governing Korea would then become extremely difficult. Despite these beliefs, however, Koiso thought the first priority was to achieve a clear victory on the battlefield. If that could be accomplished, it would be easier to initiate steps toward a peace negotiation. Admiral Yonai agreed, although, according to Koiso's memoirs, Yonai was more explicit that actual peace negotiations should be handled by the next cabinet, that the Koiso-Yonai ministery was merely transitional.[47] In any event, both of them considered the impending battle in the Philippines of crucial importance. If Japan won even one engagement in the battle, it could then prepare for a truce arrangement.

Although in the past prime ministers had been excluded from strategic and operational planning, Koiso considered it imperative, given the extraordinary conditions of wartime government, that he be authorized to participate in deliberations by the supreme command. This request was rejected out of hand by the military as unorthodox and as compromising the integrity of the supreme command. They were technically right, and Koiso's request may have violated the emperor's wish that he abide by the constitution. But the military leaders shared Koiso's sense of urgency and were willing to share power to the extent of replacing the cabinet–supreme headquarters liaison conference with a new supreme war council. Representatives from the civilian and military branches had used the liaison conference to discuss matters of importance, but its status was rather ambiguous and it had not affected military autonomy. The supreme war council, on the other hand, was to consist of the prime minister, the ministers of foreign affairs, war, and the navy, and the chiefs of staff of army and navy. These six, plus some military staff officers, would sit in the presence of the emperor to determine important policy matters. Unlike the liaison conference, the new council was authorized to be convened without staff personnel from the service ministries or supreme headquarters. At least in theory, these six leaders sitting together with the emperor would have ultimate power. In retrospect, the supreme war council did much to facilitate decision making, although as earlier, the chiefs of staff continued to guard their secrets so that the prime minister and his civilian colleagues remained ignorant of crucial military developments.[48]

Despite these institutional innovations and Koiso's serious determination to work for an eventual peace and despite the senior statesmen's increasing frankness about ending the hopeless war, nothing new was in fact undertaken by the Koiso-Yonai ministry.

The leaders persisted in viewing Japanese policy and strategy much as their predecessors had done, instead of trying new approaches. The result was a further waste of time, while hundreds of thousands were perishing in the cause of a clearly losing battle.

On August 19 the supreme war council held its first meeting, which could have been the occasion for adopting a decisive policy of preparing for peace. Here was an opportunity to revise the decisions and guidelines adopted at the September 30, 1943, meeting of the liaison conference in the presence of the emperor. Since that time much had happened to make obsolete most of those assumptions and strategies. Not only had the "absolute defense perimeter" been breached, but the Ministry of Munitions (established in November) had just reported that the available shipping was one-third of what had been visualized at the beginning of the war and was continuing to diminish in volume. Japan's "material power" was declining because of this drastic reduction in transportation facilities, the exhaustion of goods in stock, and the difficulty of forcing further savings in civilian consumption. If shipping from the south seas were totally severed, the report warned, deterioration in national strength would accelerate, and "the prosecution of the war will be seriously affected." There were shortages in almost all consumer items, including food, clothing, and medicine. All indications pointed to a real crisis in 1945 even if the enemy did not step up bombing. The only consolation was that the population was apparently continuing to increase, because the birth rate had not declined. There was plenty of female labor available. Even so, the report admitted that the physical strength of the Japanese people was steadily declining.[49]

Given such candidly pessimistic estimates, the supreme war council might have discussed some specific ways for terminating the war. Instead, the leaders adopted merely makeshift devices, apparently believing that it was not yet time for bold action. They wanted first to give the armed forces another chance to wage a counterattack. The newly appointed war minister, former chief of staff Sugiyama Gen, and the navy minister, Yonai, both insisted that the country's total resources be mobilized to prepare for the impending battle in the Pacific closer to home, in particular the Philippines. By combating the enemy far from the American continent and by dealing a decisive blow to United Nations forces, the

Japanese army and navy would be able to frustrate their ambitious strategy, exhaust their manpower, and impress them with Japan's determination to achieve its initial objectives.

If "achieving Japan's initial objectives" meant what Kido, Shigemitsu, and other civilians believed, that is, ending the "encirclement" of Japan and returning to reintegrationism, the strategy might have made some sense. Mobilizing the nation's resources to wage a do-or-die battle might prove to be a catalyst, making it easier for the Japanese to accept defeat in the name of those objectives. On the surface, that was not what came out of the August 19 meeting. Instead, they adopted a new set of notably unrealistic "guidelines for conducting the war from now on." It called for "destroying the main force of the United States" in the Pacific, preserving control over "important regions in the south," securing the lanes of oceanic communication, maintaining the status quo in the Indian Ocean, and frustrating the enemy's use of China as a base for bombing missions over Japan. It is not clear how attainable the council members considered these goals. They may have been stated for the record, to bolster national morale. As Koiso remarked, aiming at a quick victory in the latter part of 1944 would unify the country and prevent unnecessary domestic confusion even if it did not work. The new chief of staff, Umezu Yoshijirō, agreed, saying that the impending decisive battle might not result in total victory, but at least it would demonstrate Japan's seriousness of purpose. In all such expressions it is possible to detect the feeling that the end of the war was approaching. But the supreme war council failed to link that feeling to a specific and comprehensive policy for winding down and concluding the war.[50]

One reason for this failure was the continued faith in diplomatic efforts as an important complement to actual fighting. Although nearly all such efforts had proved fruitless, the idea persisted that the military situation could be improved by timely and appropriate approaches toward Russia, China, and other Asian countries. That the emperor himself was giving top priority to the Russian issue was revealed when he commanded Koiso to "avoid provoking the Soviet Union." The August 19 "guidelines" likewise stated that Japan should never be put in the position of having to fight that country. One way to ensure this, it was thought, was to continue trying to bring about a separate ceasefire between Germany and

Russia, even though that was even less likely to happen than before. Ambassador Ōshima in Berlin saw Foreign Minister Joachim von Ribbentrop the day after the formation of the Koiso cabinet and found out that the Germans still opposed a separate peace with the Soviet Union. As Ōshima reported to Shigemitsu, who was retained as foreign minister in the Koiso cabinet, the successful United Nations landing at Normandy had forced the Germans to deploy more divisions eastward to stabilize conditions at the Soviet front, so the fighting between the two countries was not likely to end.[51] The failure of General Ludwig Beck's assassination plot on Hitler's life on July 20 put off any possibility of peace moves for the time being, and the Japanese government was forced to recognize that with Hitler's authority unshaken, Germany would continue to fight Russia as well as the Anglo-American nations.

More important for the Koiso cabinet was the strategy of "utilizing the Soviet Union to improve the situation," as the "guidelines" put it. Although that strategy had gotten nowhere, the Japanese leaders were more than ever determined to try. Why did they do so, when they had been frustrated time and again in their attempt to maintain Soviet goodwill or at least neutrality? One important factor appears to have been power-political reasoning. To bring the war to a close, it was necessary to prevent Soviet participation. The Russians would desist from joining the Anglo-American countries in the Asian war if it was in their interest to do so, and if they could be persuaded that their participation would benefit only the United States and Great Britain. In fact the Japanese thought that the Russians and the Anglo-Americans were beginning to show their mutual antagonism openly and to be pursuing contradictory ambitions. As the supreme war council's memorandum noted, the United States was "trying to establish world hegemony," Britain was "seeking to maintain its prewar status," while the Soviet Union was "continuing its policy of global communization," concentrating on expanding its influence in the Balkans, southwestern Asia, and the Mediterranean. Under the circumstances, conflict between the two sides seemed inevitable. Foreign Minister Shigemitsu agreed with the analysis. It would be to Japan's advantage, he said, to encourage such a conflict; "it is to be hoped that Soviet penetration of Europe will take place at the expense not of Germany but of Britain and America." Intensified antagonism between the Soviet

Union and the Anglo-American powers in Europe, according to Japanese calculations, would keep Russia from paying close attention to Asian affairs and make it less attractive for the Russians to enter the war against Japan. The Japanese should encourage that trend in Soviet behavior by stepping up their overtures toward Moscow. With this in mind, the foreign minister instructed Morishima Gorō, minister at the Moscow embassy, to report to Tokyo in late August for further instructions.[52]

Here was an instance where calculations of power politics impelled the Japanese government to pursue a course of action that had no other effect than to prolong the agony of war. It might be argued that given their perception of growing antagonism between the two camps—by no means inaccurate—the Japanese leaders would certainly play one side against the other; moreover, it would have been unthinkable to justify siding with the United States and Britain, actual enemies, against the Soviet Union, a neutral. All the considerations about the domestic repercussions of taking decisive steps to end the hostilities would have restrained them from so bold a policy. An abrupt shift of diplomatic efforts from the Soviet Union to the United States and Britain might have caused a profound shock among the armed services and the people who had been fed the daily diet of anti-Anglo-Saxon pan-Asianism. Shigemitsu himself repeated the slogans of "Asian liberation" and "Asian resurrection" at the August 19 meeting of the supreme war council. With such an ideological emphasis, it would have been difficult to abandon the policy of approaching Russia first, for turning to the Americans and British would have been tantamount to seeking reconciliation with them. Tokyo's leaders judged that the time was not opportune for such a drastic step.

Nevertheless, these leaders frequently expressed their fear of a left-wing revolutionary uprising if the war was too prolonged. Those who advocated a renewed approach to Moscow were staunch supporters of the emperor system and the national polity, with little ideological affinity with communism. Moreover, even as he talked of "Asian liberation," Shigemitsu was reiterating Japan's basic war aims, which according to him remained "the establishment of the relationship of neighborly friendship throughout the world under the principles of equality and mutuality; economic cooperation and the open door; cultural progress and interchange."

Such concepts, already enunciated in 1943, remained the government's guiding ideas. They were little different from those emanating from Washington. Whether they were aware of this degree of ideological affinity with America and Britain or not, Shigemitsu and his colleagues did not recognize the futility of courting the Soviet Union.

It may be, as Koiso reminisced after the war, that he planned to utilize the Soviet contact to prepare for eventual peace negotiations. Since the Japanese embassy in Moscow was still operating, it provided a place where contact might be established with diplomats of the United States and Great Britain.[53] The view that Moscow would be the best place to initiate peace overtures and discussions remained strong throughout the rest of the war, even though such a strategy contradicted the perception of basic hostility between Russia and the Anglo-American powers. If their antagonism was as persistent as the Japanese believed, it would have made more sense to contact American and British diplomats elsewhere than on Russian territory. In all these instances of Japanese miscalculation underlying the continued emphasis on the Russian connection, they failed to think through the implications of what they were doing. Although committed to eventually bringing the disastrous war to a close, Tokyo's leaders were dedicated to a wrong strategy that was justified neither on ideological nor on tactical grounds.

While the Japanese were groping for ways to end the war and minimize risks at home, the United States government and military were proceeding with plans to defeat Japan. In contrast to the persistent Japanese attempts to divide Russia from America and Britain, American planning during the first half of 1944 was destined to frustrate such an effort.

For one thing, United States strategy was placing more emphasis on the offensive in the Pacific and less on the idea of joint operations with other powers. As late as May 1944, the joint staff planners were commenting that there was no definite policy on "British participation with large forces in the major operations against Japan from the east," or on the degree to which Chinese forces would become involved in the final war effort. Moreover, it was far from clear specifically when and how the United States and the Soviet Union would collaborate against Japan.[54] It seemed safest to assume that the United States would continue to play the most important role in the defeat of Japan, thus not only reconfirming America's unilateral initiatives in the war, but also minimizing chances of friction with Britain in Southeast Asia and, equally important, with the Soviet Union in Northeast Asia.

Regarding American-British collaboration, the joint strategic survey committee considered that "while developments have considerably altered the original strategic concept, it is still the part of logic and sound strategy that the British make the advance from the Southwest, and the United States advance from the East and Southeast." But the joint staff planners commented that "we are in the fortunate position of being able to execute these [strategic] plans without [British] assistance. We can therefore endeavor to limit British participation if that policy is desirable for other than military reasons."[55] This last sentence referred to the ongoing debate on the future of the European colonies in Asia, in particular French Indochina. Toward the end of 1943 Lord Louis Mountbatten, commander of the Southeast Asia Command, had obtained Chiang Kai-shek's endorsement of the idea that British forces would invade Indochina from the south, and Chinese troops from the north, in effect dividing the region into two spheres of operation. With the Allied invasion of France scheduled for midyear, it was quite possible that Britain would be able to release more ships and manpower for use in Asia. Moreover, a restored France would certainly insist on a role in the liberation of its Indochinese colony. Already in early April the British chiefs of staff decided to allow a French military mission to be attached to Mountbatten's headquarters. The whole of Southeast Asia seemed to be turning into a British-French theater of war, away from the earlier scheme of collaboration among the Allies, especially Americans and Chinese. The United States could presumably try "to limit British participation" in the theater, but such a plan was of less and less interest to officials in Washington, whose eyes were set on a unilateral Pacific strategy.

Similarly, the value of China was diminishing in the United States strategy against Japan. As the joint staff planners put it, "our plans are indicating a progressively decreasing importance of China, once Formosa is secured." (It should be pointed out that the liberation of Taiwan was considered more part of the Pacific strategy than of campaigns in China.) The question therefore arose, as the planners put it, "What is the minimum we have to do for China from other than military considerations?" The joint strategic survey committee answered the query by stating, "The basic idea should be to at least endeavor to prevent internal collapse of the government, with ensuing chaos on the China mainland."[56] This was an apt summary of the developing views that China's role in the war would be a passive one and that involvement of massive United States forces on the continent would not be necessary. The most that was envisaged was a landing on the southeast coast of China to cut off lines of communication with Japan proper. China's value was primarily as a base for air attacks on Japan, and even that value diminished during 1944. Ultimately, however, the most crucial thing was "to prevent internal collapse of the government." President Roosevelt's efforts to do so in the summer did little to alter the diminishing of China's overall strategic importance in the Japanese-American war.

Regarding the Soviet Union, the joint intelligence committee estimated in January that "about six months must elapse after the defeat of Germany before the USSR can feel reasonably certain of its ability to resist a Japanese attack in the Far East . . . [and] another six months would be required before an all-out offensive could be mounted with sufficient strength and reserve to enable Soviet forces to effect deep penetrations into presently held Japanese occupied territory."[57] In other words, it would be a year after Germany's surrender before Russian entry into the Japanese war could be expected, but this did not deter the joint war plans committee from recommending that plans be prepared "for combined operation in the Northwest Pacific." Accordingly, in February General John Deane, military attaché in Moscow, was instructed to find out from the Russians the number and size of airfields in Vladivostok, as well as the amounts of gasoline, oil, and bombs, that would be available to United States air forces. There was no immediate answer to these questions, but in June Stalin told Ambassador Averell Harriman that twelve airfields in eastern Siberia were suitable for heavy bombers and that Americans could use six or seven of them.[58]

Beyond that information, the United States was not able to obtain much from Russia at this time, and American and Soviet officers did not work out a joint strategy. Thus the situation in 1944, despite Stalin's promise at Teheran that Russia would enter the war against Japan, had not changed; American-Soviet collaboration would be very limited, involving the use of American air power but no ground forces in Siberia. As the joint chiefs of staff advised General Deane in early July, "We do not contemplate the use of ground combat forces in Siberia, except perhaps some anti-aircraft, since it appears that all of the ground forces available will be required to carry out our operations in the Pacific."[59]

As this last sentence indicated, the United States' basic strategic concept in 1944 was still a major and mostly unilateral offensive in the Pacific, although there was often acrimonious debate among American officials about the shape such an offensive should take. For instance, when Admiral E. J. King, chief of naval operations, met with General Douglas MacArthur and other field commanders at Pearl Harbor in January, the latter seriously questioned King's advocacy of a central Pacific strategy focused on capturing the Marianas as the next major target. King planned to use the Marianas as a base for B-29 bombers to fly over Japan and return without refueling and as a stepping-stone for an advance westward to Luzon and beyond, including Taiwan. Such an approach, however, would give weight to naval and air power and would bypass much of the southwestern Pacific. MacArthur and other commanders fiercely opposed King's ideas, urging instead a southwestern strategy, with campaigns in New Guinea, Celebes, and Mindanao on the way to reconquering the entire Philippines. The best way to frustrate the Japanese, they insisted, was to disrupt their seaborne traffic, especially in petroleum, which could be done through a concerted southwestern offensive. The Joint Chiefs of Staff's office discussed the matter throughout the spring and in the end decided on a simultaneous advance toward the Marianas and toward New Guinea and Celebes, with the ultimate destination in both instances of Luzon Island. The first approach bore more spectacular results in mid-1944, as Saipan was captured and turned immediately into an air base for "very long range" bombing missions over Japan.[60]

On July 11 the joint chiefs of staff drew up a revised plan for a final assault on Japan to bring about its surrender, calling for "concurrent advances through the Ryukyus, Bonins, and southeast China coast" preliminary to an amphibious attack on the island of Kyushu and, ultimately, "a decisive stroke against the industrial heart of Japan by means of an amphibious attack through the Tokyo plain assisted by continued pressure from Kyushu." The Bonins and Ryukyus were to be invaded between April 1 and June 30, 1945, and Kyushu on October 1. The final assault on Tokyo would come at the end of December.[61] Given the series of successes in the Pacific Ocean and the likelihood that there would be more throughout 1944, and given the decision to concentrate on advances across the Pacific, it could be argued that this timetable was extremely cautious and conservative. American strategists might have visualized landing on Japan's home islands in late 1944 rather than 1945, but they assumed that it would take one full year after Germany's defeat—scheduled for the end of 1944—to bring Japan to its knees. Because the United States would be fighting virtually alone in the Pacific, unlike the situation in the European theater of war, it would take longer to defeat Japan than Germany.

Thus strategic planning in 1944 reinforced America's unilateral initiatives against Japan. It was much less of a coalition war than in Europe. The United States, Britain, China, and presumably the Soviet Union would all fight Japan, but more individually than collectively. The absence of close coordination with the other Allies, coupled with the overwhelming role of the United States military in the Pacific, had important implications for the course of the war and for the shape of the peace. On the one hand, it helped avoid serious disputes among the Allies, but on the other, it meant that each power would pursue its own objectives in the peace settlement. Above all, it allowed the United States government to feel justified in acting assertively and unilaterally in some areas of the Asia-Pacific region. In doing so, it did encounter resistance from the other countries, as events throughout 1944 showed. Nevertheless, the trend was toward avoidance of trouble with America's actual and potential allies.

Not only would the United States play the leading role in the Pacific strategy to defeat Japan, but it would also take the lead in defining the postwar disposition of the vast ocean. By the beginning of 1944 President Roosevelt had accepted as axiomatic the military view that the United States would have to be the major stabilizer of the region after the war, which made it necessary and desirable to control some bases and islands in the Pacific. The only unresolved question was the mode of such control. The United States navy had not given up the hope of establishing outright sovereignty over some of Japan's former mandates and other islands. The State Department, on the other hand, had been loath to give the impression of United States imperialism in acquiring territory after victory. Its committee on colonial problems, established in the fall of 1943, changed its name to the committee on colonial and trusteeship problems in January 1944, and to the committee on dependent areas in March. It was here that the future of the Pacific islands was discussed. A subcommittee on the Japanese mandates reported in late May that the United States should adopt a policy "favoring an international status for these islands under the general international organization foreseen in the Moscow Declaration, with due provision for establishing upon them bases to maintain international security." The committee on dependent areas accepted this suggestion and in early June adopted a draft statement affirming that "military occupation does not give legal title to the United States [over the islands], that the islands have an international status, and that their future will be determined after the war."[62]

The State Department proceeded to make specific plans for trusteeship arrangements in the Pacific, but the military tried to delay such proceedings as much as possible and insisted on having freedom of action at least until the war was concluded. On July 4 the joint chiefs wrote to President Roosevelt to argue, once again, for United States sovereignty.[63] In response, the president told them that they "must . . . realize that we have agreed that we are seeking no additional territory as a result of this war." He assured them that there would be some scheme whereby the United Nations would ask the United States to act as the sole trustee for the Japanese mandated islands. Although that would not give America sovereignty over or ownership of the islands, the nation would be permitted to establish fortifications.[64] Roosevelt did not support the State Department's efforts to make specific plans for trusteeships and did not find it necessary to go beyond those guidelines at that time.

Despite such internal disagreement, all agreed that the United States should, in one way or another, have a decisive say in Pacific affairs after the war. Thus civilian as well as military officials responded quickly and adamantly when Australia and New Zealand issued a joint declaration in January 1944, asserting their right to

be heard concerning the disposition of Japanese territorial possessions in the Pacific and calling on the powers to apply the trusteeship
principle throughout the ocean. In addition, the two countries
would establish a south seas regional commission for the maintenance of their mutual security. The declaration, dubbed by American officials "the Australia-New Zealand 'Monroe Doctrine,'"
threatened American prerogatives and unilateral initiatives. Predictably, American officials seized the occasion to reaffirm their
position. Five days after the declaration, Assistant Secretary of State
A. A. Berle wrote that under the scheme the Australians and New
Zealanders could veto American plans to acquire air bases for defense of the Pacific and would limit American influence to areas
east of Wake Island, thus excluding the Philippines, Guam, the
Caroline Islands, the Marshalls, and others. Berle recommended
that the United States "promptly enter into discussion with the
Australian and New Zealand Governments indicating the general
lines of our interest, and arranging for clarification or delimitation
of the territorial clauses of this agreement in such fashion as will
permit the recognition of American interests and claims." He also
considered it imperative that the joint chiefs of staff state more
clearly than in the past "the military interests which we may wish
to safeguard in this area."[65] That a high State Department official,
usually aggressively committed to anti-imperialism, should have
spoken out so vigorously indicates the consensus within the government that the United States should have the leading voice in postwar Pacific affairs.

This did not mean that the idea of international cooperation
was losing its appeal; officials in Washington assumed that American
predominance in the Pacific was compatible with, indeed a guarantee
of, such cooperation. By becoming the major stabilizer in Pacific
affairs, the United States would be doing its share to ensure postwar
peace and stability in the world. Moreover, applying internationalist
principles would allow the region to enjoy both security and well-
being. It would become part of an international order in which
economic development and welfare would be promoted while the
great powers assumed responsibility for the maintenance of peace.
American leadership and initiative were seen as in no way incompatible with international cooperation.

A good example of this type of perception was a March 29

memorandum drafted by the State Department's policy committee, which along with a new postwar programs committee was created in January to replace the earlier committees and subcommittees on postwar foreign policy, most of which had been suspended in mid-1943. The newly organized committees were headed by Secretary Cordell Hull, with Under Secretary Edward Stettinius as vice chairman. Their involvement showed that the State Department was determined to play a crucial role in peacemaking and that its internationalist orientation would be tested, now that the end of the war appeared close. The memorandum, entitled, "War and peace aims of the United States," defined those aims as ensuring "peace and security in the future" and bringing about "betterment of economic and social conditions." These ideas had, of course, been reiterated time and again, most recently during the Quebec Conference. But they had become more specific now that they had a good chance of being implemented in the near future. The memorandum defined the means through which security and economic betterment were to be obtained:

> (1) maintenance of armed forces of our own adequate for our protection, creation of a worldwide security system and a general international organization . . .
>
> (2) establishment of conditions conducive to security and peace throughout the world, including (a) application of measures to control the present aggressor nations, (b) avoidance of post-war territorial settlements that would recognize changes brought about by the use of force or that would fail to accord with the wishes of the affected populations, (c) free choice by the peoples of the liberated countries, both enemy and Allied, of post-war governments, if not Fascist, Nazi or warlord in character, and (d) respect by all nations for the rights of others;
>
> (3) adoption of international standards and arrangements for the development of dependent areas in the interests both of the dependent peoples themselves and of the world as a whole;
>
> (4) collaboration between nations directed toward general economic advancement.[66]

This was a powerful reaffirmation of reintegrationism, of a Wilsonian world order in which peace and security would depend on, and be interchangeable with, economic development and political stability. America's own role, clearly, was to maintain military power and a security arrangement such as was being visualized for the Pacific region. It would also have to take a lead in expanding global economic activities to contribute to development and prosperity. As a special committee on "relaxation of trade barriers" noted, it was absolutely imperative after the war to support "vigorous trade expansion policies" as a prerequisite for effective economic cooperation, which in turn was necessary for world stability and peace. On the basis of studies by this and other groups, the postwar programs committee drew up a memorandum in March on "postwar commercial policy of the United States," which asserted that "in order to maximize the prospects of success, measures for the relaxation of trade barriers and the establishment of liberal commercial policies should be concerted and comprehensive." Protectionist tariffs and import quotas should be removed, as well as export restrictions, government subsidies, and other restraints on a liberal flow of goods and capital. To ensure cooperation among various countries, it was imperative to work out "a general multilateral convention on commercial policy."[67] The international conference at Bretton Woods, New Hampshire, in July, was one dramatic demonstration of America's determination to take the lead in establishing a multilateral economic order after the war.

Such a vision enabled officials in Washington to justify their insistence on America's dominant position in the Pacific, not only to police the ocean to prevent future aggressions, but also to make sure that the region became economically linked with the rest of the world. Networks of trade, shipping, and aviation would be established, and the United States and other advanced countries would seek to promote the economic well-being of less developed countries. For roughly the same reason, American officials were willing to let the European nations make arrangements for the future of the colonial areas, so long as they were within the broad framework of multilateralism and international cooperation. Just as American power and influence would predominate in the Pacific without undermining the framework of cooperation, so in Southeast Asia the European colonial powers would play a role after the war as part of a developing world order.

Throughout 1944 the State Department's committee on dependent areas gave much thought to the colonial region of Asia and tried to work out a scheme for a regional commission consisting of the United States, China, Britain, and the Netherlands; later Portugal, France, and Australia were added. This tentative scheme revealed that America's primary interest was in ensuring cooperation among the colonial powers, not in espousing indigenous causes for immediate autonomy or independence.[68] The stress on regional cooperation rather than colonial independence confirmed the policies of 1943 which, as seen earlier, had come to accept the return of the European colonial powers to Asia.

The course of fighting in 1944 accentuated the trend. British, French, and other European forces were expected to send fresh reinforcements to Southeast Asia, whereas United States strategy called for a reduced role for American armed forces, which certainly would not be used to prevent the return of European colonial regimes. Already in February the State Department was endorsing the idea that the Dutch East Indies be restored to its former masters. American forces under General MacArthur were to occupy the islands after the Japanese had been expelled, but the administration of the territory would be turned over to Dutch officials as soon as the military situation permitted. United States forces would be withdrawn, leaving security matters to collaboration by the major powers involved.[69]

Regarding the British and French colonies in Asia, American involvement was being similarly reduced. To be sure, officials expressed concern, as British troops began to gain an upper hand in Burma and points east in 1944, that the Southeast Asia Command under Mountbatten appeared to be acting unilaterally without consulting the Americans. Max Bishop, American consul at Colombo, Ceylon, reported in July that he had "noted a regrettable lack of any spirit of camaraderie between the British and American sections [of SEAC], or any real evidence of mutual frankness and trust." This he attributed to "the wide difference between the political policies" of the two countries in the area. An example of the lack of cooperation was SEAC's decision to drop Gaullist agents into Indochina by parachute, which was kept secret from the Americans.[70] Bishop's reports were taken seriously in Washington, but neither the president nor the State Department found it prudent to do anything about the situation. The virtual passivity of the United States in the face of British and French activities in Southeast Asia and the resultant de facto acceptance of the reestablishment of European power in the region expressed the limits of America's own designs in that part of Asia. Thus at a conference in August at Dumbarton Oaks to discuss a postwar international organization, the American delegates said nothing about the status of the European colonies after the war.[71] The United States would leave Southeast Asia primarily to European initiatives, so long as these initiatives were to be within a framework of global cooperation. Even if the United States did not involve itself in the political affairs of the colonies, it still wanted to be sure that the colonial powers would undertake "the development of dependent areas in the interests both of the dependent peoples themselves and of the world as a whole," in the words of the March 29 memo cited above.

Similar thinking characterized American views toward the Soviet Union at this time. By early 1944 it was clear that the territories and countries adjacent to the Soviet Union would soon be liberated from the Germans. Would those lands be integrated into the postwar community of interdependent nations, or would they come under Soviet power and turn away from a multilateral framework? Americans began to address themselves in earnest to this fascinating question. In a memorandum written in early March on "United States participation in economic reconstruction in eastern and southeastern Europe," the policy committee grappled with this issue and came to a view not unlike the definition of the American position in the Pacific. "There is no intention," the paper stated, "of seeking to deny or offset natural and legitimate Soviet interests in this area, but merely to endeavor to avoid a situation which would automatically force the nations and peoples of eastern and southeastern Europe to complete dependence on the Soviet Union."[72] Just as the United States was insisting on a predominant role in Pacific affairs without closing the ocean to the rest of the world, but rather keeping it as part of a new international order, it would grant Russia certain advantages and influences in Eastern Europe, the Baltic region, and the Balkans, at the same time making sure that these areas retained ties to other parts of the globe. In other words, Soviet power in Europe, like American power in the Pacific, would contribute to the preservation of peace and security and to the multilateral world order.

Such a formulation combined the power-political approach of

President Roosevelt with the internationalism of the State Department. But there had always been a tension between the two, and it did not abate in 1944. If anything, it intensified now that Soviet troops were recapturing and occupying lands adjacent to the prewar Russian boundaries. Because the American formulation assumed a compatibility, if not an identity, of American and Soviet interests and outlooks, the tension would grow if that compatibility could not be demonstrated. Ambassador Harriman in Washington in the spring was one of the first to draw attention to this predicament. He told the policy committee in May that the Soviets desired "to collaborate with us in a world security organization and to participate in world affairs." Stalin and his government, he pointed out, did not "wish to foment revolution along their borders, or to cause disorders which would threaten internal stability." However, he cautioned that the United States should have no illusion that "individual freedom or a democratic system exists in Russia." For this reason, there would be no genuine identity of ideas between the two countries.[73] Could the United States ensure that the region of Soviet influence be tied to the postwar world order through economic and other links? And if so, should it? How could this be accomplished? The use of force was out of the question. As Secretary of State Hull said, the United States should not propose to establish "by military force governments of our own choosing [in postwar Europe]. If they prefer not to accept democracy, we do not wish to ram it down their throats."[74]

But there might be other ways of influencing the course of events in the Russian-liberated areas. For instance, the United States might issue a declaration of its principles and hopes for liberated Europe. As conceived by the State Department, this statement would reiterate America's adherence to internationalist principles while recognizing Russia's paramount interest in security along its borders. Charles Bohlen, who had a hand in drafting the declaration that was later issued in modified form at the Yalta Conference, explained that "he wished to demonstrate to the peoples of Europe that, in addition to the program of the Communist Party and the program of the discredited reactionaries, there is a third alternative, a middle ground, which is left of center, non-Communist, based on civil liberties and economic and social progress." Such a declaration would indicate the United States' interest in postwar reintegrationism coupled with its acceptance of power as a fact in international affairs.[75]

Officials in Washington were confident that this approach would not provoke Soviet hostility and would in fact cement the ties between the two countries. The optimism was derived from many sources, including the wartime alliance, but it was rooted in two fundamental considerations. One was faith in the overriding importance of economics which, it was believed, could only impel the Russians to seek American cooperation. As noted in a July 15 memo by the policy committee, entitled "Survey of principal problems in Europe," the United States after the war would have a major weapon in its economic power, in particular lend-lease assistance. It should make full use of this weapon insofar as American policy "is based upon the premise that the economic well-being of a country is a prime factor in its internal stability and in its peaceful relations with other states." The United States should promote economic well-being in other countries, but it should not be a free gift. Assistance to a foreign government should be dependent on the degree "to which that Government cooperated with us in promoting our international policies," including open commercial relations throughout the world. Moreover, economic assistance could be utilized "to promote the political independence of other nations." As the paper put it, "We do not believe that an ordered and peaceful world can be created upon the foundations of an international society in which certain states are politically subject to their more powerful neighbors." The allusion was obviously to Soviet designs in Eastern Europe and the Balkans. Although they conceded Russia's special position in the area for security reasons, American officials were confident that ultimately the region would be linked with the rest of the world because the Soviet Union could not do without American economic aid.[76]

The second consideration was more power-oriented. No matter how distasteful Soviet intentions in Europe might be, American officials agreed almost unanimously that serious friction between the two countries should be avoided, not only during but also after the war. The only alternative was conflict and confrontation, necessitating American military involvement in postwar Europe. It would be far better if the United States and the Soviet Union could maintain a stable relationship, particularly since these countries were emerging as the two giants in the world. The idea of four-power collaboration still remained; at the Dumbarton Oaks Conference, it was accepted that the four would form the nucleus of a postwar international organization as the permanent members of a security council. At the same time, officials in Washington were beginning to pay more attention to U.S.-Soviet relations—an indication that cooperation between the emerging giants, rather than among "the four policemen," was considered the important key to future peace.

China was no longer considered a serious partner because of its deteriorating internal situation, but in 1944 Britain, too, came to be seen as having passed its prime. As Secretary of War Stimson noted in April, "the British really are showing decadence—a magnificent people, but they have lost their initiative."[77] Similarly, Admiral William Leahy noted in May that in contrast to "the recent phenomenal development of the heretofore latent Russian military and economic strength," in Britain "several developments have combined to lessen her relative military and economic strength."[78] The relative decline of British power did not lead Washington officials to abandon the idea of Anglo-American collaboration in war and peace. However, they were coming to believe that European (and, increasingly, Middle Eastern) issues that traditionally had been settled by the European powers, and during the war by the Soviet Union and Great Britain, were of serious concern to Washington as well; in the future the United States would expect Britain to defer to its wishes and to consult with it in all such matters. In this sense the shape of the postwar world was to depend more and more on the state of American-Soviet relations.

One important factor in those relations was that there was little actual conflict in military power terms between the two nations. The two powers were fast extending their spheres of action and influence in various parts of the world, but they were not coming into direct contact. Russian preponderance in Eastern and southeastern Europe and American predominance in the Pacific were being established simultaneously, and the two did not overlap. Recognition of this fact led Leahy to state, in the above memorandum, that there was no possibility of war between the United States and the Soviet Union so long as America was not dragged into it through a British-Russian conflict. Likewise, a State Department briefing paper spoke of the "absence of any conflict of vital interest between the United States and the U.S.S.R."[79] It was not surprising that American officials on the whole remained confident that on purely pragmatic, power-political grounds, conflict with the Soviet Union could be avoided. American policy was to stress compatibility with its allies and to lay the groundwork for the postwar world on the basis both of power considerations and internationalist principles. Although aware of tensions between these two factors, officials remained reasonably confident that America and Russia would find understanding and cooperation more advantageous than confrontation and crisis.

Thus United States relations with Britain and Russia in 1944 evolved around the theme of collaboration in terms of broadly defined objectives and responsibilities for each power. At a time when the Japanese government was banking on a growing rift between the Anglo-Americans and the Russians, American officials were seeking ways to avoid serious conflict and were hopeful that the wartime alliance could be carried over into the postwar period. The combination of power-political calculations and internationalist assumptions was confounding Japanese tactics, which sought to weaken the enemy camp's solidarity. The Japanese were correct in sensing that Soviet penetration of Europe was causing difficulties between the two sides, but they underestimated the determination of officials in Washington (and London) to minimize the danger of confrontation and to avoid wartime friction.

AVOIDANCE OF trouble also characterized American dealings with China in mid-1944, although China was diminishing in importance in the strategic picture being developed by the military planners in Washington. To be sure, Japan's major offensive—the *Ichigō* operation—alarmed them, and President Roosevelt reacted by asking Chiang Kai-shek, on July 9, to place General Stilwell in command of all Chinese forces, including the Communists. This extraordinary step was a climax to various developments in U.S.-Chinese relations. As seen earlier, Roosevelt had expressed doubts about Chinese political stability and about Chiang's leadership. In May he told the cabinet that "he was apprehensive for the first time as to China holding together for the duration of the war."[80]

His misgivings were reinforced not only by the Nationalists' generally inept response to the Japanese offensive, but also by favorable reports of the Chinese Communists that began to arrive in Washington after Yenan was opened up to observers. The American observer group under Colonel David Barrett was established in July to gather information on "the most effective means of assisting Communists to increase the value of their war effort."[81] The Americans were immediately and immensely impressed with the potentialities of the strategically located Communists in north China. It seemed to make sense for the United States to give them whatever assistance it could against the Japanese forces. Typical was a report written by John S. Service within days after arriving in Yenan with Barrett. His first impressions, he wrote, "have been extremely favorable . . . All of our party have had the same feeling . . . that we have come into a different country and are meeting a different people." In contrast to Chungking's ceremonial formality, visible oppressiveness, and cult of personality, Service found the Communists simple, informal, and hardworking. They practiced what they preached by treating men and women equally, and they emphasized "democracy and intimate relations with the common people." Service concluded, "While the Kuomintang has lost its early revolutionary character and with that loss disintegrated, the Communist Party, because of the struggle it has had to continue, has kept its revolutionary character, but has grown to a healthy and moderate maturity. One cannot help coming to feel that this movement is strong and successful, and that it has such drive behind it and has tied itself so closely to the people that it will not easily be killed."[82] Service, Barrett, and others at once began urging their superiors in Washington to give aid to the Chinese Communists directly, rather than shipping all equipment and materiel to the Nationalists. The Communist leaders themselves sought to influence United States policy by talking frequently with Service and others. They argued that by giving aid only to the Nationalists, America was not making effective use of China's war potential. Mao told Service in August that instead, the United States should work with all groups in China that were fighting the Japanese.[83]

Roosevelt's request that Stilwell be placed in command over all Chinese forces showed that he responded favorably to these pleas and that he was as interested as Service, Mao, and others in utilizing all Chinese resources, especially in view of the menacingly successful Japanese offensive. The president may have wanted the matter to remain strictly military and tactical, but he soon realized that it involved serious political questions as well. Service's favorable reports on the Communists implied that they, rather than the Nationalists, represented the revolutionary and democratic aspirations of the Chinese people. Agreeing with such views, the American embassy in Chungking urged that the United States insist on political reform in China, to influence "the Chinese leaders into political and economic paths that will lead to Sino-American collaboration and mutual benefit in the kind of post-war world for which we are striving." John Carter Vincent, new head of the Chinese affairs division of the State Department, likewise asserted that the United States had an obligation to try to broaden the base of government in China and to rekindle the nationalistic sentiment among the mass of its people. "[We] should make clear our conception of the type of Chinese Government which we believe will make possible our close collaboration with China in military, political, and economic matters," he wrote, "[and] we should use our influence judiciously and consistently . . . to guide China along democratic, cooperative paths."[84] Officials welcomed Roosevelt's initiatives regarding Stilwell as an opportunity to put pressure on Chiang Kai-shek for needed reforms and to encourage a broader-based government with Communist participation.

No one understood the political implications of Roosevelt's request better than Chiang himself. Six days after he received the request, he proposed that Roosevelt send a personal emissary to discuss the situation. In August the president appointed General Patrick J. Hurley as the special emissary with instructions "to facilitate General Stilwell's exercise of command over Chinese armies placed under his direction." But contrary to what Roosevelt must have anticipated, the Hurley mission created a serious situation both in Chinese politics and in U.S.-Chinese relations. When Hurley presented himself to Chiang Kai-Shek on September 7, Chiang stated that he was "prepared to give General Stilwell actual command of all forces in the field in China and that with this command he is also giving to him his complete confidence." At the same time, however, Chiang intimated that Stilwell would have to be under the national military council, an organization controlled by the generalissimo. Moreover, he said, "any so-called Communist troops serving under General Stilwell would have to submit definitely to the control of the Generalissimo and the National Military Council." In other words, while accepting Roosevelt's wishes, Chiang would use them to establish his own power over Communist and other groups in the country. Stilwell would in fact be functioning as an instrument of Kuomintang power. Notwithstanding this, Hurley confidently reported to Washington that there "is a good prospect for unification of command in China." Then, quite abruptly, three days later, Chiang Kai-shek presented a note declaring that he could not consent to the appointment of Stilwell, because he lacked confidence in the American general.[85]

Chiang on several occasions had expressed his lack of confidence in the American general. When Vice-President Henry Wallace visited Chungking in late June, Chiang intimated that Stilwell had become a persona non grata. Roosevelt's request seemed to indicate underestimation of the political aspect of the war. For Chiang Kai-shek it seemed self-evident that "[military] victory or defeat of a country depends on political factors." Among such factors was mutual confidence between allies, in particular between China and the United States. To maintain confidence, it was not best to impose a foreign commander over all Chinese forces, especially one whom Chiang disliked. General Ho Ying-ch'in, commander in chief of the Chinese army, agreed, saying that no foreigner understood the Chinese situation well enough to be a successful commander. Moreover, the appointment would be an infringement on sovereignty and could be used by the enemy for propaganda attacks. Above all, the Nationalist leaders were alarmed at the prospect of Communist forces being armed with American aid.[86] Chiang Kai-shek obviously reasoned that whatever military benefits might accrue from a combined command under Stilwell would be offset in so many other areas that he would risk temporarily displeasing Roosevelt in order not to undermine his own position.

Confronted with Chiang's stiff resistance, President Roosevelt at first responded in kind, telling him in a long telegram on September 16 that "my Chiefs of Staff and I are convinced that you are faced in the near future with the disaster I have feared." The president once again asked Chiang to place "General Stilwell in unrestricted command of all your forces. The action I am asking you to take will fortify us in our decision and in the continued efforts the United States proposes to take to maintain and increase our aid to you."[87] Chiang remained adamant and on September 24 told Hurley that he could not take any step that would open the gates to the spread of communism. The following day he declared that he no longer had confidence in Stilwell and wanted President Roosevelt to replace him.[88] The president decided to yield. While expressing his "surprise and regret" at Chiang's attitude, Roosevelt agreed to the request, telling him that "the United States Government should not [now] assume the responsibility involved in placing an American officer in command of your ground forces throughout China." Stilwell would be relieved of his duties as Chiang's chief of staff and as administrator of the lend-lease program.[89]

It is clear that Roosevelt chose to avoid trouble with Chiang Kai-shek because he did not want to strain their relations further. It is equally evident that the president was belatedly confirming what the joint chiefs had been telling him, that the China theater of the war was becoming less important. By withdrawing his request, he was indicating that the strategic and military importance of such a step was not worth all the turmoil that would be created in China and in U.S.-Chinese relations. He would refrain from involving the United States in internal Chinese affairs and concentrate on military action in the spheres that were unmistakably open to American initiatives. Just as the United States would not try to overtly influence British behavior in Southeast Asia or Soviet action in Eastern Europe, it would desist from attempting to influence domestic developments in China. It would focus on the Pacific Ocean and on the conquest and control of Japan.

PLANNING FOR THE defeat and control of Japan proceeded apace throughout 1944, characterized by America's unilateral initiatives. The significance of this fact cannot be overestimated. Just at a time when American officials were despairing of a closely coordinated policy with Britain, Russia, and China in various parts of the world, they were developing plans for the future of the Pacific and of Japan with the United States as the preponderant factor. Postwar cooperation among the powers, an ideal that was repeatedly confirmed, would thus take the form of an understanding among major countries with their own spheres of influence. Internationalist and reintegrationist principles would apply to those spheres as well as to the rest of the globe, but for the time each of the powers was expected to implement these principles without constant prodding by the United States or the threat of American retaliation if it failed to do so. In this developing vision, American designs for Japan were becoming more and more important, to the point that the United States soon had a clearer conception of what to do with Japan than with any other country in the world. This design in fact became a cornerstone of United States postwar policy, which, along with the policies of Britain, Russia, and China in their respective areas of concern, defined the shape of the peace.

Plans for the disposition of Japanese territories and the control of Japan proper after the war had been discussed by the State Department's numerous committees for over two years. In February 1944, those plans, and their underlying assumptions, came out into the open as a basis for action by the United States government. On February 18 Major General J. H. Hilldring, chief of the civil affairs division of the War Department, and Captain H. L. Pence, now head of the occupied areas section of the Navy Department, jointly sent a memorandum to the State Department soliciting its views on "the planning, training and organization for civil affairs administration in Japan Proper, the Mandated Islands, and the countries occupied by Japan." The sections headed by these officials had been created to prepare for the administration of liberated areas. Although Pence had earlier expressed some of the most extreme views on the future treatment of Japan, he now, studying specific policy alternatives with Hilldring, proved to be less extremist.

The memorandum enumerated many detailed questions to which they hoped the State Department would respond. Which territories should be occupied and by whom? Should the administration of occupied territories be "punitive, mild, or primarily to safeguard reparations?" With respect to Japan proper, the key questions were, should all or parts of the country be occupied, what countries should participate in the occupation, should it be "by zones or by one supreme council of interested United Nations membership," and how long should it last? Some questions touched on the nature of the Japanese polity. Should the existing political parties and organizations be dissolved? Should labor unions be permitted? "What will be the status of the Emperor? Will he be removed both as an individual and as an institution? . . . Will both remain? If so, under what measure of control?" There were also questions regarding postwar United States relations with other powers. "Who should participate in military government—the British? Chinese? Dutch? Free French? U.S.S.R. (if the Soviets enter the Far East war)?" If the Soviet Union entered the war, would South Sakhalin become "a special and exclusive concern of the Soviet" and thus be treated separately from the administration of Japan proper? In French Indochina, "should the U.S. Army plan for any degree of military government or civil affairs administration?" In Korea, would civil affairs responsibility be shared with Britain, China, and/or Russia? In Manchuria, would Chinese sovereignty be immediately restored, or would there be an interim regime in which China and/or the Soviet Union would have "a paramount interest and participation?"[90]

The State Department thus had an opportunity to spell out clearly its ideas for the postwar world. Most of the questions raised in the Hilldring-Pence note had been anticipated by the various State Department committees, and it did not take long for the recently created postwar programs committee to produce a body of memoranda in answer to the questions. Among the most important was PWC-111, drafted by Borton, D. C. Blaisdell, E. R. Dickover, and E. H. Dooman and approved by the rest of the committee on March 13. It dealt with the composition of forces that would occupy Japan, a problem of the utmost importance for the postwar status of that country and its relations with the United States. Without specifying details, the committee recommended three basic principles. First, the forces occupying and administering Japan after surrender should be multinational, representing those United Nations that had had a role in fighting Japan, in accordance with the principle of joint action that had been enunciated throughout the war. Moreover, a joint rather than American occupation of Japan would be less costly to the United States. The occupying forces should include Asiatic units, because their presence "might well produce results more beneficial to American interests than if they were either exclusively American or Caucasian." Second, although the occupation and military government were to be multinational, Japan should not be divided into distinct zones, as was being contemplated for Germany. A statement that survived numerous revisions asserted that "[the] occupation of Japan should be organized on the principle of centralized administration, avoiding the division of the country into zones administered separately by the different national contingents composing the occupation force." Third, Allied participation in the occupation of Japan should not "be so large as to prejudice the dominantly American character" of the military government. It was assumed that the whole setup would come under the command of the American theater commander.[91]

Other memoranda discussed related problems of the occupation. For instance, PWC-109 sought to impress the basically moderate nature of the occupation regime by stating, "The military government will naturally take such action as may be found necessary to safeguard the security of the occupying forces. Otherwise, its measures should not aim to be punitive in character or needlessly humiliating" to the Japanese people.[92] As a corollary, PWC 110a spelled out two different stages of the occupation. In the first phase, which would not last very long, "all of the prefectural capitals, other important cities and strategic areas" would be occupied to ensure fulfillment of the terms of surrender. The second and longer stage would aim at preventing a resurgence of militarism and at creating conditions that would "facilitate the emergence of a liberal government." These aims could be carried out through concentration of occupying troops "in those centers from which they will be able to observe developments."[93]

A substantial number of papers dealt with the occupation of territories other than Japan proper. For instance, regarding Sakhalin, PWC-121 correctly guessed that the Soviet Union would demand its retrocession if Russia entered the war against Japan. However, the memorandum proved unrealistic in asserting that "the predominantly Japanese character of the population and the close integration of the economy of Karafuto [South Sakhalin] with Japan might make it advisable, in spite of possible Soviet demands, that Karafuto be retained by Japan with provision for complete disarmament and periodic inspection to prevent its rearmament." But a serious dispute between Russia and the United States on the matter was not anticipated. The memorandum simply stated that if South Sakhalin were placed under a Soviet commander, "the competent military and political authorities of the American Government should decide whether American participation would be advisable in combat operations and civil affairs in Karafuto."[94] On the Japanese mandates in the Pacific, the State Department insisted, in PWC 123 of March 22, that although the United States, as belligerent occupant of the territory, was entitled "to exercise the rights of sovereignty" over the islands, this was "a temporary rather than a permanent status and does not transfer sovereignty to the occupant."[95]

A number of papers dealt with Korea, which was a difficult case because the United States would not be the principal power in military operations and occupation there, and because the problem of postwar Korean government had become quite complicated. The postwar committee insisted that the four major powers should be represented in these activities under a central civil affairs administration. However, it recognized the difficulty of establishing such a system if the four countries carried out military operations in separate areas, resulting in a virtual division of the country into zones. Even in that event, the memorandum pointed out, an international council would have to be organized to coordinate military government in various parts of Korea. The military government would, it was hoped, be of relatively short duration, although it might be prolonged because of anticipated difficulties in setting up an adequate supervisory authority to ease the transition to independence. In the meantime Koreans "should be utilized to the fullest extent possible . . . to train them for future usefulness in their own government."[96] If qualified Koreans were not available, another memorandum noted, Japanese in Korea might be kept in economic positions for a period after the end of the war.[97] In any event, the United States should foresee having "a responsibility for Korean affairs which would last even after the termination of military government." But it would be involved not as the sole power but as a party to a four-power arrangement which, in the words of a memorandum, would "minimize the possible effort by individual countries to control [Korean] affairs."[98]

The Hilldring-Pence memorandum had raised an important question regarding the treatment of the emperor. In 1943 the State Department's Japan specialists and others had generally come to the view that it would be advantageous, in obtaining Japan's surrender, to deal with the emperor instead of getting rid of him. Some officials had argued in favor of using the emperor system after the war to serve the cause of reform, peaceful orientation, and political stability. Now that the department had to formulate an official position on the issue, the members of the Far Eastern area committee took the unusual step of debating it among themselves and then voting on a recommendation. On April 24, to facilitate their discussion, two members, Borton and Dickover, prepared position papers outlining two contrasting viewpoints. Borton's paper cited three alternatives open to the United Nations: "1) Suspend the exercise of all of the functions of the emperor, 2) suspend none of his functions, or 3) suspend most of his functions." Under the first alternative, the military commander of the occupying forces "would . . . actually exercise the rights of sovereignty though the emperor might continue as the *de jure* sovereign of Japan." This would permit the greatest freedom of action regarding the emperor's ultimate status; on the other hand, Japanese officials might refuse to cooperate with occupation authorities, and there might ensue "a breakdown in the entire administrative structure." This disadvantage, of course, would not exist under the second alternative, with all government functions carried out through the emperor or in his name. However, this would assume that the United Nations supported the continuation of the emperor system in Japan, a position that Borton personally endorsed, but about which no early agreement among the Allies could be foreseen.

The third alternative would permit the emperor to delegate administrative duties to subordinate officials while depriving him of all other functions. Such a procedure "would tend to assure the good behavior of the Japanese people and to keep in office the maximum number of Japanese officials who would be willing to serve directly under the supervision of civil affairs officers." Borton recommended this alternative, coupled with the suggestion that the emperor and his immediate family be placed under protective custody upon Japan's surrender. This was not as moderate a view as Borton had held earlier, and it probably reflected his awareness that outside the State Department, the voices calling for harsh treatment of the emperor were becoming louder. To counter the criticism that the department was being too "soft," the Borton memo added that "if there developed a substantial movement among the Japanese people for the abolition of the institution of the emperor, the military authorities should take no action against that movement . . .

and should cease to utilize the emperor as a political instrument."[99]

The Dickover draft differed from the Borton memorandum in that it looked to abolition of the emperor institution as a desirable goal of the United Nations. As Dickover wrote, "The primary objective of our war against Japan is the assurance for ourselves and other peoples of the Pacific area of peace and security, not for a few years only, but for generations to come." To retain and make use of the emperor in administering Japan would "contribute directly toward perpetuation of the institution of the emperor, through giving to the Japanese people an assumption that we regard that institution as essentially sacrosanct and indispensable." That was a short-sighted approach, Dickover maintained. Under the circumstances, the only prudent course was "to work toward the discrediting of the institution in Japanese eyes and toward its eventual destruction." His reasoning was clear-cut:

> It is believed that peace and security in the Pacific can best be assured by creating a truly democratic Japan. (It is very doubtful if a Japan in which the people possessed control of the government would have built up a tremendous war machine or would have embarked upon the ambitious project of conquering all of East Asia.) The creation of a democratic Japan, however, is an ideal not easy of attainment . . . It is doubtful if democracy can gain a firm foothold in the country unless and until a more or less clean break with the past is made. For our own security, therefore, it would seem desirable that we assist liberal minded Japanese to rid themselves of some of the relics of the past, including the institution of the emperor . . . Otherwise a resurgence of militarism is not only possible but probable, unless the United Nations are willing to maintain strict surveillance, backed by powerful armed forces, over Japan for an indefinite period.

While agreeing with Borton that Japanese officials might refuse to cooperate with foreign masters who tried to abolish the emperor institution, Dickover nevertheless argued that such temporary setbacks should be tolerated in the interest of long-range objectives. His memorandum concluded that not only should the emperor and his immediately family be placed under protective custody but that he should "not be permitted to issue edicts or proclamations and none should be issued in his name." Moreover, "[if] any considerable section of the Japanese people indicate a desire to abolish the institution of the emperor, the occupation authorities should give that section their support and encouragement."[100]

The two contrasting papers were discussed at a meeting of the Far Eastern area committee on April 26. Of its thirteen members, only Dickover supported the memorandum he had drafted, while the other members endorsed Borton's draft. Joseph Ballantine told the postwar committee that Dickover's paper was based on a simplistic assumption that by abolishing the emperor system the United Nations would effectively get rid of Japanese militarism. On the contrary, it was possible to argue that if the emperor were kept and directed by the occupation commander to discharge minor official functions, this would advertise to the Japanese people that the United Nations considered him just a human being and not a divine figure. The resulting changes in Japanese attitudes would be far more important in the long run than an outright abolition of the institution. Ballantine added that if the Japanese could "evolve along the same democratic political lines as have the British . . . an emperor could be a source of stability and reform." Former ambassador Joseph C. Grew, who had recently been appointed director of the office of Far Eastern affairs, also disagreed with Dickover about the emperor system and asserted that "the institution of the Throne will offer a measure for the constructive development of Japan in the ways of peace and for the regeneration of the Japanese people in a direction which would conduce to the security of the United States." He believed that during the 1920s the emperor institution had in fact been "turned toward peaceful international cooperation," and that this could happen again once the military caste and cult were discredited by thorough defeat. The institution could be the source of authority from which new leadership would emerge in a reconstructed, peaceful Japan. In contrast to Dickover's historical determinism, which was skeptical of swift changes in Japan, Grew reminded the committee that the "Japanese are past masters at executing the maneuvre of right-about-face."[101]

The expectation that the Japanese attitude could change relatively easily and speedily after their defeat united most Asianists in the State Department against harsh treatment of the emperor. It is evident that their optimism was derived, as Grew's remarks suggested, from a perception of the 1920s as a decade of peaceful cooperation between Japan and the Western democracies. The postwar committee, too, accepted such suppositions. Although the Borton draft was slightly modified to take account of some of Dickover's points, the committee's final report, adopted on May 9, recommended placing the emperor under protective custody but permitting him to delegate administrative duties to subordinate officials. At the same time, the occupation authorities should "refrain from any action which would imply recognition of or support for the Japanese concept that the Japanese emperor is different from and superior to other temporal rulers, that he is of divine origin and capacities, that he is sacrosanct or that he is indispensable."[102]

The debate on the emperor system revealed a substantial sentiment for moderation toward postwar Japan among civilian officials. The basic philosophy, as in the past, was that it should not be very difficult to encourage the growth of a nonmilitaristic society under the leadership of liberal-minded men who would turn the emperor institution into an instrument of reform. This view reflected considerable optimism about Japanese character and history and also about the postwar international order.

This type of thinking is indicated in a document drafted by Borton and approved by the Far Eastern area committee on May 9. The Japanese people, he noted, would probably react to defeat by realizing that "their military leaders have led them to destruction and national disgrace." They might thus "turn to a new group of leaders." The existence of antimilitarist or nonmilitarist Japanese leaders had been accepted as a fact by State Department officials, and Borton reiterated the belief that "there exists a fairly substantial body of moderate political influence which has been rigidly suppressed and silenced since 1931 but which it is believed can be encouraged and made the nucleus of a liberal movement." This group included the "statesmen of the so-called Anglo-American school," who had been prominent during the 1920s, business leaders "whose prosperity was based on world trade rather than on the great East Asia prosperity sphere," and some if not all of Japan's Christian leaders, educators, and social and political reformers. It was to these men, Borton asserted, that the United Nations must turn to demilitarize and democratize Japan after the war. But their success would depend to a large extent on the kind of peace to be imposed on their country. The United States should encourage the growth of the liberal movement by removing restrictions on freedom of the press and by eliminating ultranationalistic societies. At the same time, the Japanese people should be told that the occupying nations intended "to allow a peaceful Japan to discharge her responsibilities as a member of the family of nations" and that Japan would be "given a share in the world economy on a reasonable basis with the hope for future betterment."[103]

Within three months after receiving the Hilldring-Pence request for information, then, State Department experts and leaders summed up their study and deliberation since 1942 and defined a fairly comprehensive approach to the whole range of issues involved in the defeat and control of Japan. By and large their approach had not changed. It emphasized America's predominant position in postwar Japanese affairs, while at the same time fitting Japan into an evolving international order. Although Secretary of State Hull did not yet give his formal stamp of approval to the ideas and recommendations in the memoranda, he consented to have them transmitted to the War and the Navy departments. There they were discussed further, and in the winter of 1944-45 they provided the core of final policy formulations adopted by the newly organized State-War-Navy Coordinating Committee. Even before then, however, some of the civilian recommendations were considered usable for stepped-up wartime propaganda. The idea was to appeal to the war-weary and potentially liberal-minded Japanese people to renounce their military masters and build a fresh and peaceful future.

On May 21, for instance, the Anglo-American combined chief of staff adopted an "Anglo-American outline plan for psychological warfare against Japan," designed to undermine Japanese morale and hasten its defeat. This paper, a product of many months' study by both American and British intelligence experts, confirmed the views of State Department officials. They all agreed that "Despite his indoctrination, the regimented fighting man of Japan is fundamentally human and has the primary instincts of self-preservation and the desire to live a normal life." The Japanese "are by nature volatile and of short enthusiasms; their war spirit and morale must be constantly revived." Accordingly, Allied propaganda was aimed at lessening the fighting will of the Japanese armed forces by destroying their confidence in their leaders. The Allies must try to "create doubt, confusion and defeatism among both the armed forces and the civil population of Japan by undermining confidence in the government and its foreign, domestic and military policies." A desire for peace could be encouraged by "quickening the consciousness of and arousing resentment against the hardships of the war; emphasizing that Japan has long since lost the initiative and is increasingly on the defensive; reiterating the hopelessness of victory." The assumption was that active propaganda could hasten Japanese defeat because the Japanese civilians as well as soldiers seemed tired of war and desirous of returning to peacetime pursuits.[104]

A note to the above memorandum stated, "For the time being, all attacks or reflection on the Imperial family must be avoided," in accordance with the recommendation of civilian experts. In a paper entitled, "Policy in regard to propaganda treatment of the institution of the emperor," the State Department's Asian specialists reiterated this policy in late June. They reasoned that "[indiscriminate] and violent attacks on the emperor and the imperial institution, which might lead the Japanese to infer that the United Nations intend to deal drastically with the Emperor after the war . . . would tend to drive the Japanese people further into the arms of the military." The best tactic, therefore, was to divide the people from the military by showing that the latter had used the emperor to bring ruin to the nation. Allied propaganda should emphasize that the Japanese military had "misled the emperor, as well as the people, in regard to the actual results of their military operations; have used the imperial institution in order to suppress democratic aspirations among the people and to cause a reversion to mediaeval processes of government."[105]

Far away from Washington, in the China-Burma-India theater, John K. Emmerson, now second secretary of the embassy in Chungking, was coming to similar conclusions about hastening the end of the war through political moves. From his observations of Japanese prisoners of war in Burma and in China, he was convinced that "[contrary] to the widely accepted opinion, the Japanese may not continue to fight bitterly after final defeat becomes certain."

As Emmerson put it, the mental change in a Japanese prisoner of war was remarkable. At first, he simply wished to commit suicide. But after a few days of "medical care, good food, and considerate treatment," he began to change. He "is filled with gratitude for treatment which he did not expect and rapidly sloughs off his veneer of indoctrinated Bushido. For him one life has ended and another has begun." The prisoner "seems to lack feelings of hatred or even personal animosity" toward Americans. He had heard of American wealth, movies, and modern appliances. "The United States is more familiar to him than any other foreign country." He would now be willing to cooperate with Americans against his own country.

From these observations, Emmerson felt confident that once the Japanese government capitulated, "the nation may undergo a mental change not unlike that taking place in the Japanese soldier . . . They may not obstruct the formation of a new government which offers them peace and rights never enjoyed before." The conclusions were obvious: "Our aim should be to salvage some of the good will still extant among the people. We need not be soft. But we can say that a new Japan will be given a place in the world of nations." The United States, therefore, should start reeducating Japanese prisoners so that they could purvey new ideas and help eradicate militarism when they returned to Japan. In addition, assuming that the mass of Japanese would react much like the prisoners of war, they must be given some hope for a better life after defeat. They should be told that "Japan will be encouraged to develop peace industries . . . She will be helped to re-establish trade with other nations [and] permitted to form her own government." Emmerson agreed with the sentiment prevalent in official Washington that the emperor "may be very useful to us in the first days following an armistice, as a proclamation of surrender by imperial rescript will probably end resistance wherever Japanese armies and navies are engaged."[106]

In the middle of 1944, then, knowledgeable officials of the United States were confirming a moderate approach to peace with Japan. There was sufficient congruence between the war and peace aims they articulated and the ideas evolving among those Japanese who were looking to the end of the war to have warranted a serious attempt to terminate hostilities then and there. If the Japanese leaders who replaced the Tōjō ministry and were intent upon preserving domestic stability had been privy to the thinking of American officials, they might have been persuaded to extend overtures for peace. And the United States government might have been receptive to such moves. America was no more irrevocably committed to Japan's unconditional surrender than the Japanese were to fighting to the very end. The two sides might have come together to define a postwar world by ending, rather than continuing, the war.

THE MAKING OF
POSTWAR ASIA

5

IN RETROSPECT THE months between September 1944 and February 1945 were a watershed in the history of the Second World War. During this period, with the war in Europe all but over, the wartime alliance among the United States, Great Britain, and the Soviet Union faced a severe strain. The Anglo-American counteroffensive in France and the Low Countries was being matched by the Soviet Union in Eastern Europe and the Balkans, so that by the end of 1944 most of Europe except for Germany, Austria, and Czechoslovakia had fallen to Allied forces. The question of the politics of the occupied areas inevitably arose, and with it the more important issue of the relationship between domestic politics in each country to overall European security. In the Middle East and Asia, too, indigenous movements were being freed from wartime constraints and were realigning into new political forces, while the major powers were trying to reinsert themselves into the situation to ensure stability.

Forces of change and of order were vying domestically and internationally. Because American-British-Russian relations were increasingly bound up with such internal developments, the future of the relationship appeared uncertain and in need of fresh definition. How could they maintain their cooperative framework, which all their leaders recognized as essential for postwar security and peace, when the war's approaching end would unleash pressures for economic and social change in all countries? Should the major powers maintain their commitment to global security, or should they concentrate on the processes of domestic change in many parts of the world? In that case, how could they ensure compatibility between domestic change and international order?

These issues intrigued American officials as they proceeded with the task of postwar planning. On September 26 Assistant Secretary of State Berle presented a memorandum to the policy committee on "principal problems in Europe," in which he noted that the Soviet army was emerging as the most powerful in postwar Europe, occupying all of Eastern Europe and most of the southeast. In these regions would be established "governments acting in substantial compliance with [Russia's] desires," and the result would be to "expand the Soviet influence far beyond the area in which she could exert actual military force." Outside of Europe, Berle wrote, the Soviet Union appeared bent on extending its influence "south to the Persian Gulf throughout its entire length, and westward to the Mediterranean . . . They propose to have an influence analogous to that which the British now have in Iraq and the Levant states, and to extend their influence in Turkey." All these trends were profoundly disquieting to the British, the memorandum noted, as they "see a threat to the empire lifeline, cutting them off from their Far Eastern interests including India, and reducing Britain from the status of a world power to the status of a strong Atlantic power." Such developments indicated the persistence of traditional power politics, with the strong nations pursuing their self-interest regardless of repercussions on world peace or on the welfare of peoples everywhere. As Berle said, Russia and Britain were still "pursuing nationalistic objectives," and power politics was continuing "today on the pattern made nauseatingly familiar by the Axis in 1935–1939."[1]

The memorandum is of interest for its expression of one main strand of civilian thinking in Washington toward the end of the war: viewing Soviet and British behavior and rivalry in the traditional framework of power and castigating both "the ruthlessness of British commercialism and the ruthlessness of Soviet nationalism." Both countries were judged against the standard of internationalism, defined in terms of unrestricted economic and political development within countries and open intercourse among nations. Such principles, the basis for the evolving concept of reintegrationism, did not mean the substitution of ideals for power. American officials were willing to concede a degree of unilateral influence to the major powers in certain areas in the interest of security and order, but they believed that this would not divide the world but would be a realistic foundation for a cooperative international system. The American role would be to promote interdependence, not to perpetuate exclusive arrangements. For this reason, the United States should not "identify its interests with those of either the Soviet Union or Great Britain," in the words of a report by a subcommittee composed of Berle and the directors of the area offices in the State Department.[2]

These officials accepted as axiomatic that America's primary weapon and main postwar policy orientation would be economic and that world peace would be founded upon economic interdependence. According to Berle, the United States should resist the perpetuation of closed economic systems and promote "the essential interests of a free access by communications, by air landing and transit rights, by the rights of our shipping to call at ports." Agreeing with him, the policy committee told President Roosevelt in October that "the future economic pattern of Europe will be largely determined by policies and procedures established during the period of reconstruction. Whether postwar conditions lead back to bilateralism, restriction and autarchy, or are resolved in a manner which will permit the progressive growth and liberalization of trade and investment will depend in no small measure on the ability of the war-torn countries to obtain outside (i.e., mostly American) help in reconstruction."[3] With American economic assistance these countries would be linked to the outside world and open to American influence with, it was hoped, favorable repercussions upon their internal situations. Without American aid they would continue to belong to closed systems, British or Russian. But these latter, too, would find open intercourse and peaceful cooperation more advantageous than the continuation of spheres of influence.

The reiteration of these familiar ideas in late 1944 seemed particularly important now that Russian troops were occupying most of Eastern and Southeastern Europe and the British were trying to control internal politics in Greece and Yugoslavia. The famous Churchill-Stalin conversations of October indicated one possible way to deal with the rapidly evolving situation in the region. The two leaders toyed with the idea of explicitly assigning spheres of influence to one another and of defining the power each would have in certain countries. In their "percentage agreement" Churchill and Stalin gave Russia 90 percent predominance in Rumania, 75 percent in Bulgaria, 50 percent in Yugoslavia, and 10 percent in Greece, with Britain getting the remaining percentages. This was precisely the kind of power-political arrangements that the State Department vehemently opposed, although few officials were privy to the percentage agreement. Edward Stettinius, who was appointed Hull's successor in November, as well as Berle and others, continued to express grave concern with Soviet and British action in the occupied areas.

The idea of postwar cooperation in atomic weaponry was also beginning to be promoted. To be sure, the State Department was virtually kept out of this secret weapons project, so that its officials did not have it in mind when they spoke of cooperation. But among the scientists and civilian officials involved in the Manhattan project, there was growing awareness of the dangerous implications of atomic bomb development. As they realized that the bombs would become available by mid-1945, some began seriously considering the effect of their use on the postwar world. Talk of international cooperation would be useless, they felt, unless something were done to ensure cooperation in the atomic field and to prevent an arms race that would be far graver than any such race in the past.

On September 30 two prominent scientists in the Manhattan project, James B. Conant and Vannevar Bush, wrote a memorandum calling attention to the vital importance of the atomic issue in any postwar planning. "There is hope," they wrote, "that an arms race . . . can be prevented, and even that the future peace of the world may be furthered, by complete international scientific and technical interchange on this subject, backed up by an international commission acting under an association of nations and having the authority to inspect." They recommended that "plans be laid for complete disclosure of the history of the development and all but the manufacturing and military details of the bombs as soon as the first bomb has been demonstrated."[4] At about the same time another scientist, Niels Bohr, was urging Roosevelt to explore the possibility of exchanging scientific knowledge and coordinating policy regarding the uses of atomic energy with the Soviet Union as well as Great Britain.[5] Obviously, these scientists were thinking of a peaceful, cooperative postwar order in which the question of atomic weaponry would be of paramount importance. Their suggestions complemented State Department views on postwar internationalism. Both were arguing for a world of free, frank, and open intercourse, leaving behind egoism, exclusiveness, and power politics.

President Roosevelt also believed in cooperation, postwar as well as wartime, but his conception was still largely based on considerations of war, military strategy, power, and postwar security. He shared others' concern about the Soviet and British actions and about the development of atomic bombs, but he sought to cope with these issues in the framework of big-power understanding. In contrast to his subordinates, who argued that the United States should not identify its interests with those of Britain or Russia, the president remained convinced that only shared interests and responsibilities would keep the big three together as the guardians of security and stability. But because the three nations were far apart in ideologies and in economic policies, Roosevelt stressed their mutual accommodation on the basis of some understanding of their respective prerogatives and rights. For him preventing the collapse of the wartime collaboration was of paramount importance, and to ensure it he was willing to go beyond his civilian aides in recognizing spheres of influence and special arrangements. For instance, he was not opposed in principle to percentage arrangements in Europe. "I am most pleased to know," he telegraphed Churchill when he heard of the Churchill-Stalin conversations on the Balkans, "that you are reaching a meeting of your two minds as to international policies in which, because of our present and future common efforts to prevent international wars, we are all interested."[6] In his concern with preventing future wars, he thus justified obviously power-political arrangements as a necessary price to ensure Soviet cooperation. Also, at the Quebec Conference with Churchill in September, Roosevelt reiterated his belief in an Anglo-American monopoly of nuclear secrets. In other words, despite the pleas of some scientists, the two countries would not share the development and deployment of atomic weapons with others. Toward the end of December, Secretary of War Stimson and Leslie R. Groves, director of the Manhattan project, discussed this point with President Roosevelt, and they agreed that the atomic partnership between the United States and Britain was "a blood partnership" and indissoluble, that the Soviet Union or any other power would not be brought into the picture for the time being.[7]

There was thus more than one American-British-Russian relationship at this time. Although civilian officials in Washington stressed America's commitment to principle and its opposition to Soviet and British policies, this was not the entire story. Another layer of ideas and policies stressed compatibility and shared interests among the great powers. Together, these relationships defined the environment in which the Asian-Pacific war was being fought and its ending being planned.

Although there was no single answer to the Russian question in Europe, virtually all American officials agreed on the desirability of bringing the Soviet Union into the Japanese war as expeditiously as possible. At the Quebec Conference American and British military planners adopted a final plan for the defeat of Japan, emphasizing sea and air blockades of Japanese territory and the invasion of the home islands. The Combined Chiefs of Staff, with Roosevelt and Churchill, estimated that the war in the Pacific would end some eighteen months after Germany's defeat. Soviet participation was reaffirmed, with Roosevelt telegraphing Stalin at the end of the conference, "Our three countries are waging a successful war against Germany and we can surely join together with no less success in crushing a nation that I am sure in my heart is as great an enemy of Russia as she is of ours."[8]

The estimate of eighteen months was based on the assumption that Russia would participate in the final stages of the Pacific war. According to the deliberations of the joint staff planners in Washington in late 1944, the anticipated recapturing of the Philippine archipelago was to be followed by an invasion of the Ryukyu Islands around March 1, 1945. There would be an attack and landing on Kyushu in June if Germany had not been crushed by then or in September if it had been. The final assault on Honshu, if it became necessary, would come after all these campaigns had been successfully executed. However, if the Russians declared war on Japan at about the time of the American invasion of the Ryukyus in the spring of 1945 and decided to attack Hokkaido, the U.S. forces might rule out the Kyushu operation and advance to Hokkaido for a joint subjugation of the northern island. The ideal development from the American point of view, according to the joint staff planners, was for the Russians to launch an offensive in Manchuria and aerial attacks on Japan proper just before the American invasion of Kyushu. Then, while U.S. forces were engaged in Kyushu and Honshu, the Russians could help by tying down Japanese strength on the continent of Asia and making it impossible for them to reinforce the defense of the home islands. "The effect of Russia's entry will be to cause the commitment and expenditure of enemy forces and resources in North China and Manchuria which might otherwise be employed in the defense of Japan and might also cause the withdrawal of forces from Japan to Manchuria," according to a late November memorandum drafted by the planners.[9]

The Soviet Union was seen as an important key to the early termination of the Japanese war. To be sure, as the above memorandum noted, the United States could assume that "the defeat of Japan may be accomplished without Russian participation in the war," but that would take considerably longer than eighteen months. Also military calculations in Washington in late 1944 contained an element of uncertainty because of the possibility of using atomic bombs. On September 30, Conant and Bush reported, "There is every reason to believe that before August 1, 1945, atomic bombs will have been demonstrated and that the type then in production would be the equivalent of 1,000 to 10,000 tons of high explosive so far as general blast damage is concerned."[10] Roosevelt, Marshall, Stimson, and a few other leaders who were privy to such information may have thought that dropping the bombs would force Japan to surrender shortly after August 1945. But most of the military planners knew little or nothing about the specifics of the project, and their Pacific strategy was based on conventional weapons. And in that strategy the Soviet ingredient was quite crucial. No matter what the state of American-Russian relations in Europe, the United States still needed Soviet cooperation in the Japanese war.

AGAINST THIS background, Japanese policy in late 1944 gives the impression of an exercise in futility. Tokyo's effort to take advantage of and encourage a rift between Russia and the Anglo-American powers had not borne any fruit. But they refused to give up, and this remained a principal tactic under the Koiso cabinet. As Foreign Minister Shigemitsu explained in his instruction to Ambassador Satō in December, "In proportion as the German threat has subsided, divergent interests of the members of the anti-Axis camp, in particular Russia and the Anglo-American nations, are becoming more and more evident. Everywhere Soviet-supported communist parties and democratic factions backed up by Britain and America are clashing in ever greater intensity—not only in Europe and the Balkans, but also in Asia Minor, Iran, Iraq, and China." Shigemitsu believed that here was an opportune moment for Japan to sharpen the conflict between the two sides by making all reasonable concessions to Russia to detach it permanently from Britain and the United States.[11]

It is not easy to determine how seriously Shigemitsu entertained these rather stale ideas. His postwar statements, as well as some other evidence during the war, suggest that he was primarily concerned with bringing the war to a close expeditiously, with a minimum loss of honor to the country and as little damage as possible to its social order. He may have reasoned that taking advantage of the growing rift between Russia and the Anglo-American countries was strictly a tactical move, to create, in his words, "a favorable international environment" for the termination of the war. All his talk about rapprochement with Moscow may have been merely a device to persuade others, and perhaps to convince himself, that such a tactic was worth experimenting with. Shigemitsu may also have felt, as did many of the *jūshin*, that attaining peace with Britain and America required taking a circuitous road through Russia to avoid domestic repercussions. The armed forces, as well as an aroused public, might cause such turmoil that the very purpose of terminating the war would be jeopardized. He may have reasoned that in order to prepare the Japanese for an eventual peace, it would be wise to initiate moves through Russia which, after all, was the only major country not at war with Japan.

All these considerations undoubtedly played a part, but to enumerate them only underscores the failure of Shigemitsu and others to clarify the ideas and assumptions on which they based their policy. For instance, the talk of creating "a favorable international environment" as late as 1944 betrayed a lack of sensitivity to the whole sequence of events after the 1930s. Japanese policy had tried, and had been frustrated in the effort, to play the power-political game to create such an environment. Neither the Axis pact nor the Soviet neutrality treaty had helped; the former, designed as a perfect instrument for ensuring Japan a place in the sun, had in fact isolated it even further. Not daunted easily, Shigemitsu was now talking about a new entente among Germany, the Soviet Union, and Japan in opposition to the rest of the Western world. There was no assurance that such an entente could be formed at that late hour or that it would create a better "environment" for Japan than a rapprochement with the Anglo-American nations. Shigemitsu sought to explain the desirability of such an arrangement in his message to Ambassador Satō, saying that Soviet and Japanese interests in East Asia were much more compatible than Soviet and Anglo-American, or Japanese and Anglo-American, interests, in part because the Japanese policy of liberating Asian peoples from Western imperialism was similar to the Soviet approach to nationality problems. It is not clear how strongly he believed in such ideas, which pointed to an Asia in which Russia and Japan would be the predominant powers, a situation certainly no more conducive to domestic stability in Japan than the persistence of Anglo-American influences. Moreover, he assumed that somehow the United States and Britain would accept such a development with equanimity. All this suggests that the foreign minister may have been simply trying to find excuses for initiating concrete steps toward peace, but it was a tremendously circuitous way of doing so, and it contributed little to speeding up the process of Japanese-American rapprochement.

Shigemitsu's views reflected the official thinking of the Koiso ministry in the fall of 1944. Just when American officials were trying to maintain a cooperative relationship with the Soviet Union, Tokyo was deciding to make one more attempt to keep them apart. The Foreign Ministry, in a policy memorandum on September 6, suggested that Japan should be prepared to pay a high price for Soviet "assistance" and the separation of Russia from its allies. Specifically, Japan should be willing to give back to the Soviet Union the Chinese Eastern Railway, the whole of South Sakhalin, and the northern Kuriles. In addition, Japan should grant Russia's spheres of influence in Manchuria and Inner Mongolia, give Russian ships the right to cross Tsugaru Strait (dividing Hokkaido and Sakhalin), give up the anti-Comintern pact and the Axis alliance, and tolerate "peaceful activities" by Russia in various parts of Asia. The two countries could also discuss possible peace arrangements between Germany and Russia, boundaries between Japan and the Soviet territories in Northeast Asia, and demilitarized zones along these borders. In return for these concessions, the memorandum stated, Japan should seek Russia's agreement to continue its neutrality and to refrain from going to war against Japan. If all went well, Moscow and Tokyo could even discuss a new convention for settling their disputes peacefully, an alliance against Britain and America, and joint action to end the war.[12]

Shigemitsu instructed Ambassador Satō in Moscow to propose to Foreign Minister Molotov that Japan send a special emissary (former prime minister Hirota Kōki was mentioned) to the Russian capital to discuss urgent issues between the two countries. Molotov, however, was cool to the whole scheme, telling Satō on September 16 that sending a special emissary would be misconstrued by the world and that Japanese-Russian relations did not seem to need further improvement.[13] Despite this setback, the supreme war council adopted on September 28 the policy that Japan should "seek cooperation with Russia, promote Russian understanding of its position as an Asian power and its responsibilities in the construction and stabilization of East Asia, and bring about Russian agreement with the basic premises of Japan's world policy." If Germany should surrender, as seemed likely, then Japan must keep Soviet attention focused on Europe to encourage tensions between it and the Anglo-American countries. Moreover, if there should be a separate peace between Germany and Russia or between Germany and the Anglo-American powers, Japan should try to conclude an alliance with the Soviet Union against Britain and America.[14]

Simultaneously, the Japanese leaders decided to undertake yet another initiative toward the Nationalist regime in China, a move that was implicit in the Russian orientation of Japanese policy at that time. If the Soviet Union continued to be neutral, presumably it would not aid the Chinese against Japan; the Soviets might even mediate between Tokyo and Chungking. Also, the prospect of Japan's offering drastic concessions to Russia in Manchuria, Inner Mongolia, and the rest of Northeast Asia might frighten Chiang Kai-shek and make him more amenable to Japanese overtures. Accordingly, the supreme war council decided on presenting to the Nationalists a scheme by which Tokyo and Chungking would send emissaries to Nanking to discuss possible peace terms, perhaps including Chiang's return to Nanking and the establishment of a unified Chinese government, Japan's noninterference in Chinese politics, and the restoration of Hong Kong to Chinese sovereignty. In return, the Nationalists would pledge neutrality in the Japanese war with America and Britain. They would continue to recognize the status quo in Manchuria, but the status of Mongolia would henceforth be considered an internal Chinese matter. Japanese forces would be completely withdrawn from China as soon as American and British forces were evacuated.

These negotiations were to be coupled with an aggressive propaganda campaign, demonstrating to Chungking that its reliance on the United States and Great Britain would ultimately lead to Chinese enslavement and Asian decay; even if Japanese troops were expelled from China through American and British assistance, that would only result in an extension of Anglo-American influence, and China would permanently lose its independence. Finally, the Japanese negotiators in Chungking might intimate that Japanese-Soviet relations were improving and that Moscow and Tokyo hoped to base a new Asian peace on cooperation by the three countries. If the Nationalists refused to join such an undertaking, Japan and the Soviet Union might work together to create a unified government in China on the basis of collaboration between the Nanking regime and the Yenan Communists.[15]

Armed with these guidelines, General Shibayama Kaneshirō, vice minister of war, went to Nanking in mid-September and met with Ch'en Kung-po and Chou Fo-hai, two senior statesmen in the Nanking government, hoping to approach Chungking through them.[16] Both Ch'en and Chou indicated that they had been in touch with Chungking and that they would expedite Tokyo-Nanking-Chungking negotiations by sending an emissary to the Nationalist capital. They also agreed that Russia might be used as a mediator.

Despite these beginnings, nothing concrete developed in Japanese-Chinese relations. All that the negotiations and policy guidelines revealed was the reluctance of Japanese leaders to work for peace except through Russia and China. Their reiteration, at this desperate stage of the war, of the theme of Asian unity against Anglo-Americanism indicated that this idea remained the ultimate rationalization for the war. Although pan-Asianism had gotten nowhere, the Japanese still had to believe in that doctrine to retain a modicum of optimism. It was wishful thinking, as it had always been, but there was little else on which to build wartime policy. The only alternative would have been a frank admission of failure and the acceptance of reintegrationism.

Some Japanese officials were beginning to come around to that acceptance. They viewed with increasing skepticism Tokyo's sanguine assumption that Russia, China, and Japan could somehow form an Asian bloc against the United States and Britain. Ambassador Satō, Minister Morishima, and other diplomats in the Japanese embassy in Moscow were dismayed by the naiveté of their superiors. From their perspective in Russia, they were convinced that Stalin would persist in his alliance with Roosevelt and Churchill, and that he would contemptuously dismiss any concessions Japan offered as a sign of weakness. They would certainly not be able to persuade Stalin to sever the advantageous ties with his allies, for he knew that the Soviet Union could get all those concessions and even more by staying on the Allies' side and eventually entering the war against Japan. Thus it was "useless," Satō frankly told Shigemitsu in November, to try to detach Russia from America and Britain. Although the ambassador had, in 1942 and 1943, been a champion of Japanese-Russian rapprochement, he was now persuaded that such a move would be effective only if Japan was on the offensive; to seek Soviet goodwill by making humiliating concessions would not work.[17] Instead of playing such a self-degrading game, Japan should maintain its dignity and "end as a great power," in other words, fight on valiantly and then admit its defeat. In Stockholm Minister Okamoto Suemasa cautioned that because Russia would need Anglo-American economic assistance after the war, it would be unlikely to respond to any overtures either to end the war with Germany or to detach itself from the Allies.[18] Although they stopped short of saying so, these diplomats were beginning to believe that the only way to terminate the war was to deal directly with Japan's principal enemies, in particular the United States.

IF THE JAPANESE had approached Washington rather than Moscow in late 1944, they would have found the United States more than ready with a peace plan. Most of the State Department's plans for Japan's surrender and afterward, which had been presented to the

War and Navy departments in May, remained little changed for the rest of the year. For a while after the spring the postwar programs committee did not concern itself with Japanese and Asian issues, being preoccupied with the increasingly urgent German problem. But the area committee on the Far East continued to reaffirm, refine, and amplify its surrender and postwar policy positions for Japan. In August it drafted a memorandum on the terms and conditions of Japanese surrender, and the paper was approved by the postwar programs committee on November 13.

The document, coinciding with Japan's furious and futile efforts to work through Moscow and Chungking, was an ironic reminder that the surest way to peace with America would have been through Washington. First, the document specified that Japan's acceptance of surrender should be through "a unilateral declaration by those Japanese authorities who exercise actual control over the Japanese armed forces." The surrender instrument itself, however, must be signed by the emperor, countersigned by representatives of the supreme command, and received by the theater commander— an American officer—"on behalf of all of the United Nations at war with Japan." Second, those countries "which have actively participated in the war against Japan" should determine the basic policies to be followed after Japan's surrender. The United States would take the lead in formulating policies, which it would then present to Britain, China, and, if it had entered the war against Japan, the Soviet Union. Third, the United Nations would declare their determination to destroy Japanese militarism but not the Japanese state. The enunciation of these intentions, the memorandum noted, "should give encouragement to whatever democratic and moderate elements still remain in Japan, as it would indicate the willingness of the occupation authorities to assist in the development of democracy in Japan."[19]

These were clearly the principles that had guided State Department thinking throughout the war, looking to the reconstruction of Japan and of U.S.-Japanese relations in a framework of 1920s internationalism. This was a far cry from a public opinion poll indicating that as much as thirteen percent of Americans polled insisted on the extermination of all Japanese after the war.[20] Civilian officials in Washington were not unmindful of public opinion but persisted in the belief that ultimately the American people would understand that the reform of Japan was a far more stable and sure basis for peace than its destruction.

At the end of 1944, in fact, the State Department resolutely stood its ground on this point, as can be seen in several other policy papers drawn up at this time. For instance, it was suggested that the emperor not be removed from Japan during the occupation and that civilian hostages should not be taken except in extreme cases as a measure of reprisal. Military government by the occupation forces should aim at the "emergence of a Japan properly discharging its responsibilities in the family of nations," and should therefore co-operate with those Japanese who supported such aims. To foster the growth of antimilitarist, democratic forces, occupation authorities should undertake educational reforms, encourage freedom of expression, permit the formation of labor organizations, and supervise the functioning of the courts. All such recommendations assumed that there would be some Japanese willing to cooperate with the occupation regime in carrying out necessary reforms. For instance, it was admitted that "there will not be available to military government the large number of competent and qualified American and other foreign personnel which would be required to carry out such fundamental reforms of the Japanese educational system as might seem desirable." Therefore it would be necessary to turn to "cooperative Japanese, themselves proponents of liberal ideas," to carry out new programs.[21]

The reiteration of these themes came at an opportune moment, for in December 1944 the State-War-Navy Coordinating Committee (SWNCC) was established as the key liaison between the civilian and service departments in drafting policy for the treatment of Japan, Germany, and other enemy countries. It was headed by the assistant secretaries of the three agencies and reported through their respective heads to the White House. It is possible to trace the evolution of this organ from December 1944 through the end of the war and the immediate postwar period, when it eventually was transformed into the National Security Council. The importance of SWNCC in U.S. policy toward Japan and postwar Asia can hardly be exaggerated. Equally significant, SWNCC created within itself a subcommittee on the Pacific and the Far East, headed by Dooman of State, George V. Strong of War, and Harold C. Train of Navy. Under them was a large staff from the three departments, consisting of those who had already been engaged in planning for Japanese surrender and occupation. Thus a degree of continuity was assured in SWNCC deliberations, and the ideas that had emerged within the State Department provided a major part of the input into the new organ.

Equally important, the last months of 1944 saw a further confirmation of the trend toward reducing American involvement, influence, and even interest in various parts of Asia. In Southeast Asia strategic and postwar policies were left largely in the hands of the British and their European allies. In a message to Chiang Kai-shek in mid-October, President Roosevelt announced that the China-Burma-India theater would henceforth be divided into two parts, China and Burma-India. This split meant a diminution of Chinese influence in Burma as well as a virtual end to U.S.-British-Chinese collaboration in the Asian theater just at the time of the Stilwell crisis, climaxing in his recall from Chungking. That episode further diminished the importance of China in the Japanese-American war from the view of American strategists. On October 10, just before he left China, Stilwell telegraphed General Marshall, "Two and [a] half years of struggling have proved to me that if China is to make any effort in this war which will contribute to overall plan for defeat [of] Japan, CKS must be pushed into doing it."[22] But time was running out. Roosevelt decided that "pushing" Chiang Kai-shek into undertaking more intensive military efforts in cooperation with an American commander would further complicate American-Chinese relations and create an undesirable political situation in China, out of proportion to any contribution that reformed Chinese forces could make to the war in the Pacific. After Stilwell's recall, General Albert C. Wedemeyer replaced him as Chiang's chief of staff and commander of U.S. forces in China, but Roosevelt no longer insisted on making him commander over all Chinese forces.

At the same time, Hurley, the special envoy, was instructed to remain in China to work for its military unification, but he had little to work with other than a sense of mission and unbounded optimism as he tried to mediate between the Nationalists and Communists. Unlike Stilwell, he could not count on the White House or the joint chiefs to put pressure on Chiang Kai-shek. Because

Hurley assumed that Chiang was still the undisputed leader of China, there was little leverage he could use. One person could not have much influence when the overall U.S. strategy was oriented less and less to the Chinese problem. In fact, some in Washington were even beginning to think that perhaps the United States should give up military involvement in China altogether. General George Lincoln, an army member of the joint staff planners, remarked at their meeting in early December that Japanese successes without efficient countermeasures by China might result in Chiang's "going out of existence." In such a situation the only Chinese forces "with which we could work would be those of the Communists in Shensi," he said. Under the circumstances, should the United States still try to hold whatever area was left to the Nationalists and build up from there, "or would it be better to pull out of China entirely? . . . If Chiang Kai-shek's Government should be eliminated, what basis would there be upon which to build a government in China, after the war?" The joint staff planners directed the joint war plans committee to study these queries.[23]

Although nothing definite was decided at this time, the fact that these questions were raised at the joint chiefs' office is significant, for it reflected a willingness to reduce American commitments in China. Combined with the yielding of preponderant influence in Southeast Asia to the British as well as the continued advances across the Pacific and planning for Japanese surrender, it revealed a pattern of American initiatives in certain areas of the Asia-Pacific region and lessening involvement in other areas. The implications of this posture for the postwar period were clearly shown when the joint chiefs around this time drew up guidelines for the temporary administration of captured and liberated lands. The personnel of military administration, they stated, "depends primarily upon the composition of the forces engaged in conducting the actual military operation." In other words, the British and Europeans, by far the largest components of the invading forces in Southeast Asia, would administer reconquered territories there, while China would be mostly left in the hands of Chinese. Even if "strategic developments bring about the occupation by American Forces of Chinese territory now occupied by the Japanese," the joint chiefs said, "the administration of civil affairs will be turned over to the Chinese governmental authorities as soon as military exigencies permit."[24] Chinese-American wartime collaboration and postwar cooperation were fast becoming an obsolete concept.

HAVING THUS roughly defined the nature of relations with Britain and China in the immediate future, it remained for the United States to reaffirm its position vis-à-vis the Soviet Union in Asia. This was one of the main objectives of the second meeting of Roosevelt, Churchill, and Stalin at Yalta, on the Crimean peninsula, during February 4–11, 1945. By then United Nations forces were fast converging upon the Rhine in the west and the Oder in the east, and the capture of Berlin seemed to be only a matter of time. In the Pacific, Luzon in the Philippines had fallen in early January, and the United States was preparing for an assault upon Iwo Jima and the Ryukyus on the way to the home islands of Japan. Under the circumstances, a meeting of the three heads of state was imperative to clarify the role of the Soviet Union in the defeat of Japan and in postwar Asia, as well as the nature of U.S.-Soviet relations in Europe after the impending German surrender.

The Asian question was settled without much difficulty. Roosevelt, Churchill, and Stalin generally followed the outlines of their previous understandings and accepted a fairly well defined framework for future action. Stalin promised once again that Russia would enter the war against Japan approximately three months after the end of the European war. As a reward for participation, the Soviet Union would regain South Sakhalin and the Kurile Islands, lease Port Arthur as a military base, establish a predominant position in the port of Dairen, which was to be internationalized, and retain preponderant interests in the railways in Manchuria. These concessions were in part those that the State Department had agreed on. Others, notably the Manchurian arrangements, had not been anticipated, but they expressed Roosevelt's continued concern for cooperation with the Soviet Union. He believed that these arrangements, coupled with American acceptance of de facto Soviet control over the areas adjoining it in Europe, would give the two great powers a stake in maintaining the stability of the postwar international order. By the same token, the Yalta agreements revealed Roosevelt's dwindling interest in cooperation with China as the cornerstone of his Asian policy. Far more crucial would be Russia's and America's acceptance of the new status quo.[25]

After the Yalta Conference the United States continued to look to the Soviet Union rather than to China for cooperation. The Russians were still unwilling to permit American survey parties to enter Siberia to determine the two countries' respective roles in the Japanese war. But this was no longer such a serious question, because United States policy was oriented toward reestablishing stability on the basis of American and Soviet spheres of power in the Asia-Pacific region. What the Soviet Union chose to do within its sphere was primarily its own business, and in the same way the United States would insist on prerogatives in certain areas. The State-War-Navy Coordinating Committee visualized that the Soviets would occupy Sakhalin, the Kuriles, and possibly Hokkaido, while the rest of Japan proper would be occupied primarily by U.S. forces.[26] There was a clear-cut division of responsibility.

China, of course, stood somewhere in between. On the one hand, the United States had been politically and economically involved in wartime China, but on the other hand, Soviet influence and interest were also ascendant there. In the words of Barney M. Giles, deputy commander of the army air force, the Soviet Union "considers China shall not become a base for aggressive action against the USSR on the part of another great power, or itself be in a position to threaten the Soviet territories in Asia." For this reason, "the USSR will aim at an influence in China that is at least equal to that of any other power."[27] The question was, should the United States do anything about the situation? President Roosevelt had already recognized Russian interests in Manchuria, and the Stilwell episode had disillusioned him about the idea of a unified, friendly, and cooperative China. There was a possibility, therefore, that in the absence of a strong and clear American policy, Russia might go beyond its spheres of influence and try to establish some control over China proper. Such a development was not in the Yalta formula, and the United States government still envisaged a power balance based on Russia and America supporting an independent China.

But the deteriorating political conditions in that country made it extremely difficult to devise an effective approach to the problem.

For instance when General Giles suggested that the United States might assist in organizing, training, and equipping a strong Chinese air force, the State Department objected, saying that no such commitment should be made until the political picture in China cleared up. As a Department memorandum of April 3 put it, "The unrepresentative character of the present government which is strictly controlled by a single party . . . the inefficiency and corruption prevalent in the present Chinese army and air force, the lack of protection accorded to persons and property and the absence of freedom of speech and freedom of the press, constitute factors which have created widespread dissatisfaction with the present National Government."[28] This situation was not considered favorable to the peace and security of East Asia, but the United States could take few specific steps at this juncture, beyond trying to persuade the Nationalists and Communists to come together. Hurley, who replaced Gauss as ambassador in Chungking, continued these efforts with less and less support from the State Department and from his own subordinates, who did not share his optimism that reform and reunification of China under Chiang Kai-shek were still possible. As a result the trend continued toward further withdrawal of America from Chinese affairs and the tendency to do nothing against Soviet power in China. Whereas in the weeks after Yalta America expressed misgivings over Soviet behavior in Eastern Europe, where domestic divisions were intensifying, there was a greater sense of equanimity with respect to China. This may have reflected Roosevelt's and his aides' basic optimism that the Chinese would never accept alien rule and that in some distant future, they would unify themselves and be a major stabilizing force in Asia. In the meantime, the American government was satisfied that the Yalta framework was the best guarantee of Asian peace and security. By allowing the Russians some rights in Manchuria, but within the framework of American-Soviet understanding, the United States was hoping to create a new status quo in postwar Asia.

In Southeast Asia, Yalta and its aftermath further contributed to the diminution of China's role. During the Yalta Conference the question of Europe's Asian colonies was settled through silence; with no formal decision, the way was left open for the return of the metropolitan powers. Moreover, Roosevelt, Churchill, and Stalin agreed that the new trusteeship scheme was to be established only over former mandates, enemy territories, or those lands that the victorious Allies voluntarily gave up. Such a policy clearly legiti-mized the reestablishment of the European colonies and could only mean a further decline of American power in the region. It also implied that China's role would likewise diminish, in that the num-ber of its trusteeships would be drastically curtailed.

Indochina was an example. In 1942 Roosevelt had proposed and Chiang Kai-shek had accepted that China would participate in a trusteeship for the former French colony, but after Yalta the whole scheme was a dead letter. American willingness to let French mili-tary personnel return to the peninsula, already evident in late 1944, turned into eagerness when the Japanese overthrew the Vichy regime in Indochina and supported its "national independence" in early March. The joint chiefs in Washington authorized General Wede-meyer to coordinate military strategies with a French general. Wedemeyer, temporarily in the United States in mid-March, was told by Admiral Leahy and other military planners that the new United States policy was "to aid French, providing such assistance does not interfere with operations now planned [for China and the Pacific]." That definition, noted the Far Eastern subcommittee of SWNCC, indicated "the possibility of a change in United States policy relative to assistance to the French in Indochina."[29] For the first time the United States was ready to deal with and assist the French in Indochina, with the consequence that the future of the peninsula was determined primarily by French military action.

As the United States reduced, and in some areas even with-drew, its power and influence from China, Southeast Asia, and Northeast Asia, it sharply defined its own spheres of influence. It would control affairs over most of the Pacific Ocean and would have a predominant say in the occupation of Japan. As earlier, America's position combined power arrangements with internation-alist principles so that in these areas, at least, the State Department plans could be put into effect. Their input was particularly notice-able with respect to Japan through SWNCC's Far Eastern subcom-mittee.

Soon after Yalta, on February 19, the subcommittee was charged with analyzing various Pacific and Asian problems, includ-ing "basic policies and objectives of the United States in the Pacific and the Far East," "basic directives for pre-surrender military

government in Japan proper," "military occupation of Japan including the extent of United States and allied participation, and
the national composition of forces," and "post-surrender military
government of Japan"—dealing with the Japanese political structure under military government, the treatment of the emperor, and
measures for abolishing militarism and strengthening democratic
tendencies.[30] Although the study of most of these issues was not
completed until May 1945, the basic position regarding Japanese
surrender was by now quite clear and specific, as shown in a number
of subcommittee documents. The emperor was to proclaim the
nation's unconditional surrender and order the armed forces to
cease military activities. The supreme commander of the Allied
powers was to assume all legislative, judicial, and executive power
and authority over Japanese territory. However, he would order
all Japanese officials, civilian and military, to remain at their posts
and perform their normal functions to maintain law and order.
Most of these ideas had been reiterated within various groups and
committees of the State Department, but they gained more formal
status through the policy-drafting process undertaken by SWNCC.
Thus little change in policy toward Japan was anticipated. Because
it would be under United States control, it could be fitted into
the State Department's reintegrationist scheme more easily than
other parts of Asia.

IT WAS LEFT TO THE Japanese to decide whether to seek reintegration through a timely cessation of the hostilities. Through various
intelligence reports gathered in neutral territories such as Sweden,
Switzerland, and the Vatican, and by merely reading the Western
press, Japanese leaders were able to grasp the outlines of the Yalta
deliberations. All available information pointed to possible Soviet
entry into the Asian war. As the supreme war council noted at its
meeting of February 15, Russia had every intention of joining its
allies against Japan in order to influence postwar dispositions. The
United States would continue to put pressure on the Russians to
do so, at the same time advancing its own forces, after the Philippine
operation, toward the China coast and the islands adjacent to Japan
proper. Those islands would probably be invaded by August or
September at the latest, possibly even in June or July, with the
assistance of British and Chinese forces.[31] These accurate observa-

tions obviously contradicted Tokyo's policy of turning Chungking and Moscow against the Anglo-American powers. February 1945, therefore, should have been the point when the Japanese leaders clearly recognized the futility of their approach and began to explore alternative ways of speedily terminating the war. Unfortunately, it took another half year before they were able to develop a unified policy for peace.

At least two men were willing to express in clear language what the nation should do in the aftermath of Yalta. On February 14 Konoe had an audience with the emperor and presented to him a memorial written in collaboration with Yoshida Shigeru, the veteran diplomat. The audience was a result of the emperor's wish, expressed to Kido in January, to see the *jūshin* individually to discuss the deteriorating military situation. They went to see him one after another, but only Konoe was willing to state his views frankly and unambiguously. According to his memorial, Japan's defeat was "unfortunately inevitable," and the war must be brought to an end as quickly as possible. Although others who shared his pessimism hesitated to approach the United States and Britain directly to sue for peace, Konoe and Yoshida saw no alternative. This was Japan's only choice, for the Anglo-American powers (and possibly China) would be much less vindictive, avaricious, and dangerous as victors than the Soviet Union. Public opinion in America and Britain, the memorial pointed out, did not seem to be demanding a fundamental change of Japan's national policy as a condition of peace; therefore, "defeat alone would not seriously affect the national polity." Moreover, although the United States, Britain, and China were calling for the destruction of Japanese militarism, this did not mean that they intended to annihilate Japan's armed forces. Instead, they might be willing to consider peace if the Japanese military establishment changed its orientation and got rid of some extremist elements.

In sharp contrast to these powers, the Soviet Union was a far more serious menace to Japan, Konoe asserted. The Russians had not given up their ambition of turning the entire world to communism and had every intention of interfering in Japanese politics to bring about a communist revolution. Should Japan fall under communist and Russian influence, the polity and domestic stability could not be preserved. The result would be further turmoil, a possibility that must be taken seriously because the war had created domestic conditions ripe for it. "Declining standards of living, increasing influence of laborers, extreme hostility toward America and Britain, a corresponding sentiment of friendship for Russia, radical movements within the armed forces, the new bureaucrats who are taking advantage of them, and the leftists who are manipulating all these forces behind the scenes"—all these factors were creating conditions favorable for a communist takeover, and they would become more grievous as the war went on. In this sense, those who called for continued resistance to the enemy in the name of preserving the national polity were playing into the hands of the revolutionary conspirators. Those who were committed to domestic stability must therefore be aware of right-wing as well as left-wing movements and resolve to terminate the war as quickly as possible. Actually, it was those who wanted to fight to the bitter end who were preparing the ground for communist revolution. The most important thing was to "sweep away" military fanatics and to isolate their civilian sympathizers, so that the government could approach the United States, Britain, and China about concluding the war. That was the only way to save domestic order.[32]

This was a clear expression of one type of thinking that had persisted among civilian leaders, even though submerged under the rhetoric of enmity toward the Anglo-American powers. It articulated what others had referred to only indirectly, namely, the idea that Japan's salvation lay in returning to the framework of cooperation with the Anglo-American powers, not in opposing them. Although the government had often expressed concepts that harked back to the internationalist framework of the 1920s, official policy had not yet endorsed reconciliation with these powers. The Konoe memorial argued that the strategy of ending the war through Russia and China was doomed to failure and urged Japan to return to the earlier framework. In making explicit the connection between domestic social order and political stability, on one hand, and international peace and accommodation, on the other, the memorial was reflecting views widely held in Washington. The United States could not have asked for a better vindication of the assumptions underlying its planning for Japan.

If Konoe had had his way, the Japanese government would then and there have decided to concentrate on peace moves, seeking direct contact with the United States as the principal antagonist and ending all other pursuits. Foreign Minister Shigemitsu was ready to go in that direction. At a meeting of the Privy Council on February 28, he admitted that all his attempts at "detaching the Soviet Union from America and Britain" had failed and that the only available option was to deal directly with the other powers.[33] He asked Swedish Ambassador Widor Bagge, just before the ambassador left for home in late March, to intercede on Japan's behalf and obtain peace terms from the United States and Britain.[34] Before anything more came of this, however, the Koiso cabinet fell from power, and Shigemitsu left office.

During the two months between Yalta and the downfall of the cabinet, in spite of growing awareness of the futility of existing strategies, Prime Minister Koiso was not yet ready to do what Konoe, Shigemitsu, and others were urging. Instead, he gambled on two tactical moves. One was to do away with the Vichy regime in Indochina and open the way for the area's independence. This was a desperate attempt to prevent the return of British and Free French forces to the peninsula, but such a transparent courting of indigenous nationalism was spurned by Ho Chi Minh and other native leaders, who declared that they would continue to cooperate with the United Nations to get rid of the Japanese regime.[35]

Second, Koiso sought to carry out the supreme war council's earlier decision to approach Chungking by making use of Miao Pin, the former leader of the Hsin-min Hui, who resided in Shanghai but reportedly had contacts with men close to Chiang Kai-shek. Anticipating opposition from the military and other members of the cabinet, the prime minister decided to act alone. He arranged, through his personal confidants, for Miao to fly to Tokyo to initiate peace moves. According to Tamura Shinsaku, an *Asahi* correspondent who had kept in close touch with Miao in Shanghai, Chiang authorized Miao to go to Tokyo and to express willingness to discuss peace on condition that the Nanking regime be dissolved and Japanese troops withdrawn from China. Miao himself believed that these were sound bases for a Chungking-Tokyo rapprochement and would lead ultimately to peace between the United States and Japan, thereby preventing a Soviet takeover of Manchuria.

Miao arrived in Tokyo on March 16, but Koiso kept him waiting while he maneuvered to have himself appointed war minister so that all diplomatic and military decisions would be unified as the country prepared for peace. Unfortunately, the army adamantly opposed his appointment, and Shigemitsu was skeptical of the Miao scheme. On March 21 the supreme war council failed to endorse the scheme, and when Koiso on April 2 appealed for support directly to the emperor, the latter refused to go against the council's wishes.[36] Facing these failures, Koiso had no choice but to resign his office. It was a coincidence filled with irony that on the very day he submitted his resignation, April 5, the Soviet Union notified the Tokyo government of its intention not to renew the neutrality treaty, which was to expire in one year. All of Japan's efforts to work through China and Russia to end the war had come to nothing.

Within a week of Koiso's resignation, President Roosevelt died, and a month later Germany finally surrendered. It is regrettable that the Japanese leaders had failed to approach the United States directly in February or March to initiate cease-fire discussions, for if the United States had responded to such overtures— and the available evidence makes such speculation plausible—the plans that had been worked out over the years would have been implemented. The resulting peace would have approximated what the Konoe memorial anticipated, a humiliating defeat for Japan but far less destruction of the homeland. For the United States the peace would have confirmed the outlines of the Yalta agreements and might have made the Chinese question less complicated, in that Soviet forces might not have penetrated deeply into Manchuria if the war had ended before the German surrender.

THE PEACE COULD have been negotiated by Roosevelt and Koiso, but instead, the main actors changed to Harry S. Truman and Admiral Suzuki Kantarō. The change was more than a matter of personnel. Each leader had his own conception of how to end the war, and while they hesitated to act expeditiously soon after entering office, the fighting at sea, on the ground, and in the air continued, resulting in additional and, in retrospect, unnecessary casualties.

The change in leadership necessitated strategic reconsiderations and reformulations in both Tokyo and Washington. In Tokyo a conference of elder statesmen was convened on the afternoon of April 5, immediately following Koiso's resignation. All of Japan's former prime ministers who were then living gathered at the Imperial Palace and talked for three hours. Tōjō noted that the next cabinet would be the last wartime cabinet; therefore, the *jūshin* would have to decide whether to go on fighting or to end the hostilities immediately by accepting an unconditional surrender. Most members were reluctant to consider surrender, with some, such as Hiranuma and Hirota, insisting that Japan had no choice but to fight on to win. Kido remarked that conditions inside the country were indeed "quite grievous." The people did not seem to be cooperating enthusiastically with the government at a time when the homeland was about to be invaded, and there were even signs of antimilitaristic sentiment. It was therefore imperative, he said, to organize a cabinet in which the people could place their trust.

Although Hiranuma, Hirota, and others agreed, they insisted that the next cabinet be led by men who were wholeheartedly devoted to prosecuting the war, not by advocates of peace. Even Konoe, in spite of his advocacy of peace, as expressed to the emperor in February, said that Koiso's successor should be a military person who was committed to fighting. He may have felt that Japan should fight for the time being and then seize a right opportunity to call for peace; otherwise the nation might be split even before peace initiatives were undertaken. In any event, all were agreed on the appointment of a military leader. Tōjō suggested General Hata Shunroku, saying that an army general would be the best choice insofar as the next cabinet would have to be concerned with the defense of the home islands. But he was overruled by other *jūshin* who preferred Suzuki Kantarō, a retired admiral who had served as lord privy seal. Their reasoning was that appointment of an army general on active duty could tie the new government too closely to military vicissitudes and reverses, while Suzuki would ensure separation of the government from military operations. In this sense the admiral's appointment was a modest victory for those senior statesmen who wanted to ease themselves back into positions of influence while avoiding an open rift with the military. The Suzuki cabinet, established on April 7, was to abide by the supreme command's strategic decisions but it was to gradually remove the military from the position of ultimate authority on questions of peace.[37]

The new prime minister replaced Shigemitsu with Tōgō as foreign minister, agreeing with Tōgō that ending the hostilities should be their goal. At the same time, Suzuki, like the *jūshin*, was well aware that domestic groups, especially the armed forces, would have to be persuaded to accept peace or at least to desist from sabotaging peace negotiations. Hoping that strong military leaders would be able to check extremists, Suzuki persuaded Yonai to remain as navy minister and promoted Vice War Minister Anami Korechika to succeed Sugiyama, who had been too closely identified with the war, as war minister.

Thus reconstituted, the Japanese government might have immediately begun laying the groundwork, domestically and abroad, for an eventual peace. Unfortunately, during its first month the new cabinet took almost no initiatives. This was the period of the gruesome fighting in Okinawa, while in Europe the fall of Germany was only a matter of days. The government and the supreme command in Tokyo were preoccupied with the possibility of an invasion of the Japanese homeland by the enemy countries with large reinforcements from the European theater. Plans had to be drafted to provide for the nation's essential needs in a state of siege, to prevent domestic turmoil, and to secure any shipping that was still available for military use. Still, in retrospect it seems that it should have been possible to reorient Japanese policy away from continued warfare, toward a few steps for peace. Foreign Minister Tōgō, in particular, might have at least followed up his predecessor's initiatives and explored whether the American and British governments could be contacted through Sweden, but he showed little interest in the Swedish connection.

About the only overt step he took in April was convening a second East Asian conference in Tokyo, as a sequel to the 1943 conference. Since it was physically impossible for the Asian heads of state to participate, their ambassadors met for a day on April 23 to demonstate Asian solidarity at the time of the United Nations conference in San Francisco. Just like the 1943 conference, however, the second meeting failed to enunciate anything distinctively "Asian." Tōgō, in his keynote address, called for the establishment of a world order based not on imperialism but on justice. The conferees made the idea specific by adopting a seven-part declaration, reiterating their adherence to such principles as political equality, economic reciprocity, equal opportunity, international cooperation, cultural exchange, armament reduction, and peaceful modifications of the international system. These principles, which Tōgō later characterized as his conception of "Japan's war aims," went several steps beyond those adopted at the 1943 conference and marked an almost complete return to Wilsonian internationalism. The mention of armament reduction and peaceful changes, in particular, made the 1945 declaration virtually interchangeable with the Atlantic Charter and all other wartime enunciations by the United Nations.[38] By taking pains to have the delegates issue such a declaration, Tōgō may have hoped to signal to the enemy countries that their war objectives were the same. More important, however, he wanted to convey to his countrymen that they had little to lose by embracing these principles. Peace would not necessarily be a disgrace; it would simply mean an agreement with the enemy about an acceptable framework for Japanese foreign affairs. This was what the United Nations had been insisting upon.

The trouble was that such efforts were not well coordinated with other activities of the Japanese government in late April and early May. Instead of even tacitly acknowledging the need for a peace strategy, the supreme war council determined at its meeting of April 30 that in the event of Germany's defeat, the Japanese would "have to be unified to the last man, to ensure victory, protect the fatherland, and carry through the war." More specifically, the government was to try to alienate the Soviet Union from the Anglo-American powers, "orient our policies toward the Soviet Union," and suppress pacifist sentiments at home, all futile measures that had already been tried. The fact that they had nothing else at this stage was an indication of the utter failure of leadership.[39] When Germany surrendered on May 8, the Japanese government had made no serious preparations to seize the opportunity for terminating the Asian war. Prime Minister Suzuki exhorted his countrymen to redouble their determination to fight on in the faith that ultimate victory would be theirs. If, as he later claimed, he was then secretly working for peace, he failed to send any encouraging signal either to people at home or to the enemy countries.

Interestingly enough, while the Japanese leadership was paralyzed, fixing its gaze on the illusory goal of detaching Russia from American and Britain but actually doing little to reach it, the new presidency of Harry S. Truman was undertaking a reassessment of the wartime alliance between the United States and the Soviet Union. While the Japanese persisted in the idea of gaining mediation and support from Russia, American officials in Washington and elsewhere were beginning to consider that war with Japan might be ended without Soviet help. Some were even skeptical that Soviet participation would be in the best interest of the United States, which should, if at all possible, try to end the war before the massive infusion of Russian troops. Inevitably, the issue transcended the merely strategic question of how to bring Japan to its knees and involved the future of American-Russian cooperation. With the passing of Roosevelt, the most ardent champion of such cooperation, Truman's presidency was already beginning to show signs of drift on the question. But Tokyo exhibited no overt interest in peace. If Tokyo had approached Washington, not Moscow, for peace, it might have encouraged those in America who wanted to end the war before the Soviets could enter it. Such, however, was not to be the case.

On April 12, the day Roosevelt died, General Marshall cabled General MacArthur and Admiral Chester Nimitz, who had just been named commanders of all United States army and navy forces, respectively, in the Pacific, and apprised them of a division of views among the military strategists in Washington. One school, said Marshall, continued to believe that Soviet entry into the war was essential before the American landing on Japan proper, tentatively scheduled for December. According to this view, while Soviet forces tied down Japanese troops on the Asian continent, U.S. troops would invade the homeland. Only then would the Japanese come to their senses and surrender.

A contrasting view held that an air-sea blockade and bombardment would be a more effective means of subduing Japan, and must in any event be undertaken before a landing was attempted. This view, which was gaining influence within the joint chiefs' office, was elaborated in a memorandum by the joint intelligence committee on April 18. "Effective air and sea blockade of Japan Proper," it pointed out, "combined with large-scale strategic bombing, within Allied capabilities, will reduce progressively Japanese capability to resist Allied attack." The Japanese navy and air force would be neutralized, while the army would lose its mobility. Since Japanese industry was concentrated on a few metropolitan areas, sustained bombing would destroy most of it. A critical food shortage would develop, with the result that "the psychological effects upon the Japanese people as a whole will be most detrimental and will progressively undermine their confidence in victory or even confidence in the hope of avoiding complete and inevitable defeat." Although the authors of the memorandum cautioned against expecting a quick victory as a result of the blockade-bombardment strategy, they were optimistic that "eventually there will come the time when the Japanese Emperor and many other leaders, probably influenced by Germany's experience, will seek an end to hostilities prior to complete destruction of their country."[40]

This second view, it is clear, accurately assessed the situation in Japan and anticipated what was to take place. Nevertheless, the Japanese government and high command were still hesitating to take the first necessary and explicit step for peace. Some American officials recognized that the Japanese might be induced to do so if intensified military operations were combined with political initiatives. The above memorandum suggested that "a clarification of Allied intentions with regard to the Japanese nation might bring nearer the possibility of unconditional surrender." Then the Japanese government, backed by the emperor, might decide to "accept a rationalized version of unconditional surrender before the end of 1945." If the formula could enable Tokyo's leaders to surrender without the stigma of unconditional surrender, "we believe that Japan might surrender without the invasion of Japan Proper." This last point was hotly debated by the top military strategists, with both MacArthur and Nimitz insisting that invasion of the homeland was still the best way to bring about Japan's defeat.[41]

Taking their advice, the joint staff planners adopted a recommendation on April 24 for invading Kyushu and the Kanto plain (code-worded Olympic and Coronet, respectively) "at the earliest practicable date"—presumably starting with Kyushu in November. The planners asserted that the blockade-bombardment strategy, coupled with the Olympic-Coronet operations, would bring about Japan's "decisive military defeat and the results equivalent to unconditional surrender, similar to the present situation in Germany." They argued that Japanese surrender could be hastened if the Japanese were shown that "destruction or national suicide is not implied" by their acceptance of an "unconditional surrender." Once persuaded that their nation would be spared total annihilation, they might be willing to sign and enforce a surrender instrument.[42]

Clearly there was an interest in redefining an unconditional surrender formula "in terms understandable to the Japanese," so that the war could be terminated without prolonged and costly fighting and without destroying Japan. The best approach, according to the joint chiefs, would be for the United States to issue "a declaration of intentions" to clarify the meaning of unconditional surrender to the Japanese. They drafted such a declaration on May 3, stating that the president was to explain that unconditional surrender meant "the termination of the influence of the military leaders who have brought Japan to the present brink of disaster," as well as "not prolonging the present agony and suffering of the Japanese in the vain hope of victory." However, "Unconditional surrender does not mean the extermination or enslavement of the Japanese people. On the contrary, it does mean that the people of Japan, after eliminating the burdens of militarism, can begin to earn their way back into the fellowship of peace-loving and law-abiding nations."[43]

It is interesting that nothing was said about coordinating action with, or even consulting, the other Allies before issuing such a statement. The United States planned to act unilaterally in getting the Japanese to surrender. In contrast to the war in Europe, which was winding down, in the Asian-Pacific war America had greater freedom of action because of its predominant role. Again it is clear that the Japanese were making a serious miscalculation in trying to end the war through the Soviet Union. This point becomes even clearer when one studies Washington's plans for the occupation of Japan. On May 1 Dooman, the State Department member in SWNCC's Asia-Pacific subcommittee, wrote a lengthy memorandum on the subject, summing up the department's deliberations going back to 1943. The memorandum did not explicitly call for unilateral occupation. "Any plan for the occupation and control of Japan solely by American forces would be diametrically opposed to [the] basic United States policy of international collaboration on security matters arising out of this war." Apart from the fact that such an undertaking would be too costly, much good would be accomplished if Chinese and other Asiatic troops participated in the occupation. "This use of Asiatic units would force the Japanese to realize that the greater part of the world, both Occidental and Oriental, is against them and would afford them no basis for interpreting the war in the Pacific as a racial war and as one designed to spread 'white imperialism' throughout Asia." But Dooman unequivocally supported what by then had become the basic guidelines for the occupation: "The representation of countries other than the United States in the forces to occupy Japan and therefore in the military government of Japan should not be so large as to prejudice the predominantly American character of that Military Government." Unlike Germany, which was to be divided into zones of separate military administration by the different occupying countries, Japan "was basically a single geographic, ethnic, sociological, economic and political unit," and it would be more practicable to treat it as a single unit.[44] This principle, of course, was predicated upon the predominant role to be played by United States forces and thus constituted an integral part of the general wartime policy that Japan was part of the American sphere of power.

There were additional reasons why Tokyo's leaders should have taken definite steps toward peace in April and May. One was the successful development of atomic weapons by the Manhattan Engineering District. On April 25, the key men who knew about the secret project—Marshall, Stimson, and Groves—visited the White House and told President Truman for the first time about the atomic bomb undertaking, which was nearing completion. Two days later the project's target committee had its first meeting to discuss possible targets for the bombs. At that meeting a representative of the air force recommended Hiroshima as a primary target. He also noted that the Twentieth Air Force was "systematically bombing out" Tokyo, Yokohama, Osaka, and other major cities "with the prime purpose in mind of not leaving one stone lying on another." He informed the committee that the air force planned to drop 100,000 tons of bombs on Japan per month by the end of 1945. The target committee endorsed these ideas at its second meeting on May 10 and approved a recommendation that Kyoto, Hiroshima, Yokohama, and the Kokura Arsenal be the four preferred locations for the use of atomic bombs.[45] If the Japanese had been aware of such plans, they might have decided at once to come to terms with the United States; in the event, however, the Suzuki cabinet during April and May made elaborate plans for the defense of the home islands in preparation for expected Allied landings.

The development of atomic bombs also meant that Soviet

participation in the war might be even less essential. On April 24 the joint staff planners concluded that "because of our estimated ability to interdict Japanese movement between the Asiatic main- land and Japan proper, early Russian entry into the war against Japan and attendant containing of the Kwantung army is no longer necessary to make invasion feasible." The planners lacked precise information about the atomic bomb project, but the joint chiefs, who did know, endorsed their recommendation on May 10, thus putting an official seal of approval on the idea that as far as strategic considerations were concerned, the United States no longer needed the Soviet Union as an ally against Japan.[46]

Some officials in Washington went a step farther and ques- tioned the wisdom of Soviet entry into the Japanese war. The above memo by the joint staff planners was one of the first wartime docu- ments to establish a connection between the strategic and the politi- cal implications of Soviet participation. "It should be noted," they pointed out, "that the Cairo Declaration included provision that Manchuria be returned to China and that Russia has not yet sub- scribed to the principles of this declaration. If Russia enters the war her forces will probably be the first into Manchuria. This will raise the question of introducing at least token U.S. forces in China." Here was the beginning of a tendency, which became stronger among the military and eventually among civilian authorities as well, to decide China policy not solely on strategic grounds of the war against Japan, but on political considerations dictated by Russia's expanding power in Asia. Already on May 1, Secretary of the Navy James V. Forrestal, at a meeting of SWNCC, had asked whether it might not be necessary for the United States to revive Japan's power to counterbalance that of the Soviet Union.[47] Al- though few others went so far at this time, enough officials were troubled by the apparently increasing difficulties in effecting Ameri- can-Russian cooperation in Eastern Europe that they expressed some doubt about the wisdom of such cooperation in the war against Japan. It is ironic that just when the Japanese were desperately trying to prevent Soviet entry into the war, Americans were losing their enthusiasm for Soviet participation.

This did not mean, however, that the United States was re- orienting its policy toward the Asia-Pacific region. Rather, the skepticism about Soviet participation, the development of the atomic bomb, and the stress on political initiatives toward Japan all confirmed what had been a pronounced characteristic of the war, namely, the American tendency to unilateralism and to claiming certain areas of the region as its primary responsibility. The war in the Pacific would continue to be predominantly an American affair, with far less inter-Allied cooperation than elsewhere. By the same token, the United States was willing to let other countries have their own spheres of influence. It did not redefine its war objectives to resist Soviet encroachment on Manchuria; rather, it let the Russians help themselves to the rights they had been promised there, as part of the arrangement for maintaining postwar equilibrium.

Likewise, in Southeast Asia, where Britain and France were fast regaining their lost colonies, the United States took no step to stop them. In Indochina the State Department and the joint chiefs of staff now definitely retreated from their earlier espousal of a trusteeship policy. In a memorandum written in late April the State Department noted that there was "not the slightest possibility at the present time or in the foreseeable future that France will volunteer to place Indo-China under an international trusteeship, or will consent to any program of international accountability which is not applied to the colonial possessions of other powers." For the United States to put pressure upon France would "run counter to the established American policy of aiding France to regain her strength in order that she may be better fitted to share responsibility in maintaining the peace of Europe and the world." The department recommended to the new president that the United States "should neither oppose the restoration of Indo-China to France . . . nor take any action toward French overseas possessions which it is not prepared to take or suggest with regard to the colonial possessions of our other Allies." The joint chiefs concurred with these views, and thus the Indochina question was closed as far as the United States was concerned. It would aid the French resistance movement and help France recover Indochina, but the future of that land would be in the hands of French authorities.[48] There could be no more telling epitaph for the once-enticing idea of turning Indochina into a trusteeship or of establishing a regional scheme in the colonial region. Instead, the return of the European powers to Southeast Asia was to be part of the postwar arrangements, just like the Soviet position in Northeast Asia and American predominance in Japan and the Pacific. Postwar Asia was already in the making, and it was only a matter of time before the Japanese would decide to fit themselves into the scheme.

ON MAY 8, THE DAY Germany surrendered, President Truman called on the Japanese to lay down their arms. The statement, which incorporated the draft that had just been prepared by the joint chiefs' office, assured the Japanese that unconditional surrender did not mean their "extermination or enslavement," but on the contrary paved the way for their reintegration into "the fellowship of peace-loving and law-abiding nations." As conceptualized then, this "fellowship" amounted to the Yalta formula coupled with Wilsonian internationalism. This idea should have been acceptable to the Japanese government, but it refused to believe that the most practical way to end the war was through direct contact with the United States. On May 11, 12, and 14, the supreme war council in Tokyo deliberated Japan's strategy. Those present—Prime Minister Suzuki, Foreign Minister Tōgō, and the top military officers—agreed to implement the April 30 decision of the council that in the event of German surrender Japan should "promote our policies toward the Soviet Union." More specifically, on Tōgō's insistence, this strategy was interpreted to mean "initiation of talks between Japan and the Soviet Union in order not merely to prevent the latter's entry into the war, but also to obtain its benevolent neutrality, and ultimately to have it intercede on our behalf to bring the war to an end."[49] For the first time the top leaders clearly indicated a commitment to termination of hostilities.

This much was Tōgō's signal achievement. But he was also a captive of the prevailing sentiment favoring an approach to the Soviet Union. Although the principles of international relations in which he believed—as in the declaration of the East Asian representatives on April 23—had more in common with those expressed by the Anglo-American powers than those of the Soviet Union, he delayed the end of the war by seeking Soviet good offices. According to his postwar memoirs, he believed that only Russia was in a position to influence the Anglo-American peace terms; negotiating directly with the United States or going through a neutral country such as Switzerland or Sweden would result in the enemy's insistence on unconditional surrender.[50] Just after the Japanese surrender on August 15, he defended his Soviet strategy by saying that Japan had had to seek "Russia's sincere mediation" if the nation were to obtain "a peace on the basis of something other than unconditional surrender."[51] He feared that unconditional surrender would damage the national polity and be unacceptable to the military and would throw the country into total chaos. To prevent this and to placate the army, Tōgō reasoned, Soviet good offices at least had to be tried.

This reasoning may have made some sense in the context of domestic politics. Even so, it is doubtful that Tōgō and the others really thought through the possible implications of Soviet intercession. They knew that Japan's large concessions had failed to persuade Russia to maintain its neutrality. If Japan sought their goodwill one more time, the Russians would certainly ask for even more extensive concessions, which would augment Soviet power and influence throughout Asia, particularly in Manchuria and the rest of China. Should that happen, it would be in Russia's interest to intercede on Japan's behalf only if defeated Japan were within the Soviet sphere of influence. Actually, such a scenario was not unwelcome to some Japanese officers who were dedicated to fighting the Anglo-American nations to the bitter end. They argued that making all possible concessions to Russia in China would exacerbate tensions between the Soviet Union and the United States, making the latter relatively weaker vis-à-vis Japan.[52] In that situation the Anglo-American powers might decide to preserve Japanese power against Russian expansion, or the Soviet Union might seek a Japanese alliance against them. Either way, Japan would be spared a complete defeat. But the outcome would have been very different from what Tōgō's strategem was calling for, namely, utilizing Russia to obtain a peace with America and Britain.

Another difficulty with Tōgō's postwar defense of his position is that although he justified the approach to Russia as the only alternative to an unconditional surrender, he had done very little to ascertain if that term really meant what it said. Actually, enough evidence was available to dispute that view. Apart from the Konoe memorandum of February 14 which gave a more realistic appraisal of American intentions, Tōgō had received numerous communications pointing out that the United States would not take unconditional surrender literally, that the peace terms would be open to bargaining. For instance, the political affairs bureau of the Foreign Ministry prepared a memorandum in June on possible American peace terms. According to this paper, the terms would include territorial dispositions in accordance with the Cairo declaration, American retention of the Pacific islands from which Japanese forces had been expelled, "complete wiping out of the military clique," "occupation of Japan to ensure demilitarization," and retention by the Japanese of some light industry and foreign trade. The only issue on which the United States government seemed undecided was the treatment of the emperor, because Americans were divided between those who viewed the emperor system as part and parcel of Japanese militarism and those who felt that the institution could be utilized to effect postwar reforms. The fact that Grew, who represented the second view, was acting secretary of state was significant, the paper concluded.[53] This assessment was basically accurate and should have been accepted at once by Tōgō and his colleagues. The major point that needed clarification was the status of the emperor. If they had then contacted the United States to ascertain that, it is likely that the officials in Washington would have taken such overtures seriously.

May and June would have been very propitious for such contacts, for men like Grew, as the Japanese memorandum correctly noted, were seriously endeavoring to end the war by assuring the Japanese that they could preserve the emperor system. Grew sought to persuade President Truman through Secretary of War Stimson, who shared his views, that the United States should issue a clarifying statement on this point; on May 28 he drafted such a statement, saying that if the Japanese people surrendered, they would "be permitted to determine their own future political structure."[54] Perhaps in an attempt to influence Truman indirectly, Grew also began conferring with George Sansom, a British diplomat-historian on the staff of the embassy in Washington. They shared the essentially reintegrationist view of Japan and believed that the emperor could play a positive role in reforming the country.[55]

In early June, former president Herbert Hoover also urged Truman to intimate to the Japanese what the unconditional surrender formula contained, in particular with regard to the emperor system. Grew forwarded the Hoover memo to the president and again recommended issuing a declaration of intent to speed up Japanese surrender. Such a declaration, Grew suggested, should make it clear that the United States was determined to "uproot" Japanese militarism, but that it was ready to encourage the Japanese people's "regeneration along liberal and cooperative lines" and to grant them the right to determine their own political future. This would assure the Japanese leaders that they had but to surrender, and the emperor system would be preserved. Otherwise, the war would be protracted. Grew was completely justified in stating:

> Every evidence, without exception, that we are able to obtain of the views of the Japanese with regard to the institution of the throne, indicates that the non-molestation of the person of the present emperor and the preservation of the institution of the throne comprise irreducible Japanese terms. These indications are that, whereas the Japanese would be ready to undergo most drastic privations so long as these irreducible terms were met, they are prepared for prolonged resistance if it be the intention of the United Nations to try the present emperor as a war criminal or to abolish the imperial institution. We are disposed to agree with the view that failure on our part to clarify our intentions in this regard, or the proclamation of our intention to try the emperor as a war criminal and to abolish the institution of the throne, will insure prolongation of the war and cost a large number of human lives.[56]

On June 15 Grew went to see the president and urged him to issue a clarifying statement.[57] The former ambassador was acting precisely as his Japanese acquaintances from prewar days thought he would.

Unfortunately, Grew's efforts was wasted on Foreign Minister Tōgō, who would not be diverted from trying to obtain, through Soviet intercession, "a peace on the basis of something other than unconditional surrender." Tōgō asked former prime minister Hirota to initiate talks with Soviet Ambassador Yakov Malik, which were held on June 3, 4, 24, and 29, all ending inconclusively. This was hardly surprising. Already on May 28, Stalin had told Harry Hopkins, who remained as Truman's adviser and who was visiting Moscow, that preparations for entering the Asian war were being stepped up and that Soviet forces would be ready to go to war against Japan by August 8.

Three weeks later, on June 18, President Truman formally approved implementation of the Olympic and Coronet operations, thus setting the stage for the invasion of Japan proper. Believing that Soviet help on the Asian continent would minimize American losses in these operations, Truman welcomed Stalin's assurances.[58] The two leaders agreed to meet in person with Prime Minister Churchill at Potsdam, outside Berlin, in July to discuss the Japanese war as well as European questions. By mid-June, therefore, it may be said that President Truman had put an end to speculation about the advisability of seeking Soviet participation. Although not unmindful of the political implications, Truman felt he could not rebuff Stalin's offer without doing serious damage to the war effort.

Under these circumstances the Hirota-Malik talks were doomed from the very beginning; they merely revealed to the Soviet Union the utter helplessness of Japan, giving the Russians all the more reason for joining the United Nations in the war against Japan. It certainly would not have been in their interest at this late hour to complicate matters by playing the role of mediator. All they had to do to obtain substantial territorial cessions was to deal Japan a coup de grace. Ironically, on the day that Olympic and Coronet were formally approved, the supreme war council in Tokyo met in the presence of the emperor and decided to send a special emissary to Russia to expedite the termination of hostilities. The emperor expressed his wish clearly, and for the first time in the presence of the top leaders, that peace be restored as expeditiously as possible. Still, neither he nor others at the meeting were inclined to approach the United States directly. They believed that Russia would convey Japan's interest in peace to the enemy countries.[59]

To compound the irony, on the very same day, June 18, President Truman met with Grew and the joint chiefs to discuss issuing a declaration along the lines suggested by Grew and Hoover. The president told Grew that although he liked the idea of making a public announcement on the meaning of unconditional surrender, "he decided to hold this up until it could be discussed" with Stalin and Churchill. Grew once again urged that the announcement be made as soon as possible, commenting that he "wanted to see every appropriate step taken which might encourage a peace movement in Japan."[60] But the Big Three meeting was not scheduled to take place until mid-July, which from Grew's point of view was a delay that might harden Japanese attitudes. But there was also opposition from the joint chiefs, who held that the Japanese might take such a declaration as a sign of weakness. They favored a straightforward call for unconditional surrender, and Truman sided with them.

Undaunted, Grew obtained the president's and the military leaders' support for some kind of public announcement by the three heads of state at Potsdam. The latter half of June was taken up with drafting a statement that was acceptable to the president. The fact that Secretary of War Stimson headed the drafting committee ensured at least partial acceptance of Grew's ideas. Under the war secretary's direction, Assistant Secretary John J. McCloy and others in the War Department cooperated with Ballantine and other State Department officials and completed their draft on June 29.

This new draft, submitted to President Truman on July 2, proved, if anything, more generous to the Japanese than Grew's earlier suggestions. After declaring that the United Nations were determined "to prosecute the war against Japan until her unconditional capitulation," the statement then invited the Japanese to surrender under certain conditions:

> There shall be inflexibly eliminated for all time the authority and influence of those who have deceived and misled the country into embarking on world conquest, for we believe that a new world order of peace, security and justice will be impossible until irresponsible militarism is driven from the world.
>
> The Japanese lands shall be occupied as may be deemed necessary and the exercise of our authority shall continue until there is convincing proof that Japan's war-making potential is destroyed, that she will never again threaten the peace of the world and has become fit to be admitted into the community of peace-loving nations.
>
> The terms of the Cairo Declaration shall be carried out and Japanese sovereignty shall be limited to the islands of Honshu, Hokkaido, Kyushu, Shikoku and such adjacent minor islands as we determine.
>
> The Japanese military forces shall be completely disarmed and returned to their homes and peaceful and productive lives.
>
> The Japanese shall not be enslaved as a race or destroyed as a nation, but stern justice will be meted out to all war crimi-

nals including those who have visited cruelties upon our prisoners. Democratic tendencies found among the Japanese people shall be supported and strengthened. Freedom of speech and of thought, respect for the fundamental human rights shall be established.

Japan shall be permitted to maintain such industries as are determined to offer no potential for war but which can produce a sustaining economy. Access shall be permitted to raw materials essential to this end. Eventual Japanese participation in the world economic system shall be permitted. The occupying forces of the Allies shall be withdrawn from Japan as soon as our objectives are accomplished and there has been established beyond doubt a peacefully inclined, responsible government of a character representative of the Japanese people. This may include a constitutional monarchy under the present dynasty if it be shown to complete satisfaction of the world that such a government shall never again aspire to aggression.[61]

This explicit statement of peace terms was as good an expression of wartime liberal reintegrationism as any. There is little doubt that the Japanese leaders would have found the terms acceptable. They could not have asked for a more straightforward promise regarding the emperor institution, postwar recovery, or reintegration into the international order.

The gist of the proposed proclamation survived further scrutiny within the Truman administration and was eventually issued, in modified form, at Potsdam. To be sure, some officials took strong exception to the explicit assurances about the emperor institution. The joint chiefs' strategic survey committee wondered if the "radical elements" in Japan might not be discouraged by such assurances, while "fanatical believers in the Emperor" might go to the other extreme and not be satisfied even with the proposed phraseology. Responding to such argument, Major General H. A. Craig, acting assistant chief of staff and one of the drafters of the declaration, told President Truman that the drafting committee had believed "we should not beat around the bush but should state unequivocally what we intend to do with regard to the Emperor." Whereas early in June the military had opposed anything but a straightforward call for unconditional surrender, by July, having successfully conquered Okinawa, they were more willing to use political means to end the hostilities. As Craig said, "From the military point of view there appears to be no reason whatsoever why we should not leave Hirohito himself as titular head of the [Japanese], if by so doing we make more likely acceptance of the surrender. He is primarily a symbol and if we take over completely the actual government his influence would seem to be well under our thumb. Of course the final decision with regard to Hirohito himself is largely a political one in which full regard must be had of American public opinion which has been indoctrinated for the past few years with the idea that he should be eliminated."[62]

This last sentence raised an important question. The American people sensed that the war was coming to an end and were showing signs of displeasure about reports in the press on the State Department's softening stand toward the emperor. As the department summarized American opinion in mid-July, "a large majority of the public feels that [the emperor] should be harshly treated, according to a Gallup poll."[63] Grew found himself issuing public statements denying that the government was interested in anything except unconditional surrender. But he continued to believe, as he told James F. Byrnes, who was appointed secretary of state at the beginning of July, that early surrender could be brought about if the Japanese were given "the impression that unconditional surrender may not be as bad a matter as they had first believed."[64] Archibald MacLeish, assistant secretary of state, was not sure, however, if the Japanese should be given any assurances about the meaning of unconditional surrender. "If we are modifying the announced policy of unconditional surrender to a new policy of surrender on irreducible Japanese terms" on the emperor question, MacLeish asserted, "the American people have a right to know it." Moreover, he argued, "what has made Japan dangerous in the past and will make her dangerous in the future if we permit it, is, in large part, the Japanese cult of emperor worship which gives the ruling groups in Japan . . . their control over the Japanese people." Dean Acheson, another assistant secretary of state, agreed, pointing out at a meeting of the department that "the institution of the throne is an anachronistic, feudal institution . . . To leave that institution intact is to run the grave risk that it will be used in the future as it has been used in the past."[65]

By the time the Potsdam Conference was convened on July

17, opposition to the proposed statement had become sufficiently strong that the final draft given to President Truman omitted explicit references to the emperor. One reason for this change was the growing influence within the State Department of men like Byrnes, Acheson, and MacLeish—with no expertise on Japanese affairs but keenly sensitive to public opinion—and the president's tendency to listen to them rather than to Grew and other experts. Nevertheless, the draft Truman received still assured the Japanese that their unconditional surrender would bring with it a right to choose their own form of government, which could easily be interpreted to mean retention of the emperor system.[66]

The weeks between mid-June and mid-July were also of crucial importance in confirming the earlier occupation guidelines. Combined with the ongoing deliberations on the emperor, the policy further affirmed America's determination to play the leading role in administering defeated Japan and to reform it along liberal, cooperative lines. America's preponderant role had been reiterated in the memorandum drafted by Dooman on May 1, and the Asia-Pacific subcommittee of SWNCC adopted it as its recommendation on June 23. The joint chiefs agreed and made the policy even more explicit by calling for the "control" of occupation by United States forces.[67] On June 11 the subcommittee drafted a comprehensive "initial post-defeat policy relating to Japan," which, like the draft declaration on unconditional surrender, sought to define the objectives to be accomplished by Japan's defeat. Certain themes were reiterated:

> The general objectives of the United States in regard to Japan are:
>
> 1. The unconditional surrender or total defeat of Japan;
>
> 2. The stripping from the Japanese Empire of territories, including the Mandated Islands . . . ;
>
> 3. The creation of conditions which will insure that Japan will not again become a menace to the peace and security of the world;
>
> 4. The eventual emergence of a government in Japan which will respect the rights of other states and Japan's international obligations; and
>
> 5. The eventual participation of Japan in a world economic system on a reasonable basis.

The document emphasized as additional objectives the "strengthening of democratic tendencies" in postwar Japan, the "encouragement of liberal political elements," educational reform for "making possible the development of democratic ideas," and "a wider distribution of ownership, management and control of the Japanese economic system." Nothing was said about the emperor, except that his constitutional powers "shall be suspended" immediately upon the termination of hostilities. At the same time, it was stated that the military government should "utilize the Japanese administrative machinery and . . . Japanese public officials, making these officials responsible for the carrying out of the policies and directives of the military government."[68]

These and other documents being circulated among the top echelon of the government at this time clearly indicated an agenda for reforming Japan along liberal lines so that the country could emerge once again as a peaceful, responsible member of the international community. Although nothing definite was decided about the treatment of the emperor, it was assumed that the military government would encourage liberal Japanese officials as well as private individuals to cooperate with occupation authorities in stamping out militarism and carrying out the objectives of the occupation. As a Navy Department memo noted in mid-July, there existed "numerous Japanese . . . who, through prior contacts and earlier education, will be disposed to accept and to assist in the development of . . . democratic principles." It would be a primary task of the military government, therefore, to "seek out such persons" and obtain their assistance in the programs for democratization.[69] It was no accident that around this time the Office of War Information began making a list of "friendly Japanese" who could be counted upon to cooperate with occupation authorities.

By the time of the Potsdam Conference American officials had given much thought to the meaning of Japan's unconditional surrender, which after all was the key to the question of war objectives. There was a fairly definite program for the United States to play the leading role in the occupation, to institute various reform measures, and to utilize Japanese personnel with liberal leanings. The program was far from a complete surrender. If what Japan needed was "a peace on the basis of something other than unconditional surrender," as Tōgō said, the United States could be said to be offering it. But Tōgō was still determined to send a special emissary to Moscow to seek an acceptable peace through Stalin's intercession. Former prime minister Konoe was chosen because, in Tōgō's and his colleagues' view, he was a well-known figure who could talk with both Americans and Russians. On July 12 the foreign minister instructed Ambassador Satō in Moscow to inform the Soviet government of Konoe's impending visit and its purpose. However, once again Tōgō made it clear that so long as the United States and Great Britain insisted on unconditional surrender, Japan would have no choice but to continue fighting "for our honor and survival."[70] Satō conveyed the message to the Russian government on July 13, only to find that on the following day Stalin and Molotov were to depart for Potsdam. Undaunted, Foreign Minister Tōgō kept on instructing Satō to seek something other than an unconditional surrender.

Because it was becoming all too clear that such efforts were of no avail, some Japanese officials appealed to the Foreign Ministry to deal directly with the Anglo-American nations. Many of them were convinced that Japan was wasting precious time by going through the Soviet Union. Unlike their superiors in Tokyo, they felt that Japan should take advantage of the rift between the Anglo-American powers and the Soviet Union by approaching the former rather than the latter. Consul General Kanda Jōtarō at Zurich, for instance, telegraphed Tokyo in mid-June, arguing that the United States would welcome direct Japanese overtures for peace, because an early termination of the war might obliterate the American need for Soviet participation, which could result in further extension of Russian power in Asia. Whereas some in Tokyo were saying that an extension of Soviet influence would exacerbate American-Russian tensions to the advantage of Japan, Kanda saw that no good would come out of such a development. He argued that Japanese interests could be seriously jeopardized if the whole of Asia fell to Russian domination, as the whole of Europe threatened to do.[71]

Japanese diplomats, businessmen, and others in neutral Switzerland shared Kanda's ideas. They saw what was happening in Europe: postwar chaos, social upheavals, and communist activities, abetted by the presence of Soviet troops in Eastern and Central Europe. They did not want to see this happen in Japan, and the only way to prevent it, they thought, was to deal frontally with the

Anglo-American nations. Minister Kase Toshikazu in Bern agreed with them, and a group of Japanese businessmen went ahead and secretly contacted Allen Dulles, representing the Office of Strategic Services. Unfortunately the Dulles contact got nowhere because Foreign Minister Tōgō showed no enthusiasm.[72]

But the idea of contacting the United States directly was becoming too firm to be squelched. Ryū Shintarō, an *Asahi* correspondent in Bern, in a long telegram on July 9 to his friend, Ogata Taketora, a member of the cabinet, said that if Japan failed to end the war before Russian entry, it would experience the same kind of misery and confusion as postwar Germany. Japan should end the war right away, because that was what the United States and Britain also wanted, notwithstanding their public adherence to the unconditional surrender formula. Surrender terms were negotiable, Ryū believed; all Japan had to do was to indicate its readiness to end the fighting. Otherwise, not only the nation's armed forces but also its people and its "essence" would be destroyed. So that Japan would rise again "in fifty years, in a new form," he urged Tokyo's leaders to make up their minds and move for peace.[73] Similarly, Minister Okamoto Suemasa in Stockholm appealed to his superiors in Tokyo to bring the war to a speedy conclusion "for the safety of our imperial institution, and for the future welfare of our people." He reported that the American government appeared ready to consider something other than unconditional surrender, and warned that if Japan did not take this opportunity it would face the same disaster the Germans were experiencing.[74] On July 18 and 20, Ambassador Satō in Moscow sent similarly worded messages to Tokyo, calling on the government to come to terms with the United Nations on only one condition, the preservation of the emperor system. If this one condition could be met, he reasoned, it really did not matter whether the cessation of hostilities was called an unconditional surrender or not. Japan's honor would be kept and its destruction prevented.[75]

In retrospect, these urgent messages provide additional evidence that there was sufficient interest and intelligence in both Japan and the United States in the middle of July to end the war then and there. The Americans would have called it Japan's capitulation and unconditional surrender, and the Japanese could have given it another name, but it would have amounted to the same thing. It would have spared further destruction and would have taken the same form as the actual end of the war a month later. In other words, the additional fighting between mid-July and mid-August made no difference in the peace terms.

Furthermore, the contours of postwar Asia would have been roughly the same; the Yalta framework would have been no less solidified by Japan's defeat in July. British and French forces were fast reoccupying their former colonies in Southeast Asia, and the Soviet Union was deploying its forces for use in Asia. Even if the Russians had not come into the war against Japan, they would have occupied Sakhalin, the Kuriles, and other areas assigned to the Soviet Union at Yalta. The United States, on its part, would have carried out its long-prepared occupation plans for Japan and its former territories in the Pacific. The Japanese-American war would have concluded more or less according to the scenario foreseen by American officials months in advance. But the scenario would have been one with which Japanese officials were also familiar, for its outlines were strikingly evocative of international relations of the 1920s.

CONCLUSION

6

THE POTSDAM Conference could have given the final touches to the outlines for an emerging postwar Asia. The Japanese-American war could have been terminated on the eve of the conference, and it still should have been possible to end the conflict immediately after the conference adjourned on August 2. The three heads of state—Truman, Stalin, and Churchill (later replaced by Clement Attlee when the Conservatives lost their general election in mid-conference)—did little or nothing to alter the Yalta framework for dealing with postwar problems. And as far as the Japanese war was concerned, they again confirmed America's predominant role by adopting a declaration that followed a draft prepared within the United States government. The Potsdam declaration, issued on July 26, called on the Japanese government to proclaim an unconditional surrender on these terms:

> There must be eliminated for all time the authority and influence of those who have deceived and misled the people of Japan into embarking on world conquest, for we insist that a new order of peace, security and justice will be impossible until irresponsible militarism is driven from the world.
>
> Until such a new order is established and until there is convincing proof that Japan's war-making power is destroyed, points in Japanese territory to be designated by the Allies shall be occupied to secure the achievement of the basic objectives we are here setting forth.
>
> The terms of the Cairo Declaration shall be carried out and Japanese sovereignty shall be limited to the islands of

[261]

Honshu, Hokkaido, Kyushu, Shikoku and such minor islands as we determine. The Japanese military forces, after being completely disarmed, shall be permitted to return to their homes with the opportunity to lead peaceful and productive lives.

We do not intend that the Japanese shall be enslaved as a race or destroyed as a nation, but stern justice shall be meted out to all war criminals, including those who have visited cruelties upon our prisoners.

The Japanese Government shall remove all obstacles to the revival and strengthening of democratic tendencies among the Japanese people. Freedom of speech, of religion, and of thought, as well as respect for the fundamental human rights, shall be established. Japan shall be permitted to maintain such industries as will sustain her economy and permit the exaction of just reparations in kind, but not those which would enable her to re-arm for war. To this end, access to, as distinguished from control of, raw materials shall be permitted. Eventual Japanese participation in world trade relations shall be permitted.

The occupying forces of the Allies shall be withdrawn from Japan as soon as these objectives have been accomplished and there has been established in accordance with the freely expressed will of the Japanese people a peacefully inclined and responsible government.

It is evident that the declaration faithfully followed the gist of the draft prepared by the Stimson committee in spirit and content. There were three noticeable changes, however. First, the occupation of Japan was to be limited to "points" rather than taking in the whole country, reflecting the view of the British delegation, which was apprised of the draft text only at the last moment, that occupation of the whole country would be both unnecessary and undesirable. Rather, the British felt that economic restrictions, coupled with the stationing of Allied forces in certain areas of Japan, would be sufficient. But this was a minor change; the principle of treating defeated Japan as a whole, instead of dividing it up into zones of occupation, was not modified at all. Moreover, by retaining the basic objectives of the occupation—demilitarization and democratic reforms—the Potsdam declaration implied a large-scale occupation.

The second change was the specific reference to reparations, which was inserted to approximate the treatment of Japan with that of Germany. One of the major issues the heads of state had to deal with at Potsdam was the amount of reparations the Germans were to pay. At the same time, because no reparations would be possible without economic recovery, the insertion of the reparations clause amounted to an even more explicit statement that postwar Japan would be gradually reintegrated into the world economy. Finally, the most important change was the deletion of all references to the emperor institution, replacing them with the term "freely expressed will of the Japanese people." This change indicated that President Truman accepted the advice of Byrnes, Acheson, MacLeish, and others that American public opinion would not tolerate an explicit assurance about the emperor. Nevertheless, Grew, Dooman, and others who had worked long and hard for such a guarantee could rest satisfied that the Japanese people would "freely" express their will to retain the emperor and that therefore the new phraseology endorsed the spirit of the earlier draft.[1] In this and other instances, the Potsdam declaration was clearly an American product, summing up more than three years of planning and deliberations within the United States government.

The Potsdam declaration should have been accepted immediately and unequivocally by the Japanese government, for it gave them just what they were seeking, "a peace on the basis of something other than an unconditional surrender." Diplomats like Minister Kase in Bern and Ambassador Satō in Moscow correctly understood the import of the declaration. As they told Foreign Minister Tōgō, its conditions were far more moderate than the terms the United Nations had imposed on Germany, and therefore eminently acceptable. Delay or rejection by Japan, they warned their superiors in Tokyo, would result in sure ruin of the homeland.[2] Prime Minister Suzuki and Foreign Minister Tōgō belatedly came around to accepting this advice, but unfortunately they had an exaggerated notion of the resistance, especially by the military, in Japan if the Potsdam proclamation were accepted right away. They believed they needed time to persuade the military and the people that acceptance of the Potsdam terms would be best for the country and for the imperial institution. Hoping to demonstrate to the people that the nation was far from being defeated, Suzuki told the press that "it would not be necessary to take the declaration seriously." Such a statement was broadcast abroad as indicating Tokyo's lack of interest: almost the opposite of what he intended. It was only after the dropping of atomic bombs on August 6 and 9 and the Soviet declaration of war on August 8, that the Suzuki cabinet finally and decisively set about bringing the war to a close through direct negotiation with the United States.

Japan's failure to accept the Potsdam terms literally altered the surface of the earth. Ending the war in late July or at the beginning of August would have brought about a conventional peace along the lines defined at Yalta. It would have caused serious domestic dissension and disorder in Japan, but the country would have been occupied by United States forces, and in the end "liberal" and "cooperative" Japanese would have come forward to ease internal tensions and work with the occupation authorities for a smooth transition to a more peaceful orientation. Russia, Britain, France, and China would in the meantime have divided up East and Southeast Asia into their respective spheres of influence. The United States would have established control over most of the Pacific Ocean and reduced its commitments in the Philippines, China, and elsewhere on the Asian continent. In the postwar period the American government would have tried to work for some regime of international cooperation, offering its rich economic resources to other nations in return for their willingness to join forces for the creation of a more open international economic order.

All these policies and orientations remained after early August, and it is possible to argue that they continued to define postwar Asian politics until the onset of the Cold War in Asia in 1949.[3] Nevertheless, the Japanese-American war, indeed the whole of Asia and the entire world, entered a novel stage when the first atomic bomb was dropped over Hiroshima on August 6. The war as a conventional phenomenon came to an end that morning, and a new phase began that lasted not merely for the eight days until Japan's formal surrender, but for many more years and even decades.

Not that the political significance of the new weapon was recognized clearly from the beginning. The United States government considered it almost entirely in strategic terms. When President Truman was told about the successful tests at Alamogordo on July 16, while he was in Germany, he immediately authorized the use of the bombs (two were available right away) to speed the end of hostilities. The Japanese viewed the Hiroshima bombing as something unprecedented and far more destructive than conventional attacks and hastened to contact the United States government to bring the conflict to an end. But even then, the two sides dealt with one another as if nothing unusual had taken place, the Japanese still insisting on keeping intact "the prerogatives of His Majesty as a sovereign ruler," and the United States assuring them that the "ultimate form of government of Japan shall, in accordance with the Potsdam Declaration, be established by the freely expressed will of the Japanese people." The formula was vague enough to be acceptable to both sides, and Tokyo decided to surrender on August 14.[4] These exchanges could have taken place when the Potsdam declaration was first issued, and it could even be argued that they could have been held long before the Potsdam Conference.

In a way it was symbolic that the Japanese-American differences came down to a matter of a few words on the institution of the emperor and that on almost all other issues Tokyo and Washington were in essential agreement. This was ultimately because the two governments included leaders with a shared past who had once worked together for similar goals and in accordance with the same principles, but who had gone separate ways to experiment with alternative solutions to global and domestic problems. The war's end showed that Japanese-American cooperation and interdependence were a more desirable framework than rivalry and conflict. In that sense, the defeated Japanese, as well as victorious Americans, were ready to return to an earlier period and resume their partnership in the world arena while removing those elements in Japan that had undermined that partnership.

The dropping of the atomic bomb changed the picture. It ensured that whatever the two countries' desires and intentions, they could no longer go back to the past, to restore the familiar framework of international relations. They were now faced with an uncertain future. It was ironic that Minister Kase, who had done more than any other diplomat to urge the Tokyo government to end the war by accepting the Potsdam declaration, was also the first to note the profound implications of the Hiroshima bombing. Although he had worked hard to bring about reconciliation between Japan and the United States, he telegraphed Tokyo on August 8, he now feared that the new weapon would most surely bring about a third world war and that by using it America had transformed itself into something unknown, something far more fearful than before.[5] Ironically, in response to this telegram Kase received an instruction to communicate to America Japan's acceptance of the Potsdam declaration. Here, in one person, one era was ending and another beginning.

The onset of the atomic age made it certain that the world would not go back to the prewar status quo, that something was being added to hitherto familiar conceptions of international order. To be sure, the nations of the world went about the business of reconstruction and of restoring world peace and stability as if conventional wisdom were sufficient. The Yalta framework of power relations was solidified in Asia, and Wilsonian principles informed the thrust of America's economic policy after the war. At least for the Japanese, these arrangements were something they had to live with, and gradually they accepted them as the best means for ensuring domestic peace, prosperity, and welfare. The postwar changes required no drastic departure from tradition; they could be fitted into their conception of some forces in modern Japan, forces that had stressed economic development, political liberalism, and intellectual openness. Because these were the objectives the occupation authorities emphasized, and because the United States remained the predominant occupier, postwar reforms became bound up with U.S.-Japanese relations.

To the extent that the Japanese welcomed and promoted domestic transformation, they developed a stable view of their relations with the United States. This perception of shared economic interests and cultural aspirations was essentially a moderate, reintegrationist, and conservative one. Japan's internal and external orientations were based more on familiar concepts and on the tradition of cooperation and interdependence across the Pacific than on sweeping new definitions of national life or international objectives. In time, therefore, Japan emerged as a symbol of the old order—the old order that had shaped international relations during the Wilson years and the 1920s. It was an order defined by the Atlantic Charter as well as by the declaration of the East Asian Conference. It was oriented toward world interdependence and stability, and assumed a balance between these objectives and domestic arrangements so that interest groups would have a stake in an open and stable world order.

But while these traditional forces were at play at one level, atomic weapons were ushering in an unprecedented stage of international affairs at another. Already in October 1945, barely two months after the end of the war, the United States initiated a study of atomic warfare, with the joint war plans committee of the joint chiefs charging another committee to "select approximately 20 of the most important targets suitable for strategic atomic bombing in the U.S.S.R. and Soviet-dominated territory."[6] One should not attribute too much literal significance to these plans. After all, hypothetical plans for war had always existed, even among friendly nations. Moreover, in the fall of 1945, planning for atomic raids would have been unthinkable but for the appearance of the Soviet Union as a major military power and potential adversary occupying vast areas of Europe, the Middle East, and Northeast Asia. Even without the atomic bomb, the emergence of America and Russia as the two strongest military powers would have made postwar international and Asian affairs drastically different from the situation prevailing in the 1920s. Nevertheless, the point is that by August 1945, officials in Washington, Tokyo, and elsewhere had accepted the reality of Russian power, as exemplified by the Yalta agreements, and were seeking to incorporate it into a world order that would still be sustained by certain principles of Wilsonian internationalism. However, neither the Yalta system nor Wilsonianism had anticipated the need to accommodate atomic weapons. After 1945 the bomb developed its own momentum; it came to dominate foreign policy and strategic assumptions, and future war began to be visualized as nuclear conflict, not a temporary aberration from the norm but an end to all international and domestic order.

The irony was that possession of the new deadly weapons made the United States and later the Soviet Union and other countries extremely cautious in their use, so that the resulting "balance of terror" served to preserve an uneasy peace throughout most regions of the world for more than three decades after 1945. The peace in turn enabled Japan to recover economically and to engage in commercial activities on the global scale. Japan, having accepted the terms of peace presented by the United States, and reinforcing the principles underlying those terms through their own initiative, came to embody some of the traditional Wilsonian internationalist precepts. In this sense, there was continuity between the 1920s and the postwar years. Despite the coming of the atomic age and the accompanying confrontation between the United States and the Soviet Union, the old order of economic development and interdependence continued to characterize affairs among states. Japan no less than America contributed to the restoration and perpetuation of that order. It was only during the 1970s that the fundamental assumptions of internationalism were challenged by a global shortage of energy resources, the self-assertiveness of developing countries, and a growing skepticism among the developed nations about the virtues of unlimited growth. It remained to be seen whether Japanese and Americans would be able to cooperate with each other and with other peoples to develop a still newer conception of international relations.

NOTES
BIBLIOGRAPHY
INDEX

NOTES

Abbreviations

1. The End of Uncertainty

1. See Akira Iriye, *After Imperialism: The Search for a New Order in the Far East, 1921–1931* (Cambridge, Mass., 1965).

2. Okagawa Eizō, *Manshū kaitaku nōson no settei keikaku* (Tokyo, 1944), p. 3.

3. Manshikai, ed., *Manshū kaihatsu yonjūnen-shi* (Tokyo, 1964), pp. 124–126; Kami Shōichirō, *Manmō kaitaku seishōnen giyūgun* (Tokyo, 1973), p. 39.

4. See Nakamura Takafusa, "Japan's Economic Thrust into North China," in Akira Iriye, ed., *The Chinese and the Japanese: Studies in Political and Cultural Interactions* (Princeton, 1980).

5. Japan, Foreign Ministry, *Kakukoku tsūshō no dōkō to Nihon* (Tokyo, 1938), *passim.*

6. Uda Hisashi, *Tai-Shi bunka kōsaku sōan* (Tokyo, 1939), pp. 3, 7, 9, 17, 27.

7. Akira Iriye, "Toward a New Cultural Order: the Hsin-min Hui," in Iriye, *Chinese and Japanese.*

8. Saitō Yoshie, *Tai-Shi keizai seisaku no aru kihon mondai* (Tokyo, 1938).

9. Japan, Foreign Ministry, "Sekai keizai no dōkō to Tōa keizai shinchitsujo no kensetsu" (April 1939).

10. The best treatment of U.S.-Japanese relations during the 1930s is Dorothy Borg and Shumpei Okamoto, eds., *Pearl Harbor as History: Japanese-American Relations, 1931–1941* (New York, 1973).

11. Iriye, "Toward a New Cultural Order."

12. Yabe Ryōsaku, ed., *Ajia mondai kōza*, 1 (Tokyo, 1939), 17–19. The best study of the Wang Ching-wei scheme is John Hunter Boyle, *China and Japan at War, 1937–1945: Politics of Collaboration* (Stanford, 1972). For a superb interpretation of German and Italian intellectuals' responses to fascism during the 1930s, see H. Stuart Hughes, *The Sea Change: The Migration of Social Thought, 1930–1965* (New York, 1975). It is clear that Japanese writers were strongly influenced by the views of Germans and Italians who condemned modern capitalist civilization and bourgeois values.

13. Yatsugi Kazuo, *Shōwa dōran shishi* (Tokyo, 1971), 1, 240 and following.

14. *Matsuoka Yōsuke: Sono hito to shōgai* (Tokyo, 1974), pp. 730–736.

15. Ibid., pp. 747–748.

16. The best study of Japanese-American negotiations in 1941 is Robert J. C. Butow, *John Doe Associates: Backdoor Diplomacy for Peace* (Stanford, 1974). For the Japanese army's interest in the talks, see Satō Kenryō, *Daitōa sensō kaikoroku* (Tokyo, 1966), pp. 118–151.

17. A good record of navy indecision can be read in the transcripts of informal talks held immediately after the war by Japan's top former naval leaders, contained in Shinmyō Takeo, ed., *Kaigun sensō kentō kaigi kiroku* (Tokyo, 1976). The participants recalled that the navy in 1941 was driven by two contradictory sentiments: fear of the United States and need to avoid war with it, on one hand, and the fatalistic view that such war was inevitable. None of them could remember that the army and the navy had worked out a comprehensive strategy toward the United States before mid-August of 1941.

18. Ōshima to Matsuoka, May 18 and 22, 1941, JFMA.

19. Satō, *Daitōa sensō*, pp. 132–134; Shinmyō, *Kaigun*, pp. 129–131.

20. Benjamin Kidd, *The Control of the Tropics* (London and New York, 1898).

21. Akira Iriye, *Pacific Estrangement: Japanese and American Expansion, 1897–1911* (Cambridge, Mass., 1972).

22. Robert Freeman Smith, *The United States and Revolutionary Nationalism in Mexico, 1916–1932* (Chicago, 1972), p. 35.

23. Charles A. Beard and G. H. Smith, *The Open Door at Home* (New York, 1934), pp. 273–274.

24. Arnold A. Offner, *American Appeasement: U.S. Foreign Policy and Germany, 1933–1938* (Cambridge, Mass., 1969), chaps. 7–8; Robert Dallek, *Franklin D. Roosevelt and American Foreign Policy, 1932–1945* (New York, 1979), chap. 7.

25. Offner, *American Appeasement*, p. 269.

26. The best study of the Western powers' attitudes during the Manchurian crisis is Christopher Thorne, *The Limits of Foreign Policy: The West, the League and the Far Eastern Crisis of 1931–1933* (London, 1972). See also Gary B. Ostrower, *Collective Insecurity: The United States and the League of Nations during the Early Thirties* (Lewisburg, Pa., 1979). For United States policy toward China after 1937, see Michael Schaller, *The U.S. Crusade in China, 1938–1945* (New York, 1979).

27. No full story of Chinese-Japanese contacts during the war has been published. Some details are provided in the essays by Susan Marsh and Lloyd E. Eastman in Iriye, *Chinese and Japanese;* Boyle, *China and Japan at War;* and *Matsuoka Yōsuke,* pp. 818–842.

28. Lloyd E. Eastman, *The Abortive Revolution: China under Nationalist Rule, 1927–1937* (Cambridge, Mass., 1974), chap. 4.

29. Ōshima to Matsuoka, June 22, 1941, JFMA.

30. Tsutsui to Matsuoka, June 24 and 27, 1941, ibid.

31. *Matsuoka Yōsuke*, pp. 1016–1037.

32. Satō, *Daitōa sensō*, pp. 135–141, 144–149. The navy seems to have endorsed the occupation of southern Indochina in part to retain its role in Japanese strategy; war with Russia would make the army predominant, whereas a southern strategy would bring about an equitable distribution of influence and, even more important, funds. See Shinmyō, *Kaigun*, pp. 133–134.

33. Imai Seiichi et al., *Taiheiyō sensō-shi*, 4 (Tokyo, 1972), 97.

34. Ibid., pp. 87–88.

35. Satō, *Daitōa sensō*, pp. 149–150; Shinmyō, *Kaigun*, pp. 130–131.

36. For details, see the excellent discussion in Irvine H. Anderson, *The Standard-Vacuum Oil Company and United States East Asian Policy, 1933–1941* (Princeton, 1975). Dallek, *Roosevelt*, pp. 274–275, reveals that the president had no intention of embargoing all oil shipments to Japan. But American officials established a de facto embargo, and Roosevelt eventually—by early September—accepted the policy. It is conceivable that if his intentions had been clearly signaled to Tokyo, those Japanese who wanted to lessen chances of war in the Pacific might have felt encouraged.

37. Satō, *Daitōa sensō*, pp. 150–154. Historians disagree as to whether Japan considered the United States or Great Britain its chief antagonist before the war. For a forceful presentation of the view that the crisis essentially involved Japanese relations with Britain, see Chihiro Hosoya, "Japanese Views of the International System, 1919–1941," paper presented at the Anglo-Japanese conference on World War II (London, 1979).

38. Dallek, *Roosevelt*, p. 274.

39. The best discussion of the making of the Atlantic Charter is

Theodore A. Wilson, *The First Summit: Roosevelt and Churchill at Placentia Bay, 1941* (Boston, 1969).

40. Ōshima to Toyoda, Sept. 4, 1941, JFMA. The feeling that the nation had to choose either war with or submission to the Anglo-American powers was widespread among Japan's military officials. See, for instance, the supreme headquarters' "secret diary" in Japan, Defense Agency, *Daihonei rikugunbu*, 2 (Tokyo, 1968), 409–410.

41. Ishii to Toyoda, Sept. 2, 1941, JFMA.

42. Japan, Foreign Ministry, ed. *Nihon gaikō nenpyō narabi shuyō bunsho* (Tokyo, 1955), 2: 544–545.

43. Ōshima to Tōgō, Oct. 29, 1941, JFMA.

44. Kamimura to Tōgō, Nov. 21, 1941, ibid.

45. See, for instance, the articles by Okazaki Saburō and Sakamoto Tokuma in *Chūōkōron*, 56.10 (Oct. 1941).

2. Abortive New Order

1. Agawa Hiroyuki et al., eds., *Taiheiyō kaisen* (Tokyo, 1964), pp. 192–234.

2. Ibid., pp. 235–245.

3. Roosevelt to Chiang, Dec. 8, 1941, *The Collected Wartime Messages of Generalissimo Chiang Kai-shek, 1937–1945* (New York, 1945), 2: 640.

4. Far Eastern division memo, Jan. 26, 1942, 740.0011 PW/2037 3/8, SDA.

5. Japan, Defense Agency, *Hoku-Shi no chiansen*, 2 (Tokyo, 1971), 6–7, 9–10, 22, 24.

6. See Thomas Havens, *Valley of Darkness: The Japanese People and World War Two* (New York, 1978).

7. Okumura Kiwao, *Sonnō jōi no kessen* (Tokyo, 1943), pp. 250–262.

8. Alfred Vagts, *A History of Militarism* (New York, 1959), p. 451.

9. Defense Agency, *Hoku-Shi*, 2: 72–73.

10. Defense Agency, *Daihonei rikugunbu*, 5: 9.

11. Defense Agency, *Hoku-Shi*, 2:88.

12. Ibid., 2: 89–90.

13. Ibid., 2: 75, 257.

14. Ibid., 2: 256–258.

15. Ibid., 2: 48–50, 175.

16. Ibid., 2: 94–95.

17. Nashimoto Yūhei, *Chūgoku no naka no Nihonjin* (Tokyo, 1958).

18. Hidaka to Tōgō, Dec. 21, 1941, JFMA.

19. Ibid., and Defense Agency, *Hoku-Shi*, 2: 81.

20. Shigemitsu to Tōgō, Feb. 17, 1942, JFMA.

21. Hidaka to Tōgō, Dec. 17, 1941, ibid.

22. Shigemitsu to Tōgō, March 9, 1942, ibid.
23. Shigemitsu to Tōgō, May 25, 1942, ibid.
24. Nashimoto, Chūgoku, 2: 228–238.
25. Shigemitsu to Tōgō, June 14 and 25, Aug. 5, 1942; Horiuchi to Tōgō, April 27, May 7, June 4, 8, and 16, 1942, JFMA.
26. Far Eastern division memo, Jan. 23, 1942, 740.0011 PW/2037 2/8, SDA.
27. Far Eastern division memo, Jan. 20, 1942, 740.0011 PW/1891, ibid.
28. Gauss to Hull, March 10, 1942, 740.0011 PW/2101, ibid. Louis Allen, Singapore, 1941–1942 (London, 1977), pp. 259–260.
29. Hornbeck memo, Jan. 21, 1942, 740.0011 PW/1891, SDA.
30. See note 26.
31. Far Eastern division memo, Jan. 26, 1942, 740.0011 PW/2037 3/8, SDA.
32. Maurice Matloff and E. M. Snell, Strategic Planning for Coalition Warfare, 1941–1942 (Washington, 1953), p. 205.
33. Memo of White House conference, June 1, 1942, in United States, Department of State, Papers Relating to the Foreign Relations of the United States 1942, 3 (Washington, 1961), 578–583.
34. Chiang Tsung-t'ung yen-lun hui-pien (Taipei, 1956), 16: 13–22.
35. Memo of White House conference, May 29, 1942, State Department, Foreign Relations 1942, 3: 568, 574.
36. Hornbeck to Hull, May 20, 1942, Stanley K. Hornbeck Papers.
37. Milton E. Miles, A Different Kind of War (New York, 1967), pp. 16–24. Schaller, U.S. Crusade, chap. 7.
38. See note 31.
39. Nathaniel Peffer, "The Roots of the Pacific Conflict," Asia, 42.2 (Feb. 1942): 79–80. For a similar contemporary view by a French journalist, see Robert Guillain, Le peuple japonais et la guerre (Paris, 1947).
40. Far Eastern division memo, Feb. 5, 1942, 740.0011 PW 2307 6/8, SDA.
41. Hornbeck to Washburn, July 28, 1942, Hornbeck Papers.
42. See note 31.
43. P minutes 20, Aug. 1, 1942, Harley Notter Papers.
44. Hornbeck memo, July 31, 1942, Hornbeck Papers.
45. Hornbeck memo, July 8, 1942, ibid.
46. Ministry of Education, Daitōa shinchitsujo kensetsu no igi (Tokyo, 1942), pp. 55–56.
47. Okumura, Sonnō jōi, pp. 337–338. For an example of a distinguished academic figure swallowing this propaganda, see Takada Shinji's essays in Asahi, Jan. 1, 2, 3, 1942. Takada, a Tokyo University professor, argued that Japanese victory over Anglo-American "materialism" was inevitable because the former embodied the "spiritual culture" of the East.

48. Suzuki Yasuzō, *Seiji bunka no shinrinen* (Tokyo, 1942), p. 30.

49. Ministry of Education, *Daitōa*, pp. 255–259.

50. Ishikawa Junkichi, *Kokka sōdōin-shi: Shiryō-hen*, 4 (Tokyo, 1976), 848.

51. Defense Agency, *Daihonei kaigunbu*, 2 (Tokyo, 1975), 216–219. An interesting account of a Ministry of Communication official who was sent to Java is provided by Utsumi Nobuo, *Java shinchū no omoide* (Tokyo, 1969). He writes that when Japanese went to the East Indies in 1942 they were overwhelmed with strong Western influences there: highways, horseracing, air-conditioning, golf. Far from rejecting these amenities, Japanese occupiers avidly took to them.

52. General Staff memo, March 1941, JDAA.

53. Defense Agency, *Daihonei rikugunbu*, 2: 572–573, 642–644, 650–652; Defense Agency, *Daihonei kaigunbu*, 2 (Tokyo, 1975), 209–216.

54. Waseda University, ed., *Indonesia ni okeru Nihon gunsei no kenkyū* (Tokyo, 1969), p. 120; *Sugiyama memo*, 2 (Tokyo, 1967), 107–108; Ishikawa, *Kokka sōdōin-shi*, 3: 1174.

55. Japan, Foreign Ministry, *Gaimushō no hyakunen* (Tokyo, 1969), 2: 684–757.

56. Tōgō Shigenori, *Jidai no ichimen* (Tokyo, 1952), pp. 293–298; Fukai Eigo, *Sūmitsuin jūyō giji oboegaki* (Tokyo, 1953), p. 259.

57. Foreign Ministry, *Gaimushō no hyakunen*, 2: 750.

58. *Kido Kōichi nikki*, 2 (Tokyo, 1966), 980–981.

59. *Nihon keizai nenpō 1942* (Tokyo, 1942), pp. 165–175.

60. Suzuki, *Seiji bunka*, pp. 43–53.

61. Ibid., pp. 67–79. For some documentation on private industry's attitudes, see Nihon Kokumin Undō Kenkyūjo, ed., *Nihon kokumin undō nenshi*, vol. 1 (Tokyo, 1943).

62. Hamilton memo, Jan. 6, 1942, 740.0011 PW/2030 1/2, SDA.

63. John Morton Blum, *V Was for Victory: Politics and American Culture during World War II* (New York, 1976), chap. 1.

64. *Asia*, 42.3 (March 1942): 153–155.

65. Ibid., 42.5 (May, 1942): 324–326.

66. W. Roger Louis, *Imperialism at Bay: the United States and the Decolonization of the British Empire, 1941–1945* (New York, 1978), pp. 134–135.

67. Ibid., pp. 27–43.

68. Christopher G. Thorne, *Allies of a Kind: The United States, Britain, and the War against Japan, 1941–1945* (London and New York, 1978), p. 206.

69. See note 33.

70. Welles to Foote, March 12, 1942, 740.0011 PW/2137, SDA.

71. Foote to Hull, May 29, 1942, 740.0011 PW/2137, ibid.

72. P minutes 20, Aug. 1, 1942, Notter Papers.

73. P minutes 23, Aug. 15, 1942, ibid.
74. T document 137, Oct. 23, 1942, ibid.
75. Louis, *Imperialism at Bay*, chap. 11.
76. See note 72.
77. Ibid.
78. Hornbeck memo, Sept. 7, 1942, Hornbeck Papers.
79. *Sugiyama memo*, 2: 61–63.
80. Defense Agency, *Hoku-Shi*, 2: 62.
81. Imai, *Taiheiyō sensō-shi*, 4:178; Chalmers Johnson, *An Instance of Treason: Ozaki Hotsumi and the Sorge Spy Ring* (Stanford, 1964).
82. Hayashi Saburō, *Kantōgun to Kyokutō Sorengun* (Tokyo, 1974), pp. 218–223.
83. *Sugiyama memo*, 2: 4.
84. Satō to Tōgō, April 14, 1942, JFMA.
85. *Sugiyama memo*, 2: 70.
86. Satō to Tōgō, May 5 and June 30, 1942, JFMA.
87. *Sugiyama memo*, 2: 68, 79.
88. Ibid., 2: 53.
89. Tōgō, *Jidai*, p. 288.
90. Foreign Ministry, *Gaimushō no hyakunen*, 2: 630; *Sugiyama memo*, 2: 134–138.
91. Ōshima to Tōgō, Aug. 9, 1942, JFMA.
92. *Sugiyama memo*, 2: 158–174.
93. Matloff and Snell, *Strategic Planning*, 1: 144.
94. Strong memo, May 21, 1942, OPD 381 Japan, in United States, JCSD.
95. Military intelligence division memo, March 8, 1942, WPD 380.3, OPD 381 Japan, ibid.
96. Givens memo, May 21, 1942; Strong memo, May 21, 1942, OPD 381 Japan, ibid.
97. War plans division memo, March 8, 1942, WPD 380.3, OPD 381 Japan, ibid.
98. Matloff and Snell, *Strategic Planning*, 1: 145.
99. Standley to Stalin, June 19, 1942, State Dept., *Foreign Relations 1942*, 3: 597.
100. P document 34, Aug. 12, 1942, Notter Papers.
101. P document 118, Oct. 12, 1942, ibid.
102. Security subcommittee memo included in P memo dated Dec. 13, 1943, ibid.
103. International organization subcommittee memo included in above P memo, ibid.
104. S document 50, Dec. 7, 1942, ibid.
105. S document 50a, Dec. 17, 1942, ibid.

106. Blum, V Was for Victory. See also Richard Polenberg, War and Society: The United States, 1941–1945 (Philadelphia, 1972).
107. See note 47.

3. Redefining War Aims

1. Sugiyama memo, 2: 187–302; Imai, Taiheiyō sensō-shi, 5 (Tokyo, 1973), 43–48.
2. Sugiyama memo, 2: 306–308, 321, 323.
3. Ibid., 2: 314–318.
4. Ibid., 2: 344–347.
5. Ibid., 2: 379–386.
6. Defense Agency, Hoku-Shi, 2: 298–311.
7. Tajiri to Aoki, June 9, 1943, JFMA.
8. Shigemitsu to Aoki, Jan. 27, 1943, ibid.
9. Defense Agency, Hoku-Shi, 2: 313, 316–317.
10. Ibid., 2: 314–315.
11. Ibid., 2: 305.
12. Ibid., 2: 318–319, 336–339.
13. Ibid., 2: 380–382.
14. Ibid., 2: 339, 382.
15. Ibid., 2: 426–430.
16. Kiyosawa Kiyoshi, Ankoku nikki (Tokyo, 1971), 1: 35.
17. Wartime Messages of Chiang, 2: 734–737.
18. Chiang Tsung-t'ung, 16: 193–204.
19. Defense Agency, Hoku-Shi, 2: 315, 402.
20. Ibid., 2: 404. For further details about wartime Communist activitives, see Mark Selden, The Yenan Way in Revolutionary China (Cambridge, Mass., 1971); William Hinton, Fanshen: A Documentary of Revolution in a Chinese Village (New York, 1966).
21. Sugiyama memo, 2: 458–463.
22. Ibid., 2: 470–485.
23. Fukai, Sūmitsuin, pp. 328–335.
24. Ta Kung Pao, Dec. 7, 1942.
25. Sugiyama memo, 2: 352–353.
26. Ibid., 2: 386–393.
27. Ōta Jōtarō, Biruma ni okeru Nihon gunsei-shi no kenkyū (Tokyo, 1967), pp. 354–373.
28. Sugiyama memo, 2: 440–442.
29. Ibid., 2: 354.
30. Ibid., 2: 414–417, 432–436.
31. Ibid., 2: 414–425; F. C. Jones, Hugh Borton, and B. R. Pearn, The Far East, 1942–1946 (London, 1955), pp. 72–81.
32. Sugiyama memo, 2: 470–479.

33. Ibid., 2: 497.
34. Ibid., 2: 504.
35. Kiyosawa, *Ankoku nikki*, 1: 179–180, 214.
36. Shigemitsu Mamoru, *Shōwa no dōran* (Tokyo, 1952), 2: 179.
37. Kiyosawa, *Ankoku nikki*, 1: 198; *Asahi*, Dec. 7, 1943, p. 1.
38. Dallek, *Roosevelt*, pp. 373–376.
39. Tony Sharp, *The Wartime Alliance and the Zonal Division of Germany* (London, 1975), pp. 3–4.
40. ST minutes, May 7, 1943, Notter Papers.
41. ST minutes, May 12, 19, 26, 1943, ibid.
42. ST minutes, May 19, 1943, ibid.
43. Coville memo, May 25, 1943, ibid.
44. Fearey memo, T 341, June 21, 1943, ibid.
45. ST minutes, May 26, 1943, ibid.
46. Louis, *Imperialism at Bay*, pp. 267–271.
47. Thorne, *Allies*, p. 281.
48. P 123-b, Dec. 8, 1943; P 236, July 2, 1943, Notter Papers.
49. P minutes, April 10, 1943, ibid.
50. P 34, Aug. 12, 1943, ibid. (This document was identical to P 214, March 12, 1943, ibid.)
51. United States, Department of State, *Postwar Foreign Policy Preparation, 1939–1945* (Washington, 1949), pp. 471–472.
52. P 236, July 2, 1943, Notter Papers.
53. ST minutes June 16 and July 2, 1943, ibid. For a discussion of wartime United States policy toward Indochina, see Christopher Thorne, "The Indochina Issue between Britain and the United States, 1942–1945," *Pacific Historical Review*, 45.1 (Feb. 1976).
54. P 214, March 12, 1943, Notter Papers.
55. State Dept., *Postwar Foreign Policy Preparation*, p. 553.
56. Ibid., pp. 189–190.
57. Martin J. Sherwin, *A World Destroyed: the Atomic Bomb and the Grand Alliance* (New York, 1975), pp. 85–86.
58. Dallek, *Roosevelt*, pp. 414–415.
59. Churchill memos, April 12, 1943, and others undated, in PREM 4, 30/11, in Great Britain, Prime Minister's Office Files.
60. T memo, April 27, 1943, Notter Papers.
61. U.S. Department of Defense, "The Entry of the Soviet Union into the War against Japan: Military Plans, 1941–1945" (1955), mimeographed, p. 16, JCSD.
62. Ibid., p. 20.
63. Masland memo, T 321, May 24, 1943, Notter Papers.
64. Hornbeck to Berle, Feb. 20, 1943, Hornbeck Papers.
65. Walter LaFeber, "Roosevelt, Churchill, and Indochina, 1942–1945," *American Historical Review*, 80.5 (Dec. 1975).

66. Dallek, *Roosevelt*, p. 391.

67. Joint intelligence committee memo, Jan. 20, 1943, 28/5, JCSD.

68. Strong to Marshall, Feb. 27, 1943; Handy to Marshall, March 15, 1943, OPD 381 Japan, JCSD.

69. Dallek, *Roosevelt*, p. 392.

70. LaFeber, "Roosevelt."

71. Ibid.

72. P minutes 47, March 13, 1943, Notter Papers.

73. Hamilton memo for Acheson, March 11, 1943, 740.0011 PW/ 2055 1/2, SDA; Hornbeck to Hull, Feb. 4, 1943, Hornbeck Papers.

74. ST minutes, May 7, 12, 19, 1943, Notter Papers.

75. Chase memo, June 16, 1943, State Dept., *Foreign Relations 1943,* 3: 254–255.

76. Davies memo, June 24, 1943, ibid., 3: 258–266.

4. Japanese-American Rapprochement

1. Borton memo, Sept. 27, 1943, T 366, Notter Papers.

2. Blakeslee memo, Sept. 29, 1943, T 357, ibid.

3. State Dept., *Postwar Foreign Policy Preparation,* pp. 560–564.

4. Borton memo, Oct. 6, 1943, T 381, Notter Papers.

5. Borton's conversation with Hornbeck, Oct. 28, 1943, ibid.

6. Ibid.; and Hornbeck memos, Nov. 1 and 15, 1943, Hornbeck Papers.

7. Williams memo, Oct. 9, 1943, T 391, Notter Papers.

8. Thorne, *Allies,* pp. 312, 327; Dallek, *Roosevelt,* p. 428.

9. State Dept., *Postwar Foreign Policy Preparation,* pp. 202–203.

10. *Sugiyama memo,* 2: 518–529.

11. Dallek, *Roosevelt,* p. 427–428.

12. Chin-tung Liang, *General Stilwell, 1942–44: The Full Story* (New York, 1976), pp. 169–170.

13. Gauss to Roosevelt and Hull, Dec. 9, 1943, Papers of Franklin D. Roosevelt.

14. Paul A. Varg, *The Closing of the Door: Sino-American Relations, 1936–1946* (East Lansing, Mich., 1973), p. 93.

15. Dallek, *Roosevelt,* p. 485.

16. Davies to Hopkins, Dec. 31, 1943, in State Dept., *Foreign Relations* 1943, 3: 397–399.

17. Hornbeck memo, Dec. 27, 1943, Hornbeck Papers.

18. Varg, *Closing,* pp. 93–96.

19. Ibid., p. 94; Liang, *Stilwell,* pp. 169–170; *Wartime Messages of Chiang,* 2: 776–781.

20. Defense Dept., "Entry of Soviet Union," pp. 25–27.

21. Imai, *Taiheiyō sensō-shi*, 5:150–155; Koiso Kuniaki, *Katsuzan kōsō* (Tokyo, 1963), pp. 750-758.

22. Liang, *Stilwell*, p. 166.

23. LaFeber, "Roosevelt." See also George C. Herring, *America's Longest War: The United States and Vietnam, 1950–1975* (New York, 1979).

24. *Sugiyama memo*, 2: 518–520. The best treatment of German policy and strategy during the war is Klaus Hildebrand, *The Foreign Policy of the Third Reich* (Berkeley, 1973).

25. Matsumoto Shun-ichi and Andō Yoshirō, eds., *Nihon gaikō-shi*, 25 (Tokyo, 1972), 29–31.

26. Kiyosawa, *Ankoku nikki*, 1: 191–192, 198; *Asahi*, Dec. 1, 2, 1943.

27. Ibid., Dec. 3, 1943.

28. Shigemitsu, *Shōwa*, 2: 189–190.

29. *Kido nikki*, 2: 1075: Kiyosawa, *Ankoku nikki*, 1: 174–219. The Dec. 3, 1943, issue of *Asahi* contains two articles by a Japanese student who had recently returned from the United States.

30. Tōgō, *Jidai*, p. 302. According to Okada's son-in-law, Sakomizu Hisatsune, some time in 1943 Okada initiated a plot to oust Navy Minister Shimada Shigetarō as a preliminary step to cause Tōjō's downfall. Although the conspiracy did not gain momentum until June 1944, the tactic of assailing Tōjō's navy minister was one of the means the *jūshin* actually used to bring down the cabinet. See Etō Jun, *Mōhitotsu no sengo-shi* (Tokyo, 1978), pp. 20-22.

31. Kerr memo, Nov. 25, 1943, 740.00119 PW 1939/28, SDA.

32. Hiss to Hornbeck, Dec. 3, 1943, contained in above document.

33. OWI memo, Dec. 3, 1943, JPS 286/2/D, JCS Papers.

34. T minutes, Dec. 17, 1943, Notter Papers.

35. *Yabe Teiji nikki*, 1 (Tokyo, 1974), 679.

36. Kiyosawa, *Ankoku nikki*, 2: 6.

37. *Kido nikki*, 2: 1078–1079.

38. Sugiyama memo, 2: 531; Japan, General Staff, ed., *Haisen no kiroku* (Tokyo, 1967), pp. 27–28. *Matsuoka Yōsuke*, pp. 1111–1112.

39. *Haisen no kiroku*, pp. 28–29.

40. *Kido nikki*, 2: 1084; Imai, *Taiheiyō sensō-shi*, 5: 279.

41. *Imai, Taiheiyō sensō-shi*, 5: 283–285; Satō, *Daitōa sensō*, pp. 258–260.

42. *Kido nikki*, 2: 114–120; *Yabe nikki*, 1: 726–727.

43. Kiyosawa, *Ankoku nikki*, 2: 153; Satō, *Daitōa sensō*, pp. 297–303.

44. Hosokawa Morisada, *Jōhō tennō ni tassezu* (Tokyo, 1953), pp. 248, 154.

45. *Kido nikki*, 2: 1122–1127.

46. Ibid., pp. 1120–1121.

47. Koiso, *Katsuzan*, pp. 778–793.

48. Ibid., pp. 794–797; Imai, *Taiheiyō sensō-shi*, 5: 291–292.

49. General Staff, *Haisen no kiroku*, pp. 57–65.

50. Ibid., pp. 38–57.

51. Ōshima to Shigemitsu, July 26, 1944, JFMA.

52. Foreign Ministry, *Gaimushō no hyakunen*, 2: 267.

53. Koiso, *Katsuzan*, p. 797.

54. JPS 451, May 3, 1944, and JPS 134 meeting, March 9, 1944, JCSD.

55. JPS 451, May 3, and JPS 451/1, May 19, 1944, ibid.

56. See JPS 451 and 451/1, ibid.

57. JIC 17, Nov. 11, 1944; JWPC 104/1, Feb. 28, 1944, ibid.

58. Arnold to Deane, Feb. 8, 1944, Roosevelt Papers; Defense Dept., "Entry of Soviet Union," pp. 32–33.

59. Defense Dept., "Entry of Soviet Union," p. 34.

60. See JPS files for 1944, JCSD.

61. Defense Dept., "Entry of Soviet Union," pp. 28–29.

62. CDA 165a, May 29, 1944, and CDA 164b, June 6, 1944, Notter Papers.

63. Louis, *Imperialism at Bay*, p. 373.

64. Ibid.

65. Berle memo, Jan. 26, 1944, Notter Papers.

66. PC 4, March 29, 1944, ibid.

67. PWC 56, Dec. 8, 1943, and PWC 52, March 6, 1944, ibid. The best recent study of the Bretton Woods conference is Alfred E. Eckes, Jr., *A Search for Solvency: Bretton Woods and the International Monetary System, 1941–1971* (Austin, Tex., 1975).

68. CDA 103a, March 31, 1944; CDA 57, May 2, 1944; and CTP minutes, Feb. 8, 15, and 23, 1944, Notter Papers.

69. EUR 3, Feb. 18, 1944, and accompanying memo by Far Eastern committee, ibid.

70. Bishop to Hull, July 29, 1944, and Grew to Stettinius, July 29, 1944, 740.0011 PW/7-2944, SDA.

71. LaFeber, "Roosevelt."

72. EUR 5, March 6, 1944, Notter Papers.

73. PC minutes, May 10, 1944, ibid.

74. PC minutes, April 3, 1944, ibid.

75. PC minutes, May 1, 1944, ibid.

76. EUR 13, July 15, 1944, ibid.

77. Thorne, *Allies*, p. 392.

78. State Department briefing paper, no date, in United States, Department of State, *Papers Relating to the Foreign Relations of the United States 1944: The Conference at Quebec* (Washington, 1972), pp. 190–192.

79. Ibid.

80. LaFeber, "Roosevelt."

81. Varg, *Closing*, p. 121.
82. Service to Stilwell, July 28, 1944, Roosevelt Papers.
83. Varg, *Closing*, pp. 126–127.
84. Gray to Tully, Sept. 9, 1944, Roosevelt Papers.
85. Hurley to Roosevelt, Sept. 7, 1944, ibid.; Varg, *Closing*, p. 151.
86. Liang, *Stilwell*, chap. 10.
87. Ibid., pp. 254–255; Roosevelt to Chiang, Sept. 16, 1944, Roosevelt Papers.
88. Liang, *Stilwell*, p. 259.
89. Roosevelt to Chiang, Oct. 5, 1944, Roosevelt Papers.
90. Hilldring and Pence to Dunn, Feb. 18, 1944, in State Dept., *Foreign Relations 1944*, 5 (Washington, 1965), pp. 1190–1194.
91. PWC 111, March 13, 1944, ibid, 1202–1205.
92. PWC 109, March 22, 1944, ibid., 1213–1214.
93. PWC 110a, April 17, 1944, ibid., 1230–1231.
94. PWC 121, March 21, 1944, ibid., 1211–1213.
95. PWC 123, March 22, 1944, ibid., 1217–1218.
96. PWC 125, March 29, 1944, ibid., 1224–1228.
97. PWC 126, March 29, 1944, ibid., 1228–1230.
98. PWC 124a, May 4, 1944, ibid., 1239–1242.
99. PWC 116a, April 24, 1944, Notter Papers.
100. PWC 116a (alternative), April 24, 1944, ibid.
101. PWC 145, April 26, 1944, and PWC 146, April 26, 1944, ibid.
102. PWC 116d, May 9, 1944, in State Dept., *Foreign Relations 1944*, 5: 1250–1255.
103. PWC 152b, May 9, 1944, ibid., 1257–1260.
104. CCS 539/4, May 21, 1944, JCSD.
105. FE 7, June 17, 1944, Notter Papers.
106. Emmerson to Hull, July 27 and Aug. 10, 1944, 740.0011 PW/7–2744 and 8–1844.

5. The Making of Postwar Asia

1. Berle memo, Sept. 26, 1944, Notter Papers.
2. PC 8, Oct. 23, 1944, ibid.
3. ECA 9, Oct. 26, and ECA 10, Nov. 4, 1944, ibid.
4. Conant and Bush memo, Sept. 30, 1944; Conant and Bush to Stimson, Sept. 19, 1944, United States, MED Papers.
5. Dallek, *Roosevelt*, pp. 470–471.
6. Ibid., p. 479.
7. Groves memo on White House meeting, Dec. 30, 1944, MED Papers.
8. Defense Dept., "Entry of Soviet Union," pp. 30–31, 35–36.

9. JPS meetings of Oct. 11, Oct. 25, Nov. 9, Nov. 16, and Nov. 22, 1944; JPS memo, Nov. 23, 1944, JCSD.

10. Conant and Bush memo, Sept. 30, 1944, MED Papers.

11. Foreign Ministry, Gaimushō no hyakunen, 2: 646–658.

12. General Staff, Haisen no kiroku, pp. 168-174.

13. Ibid., pp. 187–189.

14. Ibid., pp. 184–187.

15. Ibid., pp. 163–168.

16. Ibid., pp. 177–180.

17. Foreign Ministry, Gaimushō no hyakunen, 2: 651–654.

18. Okamoto to Shigemitsu, Sept. 15, 1944, JFMA.

19. PWC 284a, Nov. 13, 1944, Notter Papers.

20. Thorne, Allies, p. 657.

21. PWC 283, Nov. 10, and PWC 287a, Nov. 6, 1944, Notter Papers.

22. Stilwell to Marshall, Oct. 10, 1944, Roosevelt Papers.

23. JPS, 182 meeting, Dec. 6, 1944, JCS Papers.

24. JCS to Stilwell, Sept. 15, 1944, Roosevelt Papers.

25. For the most up-to-date discussion of the Yalta Conference, see Diane Shaver Clemens, Yalta (New York, 1970).

26. NCC 16/2, Feb. 19, 1945, SWNCC Papers.

27. Giles memo, March 21, 1943, SWNCC 83, SWNCC Papers.

28. State Department memo, April 3, 1945, SWNCC 83, ibid.

29. Wedemeyer to Chennault, March 19, 1945, ibid.; Far Eastern subcommittee memo, March 24, 1945, ibid.; State Dept., Foreign Relations 1945, 6 (Washington, 1969), pp. 297–303.

30. SWNCC 16/2, Feb. 19, 1945, SWNCC Papers.

31. General Staff, Haison no kiroku, pp. 230–232.

32. The Konoe memorial is printed in full in Japan, Foreign Ministry, ed., Shūsen shiroku (Tokyo, 1952), pp. 195–198.

33. Fukai, Sūmitsuin, p. 411; Shigemitsu, Shōwa, 2: 258–261.

34. Shigemitsu, Shōwa, 2: 262.

35. Shigemitsu to embassies in Manchukuo, China, Thailand, and Burma, March 9, 1945, JFMA.

36. Koiso, Katsuzan, p. 827; Kido nikki, 2: 1182–1185; Tamura Shinsaku, Miao Pin kōsaku (Tokyo, 1954), pp. 166 and following.

37. Kido nikki, 2: 1188–1194.

38. Tōgō, Jidai, pp. 310–311.

39. General Staff, Haisen no kiroku, pp. 254–255.

40. Defense Dept., "Entry of Soviet Union," pp. 54–55; JIC 266/1, April 18, 1945, JCSD.

41. Defense Dept., "Entry of Soviet Union," pp. 55–60.

42. Ibid., pp. 61–68.

43. JCS 1355, Appendix B, May 3, 1945, JCS Papers.

44. Dooman memo, SWNCC 70/1/D, May 1, 1945, SWNCC Papers.

45. Target committee meetings of April 27, and May 2, 1945, MED Papers.
46. Defense Dept., "Entry of Soviet Union," pp. 61–68.
47. Thorne, *Allies*, p. 660.
48. Leahy memo, April 30, 1945, SWNCC 35/10, SWNCC Papers.
49. Foreign Ministry, *Shūsen shiroku*, p. 332.
50. Tōgō, *Jidai*, pp. 319–320.
51. Tōgō memo, Aug. 15, 1945, JFMA.
52. General Staff, *Haisen no kiroku*, pp. 343–352; Foreign Ministry, *Shūsen shiroku*, pp. 329–330.
53. Political affairs bureau memo, June, 1945, JFMA.
54. Grew to Stimson, May 28, 1945, State Dept., *Foreign Relations 1945*, 6: 545–547.
55. Foulds minutes, May 31, 1945, F 3238/364/G23, Great Britain, Foreign Office Documents. For the role of Sansom, see Hosoya Chihiro, "George Sansom to haisen Nihon," *Chūōkōron*, Sept. 1975.
56. Grew to Truman, June 13, 1945, 740.00119 PW/6-1345, SDA.
57. Grew memo, June 15, 1945, 740.00119 PW/6–1545, ibid.
58. *Kido nikki*, 2: 1208–1209; Matsumoto and Andō, *Nihon gaikō-shi*, 25: 154–155; Defense Dept., "Entry of Soviet Union," pp. 72–84.
59. *Kido nikki*, 2: 1213.
60. Grew memo, June 18, 1945, 740.00119 PW/6-1845, SDA.
61. Draft proclamation, June 29, 1945, OPD 387.4, JCSD.
62. Craig to Truman, July 14, 1945, OPD 387.4, ibid.
63. Jones memo, July 16, 1945, 740.00119 PW/7-1645, SDA.
64. Grew to Byrnes, July 13, 1945, in above document, ibid.
65. MacLeish to Byrnes, July 6, 1945, 740.00119PW/7-1645, SDA.
66. Leahy to Truman, July 18, 1945, 740.00119PW/7-1845, ibid.
67. SWNCC 70/2, June 23, 1945; SWNCC 70/3D, July 18, 1945; SWNCC 70/4, July 27, 1945, SWNCC Papers; Leahy memo, July 6, 1945, JCS 1398/2, JCSD; Thorne, *Allies*, pp. 531–532.
68. SWNCC 150, June 11, 1945, State Dept., *Foreign Relations 1945*, 6: 549–555.
69. SWNCC 162/D, July 19, 1945, SWNCC Papers.
70. Foreign Ministry, *Shūsen shiroku*, pp. 424–464.
71. Kanda to Tōgō, May 21 (received) and June 11, 1945, JFMA.
72. For the Dulles episode, see Foreign Ministry, *Shūsen shiroku*, pp. 298–314; and State Dept., *Foreign Relations 1945*, 6: 481–495. See also Kase to Tōgō, July 21, 1945; Tōgō to Kase, July 23, 1945, JFMA.
73. Ryū to Ogata, July 9, 1945, JFMA.
74. Okamoto to Tōgō, July 21, 1945, ibid.
75. Satō to Tōgō, July 18 and 20, 1945, ibid.; *Shūsen shiroku*, pp. 469–473.

6. Conclusion

1. Foulds to Sterndale Bennett, July 27, 1945, F 4789/364/G23, Great Britain, Foreign Office Documents.
2. Foreign Ministry, *Shūsen shiroku*, pp. 507 and following.
3. Regarding the Cold War in Asia, see the essays in Yōnosuke Nagai and Akira Iriye, eds., *The Origins of the Cold War in Asia* (Tokyo and New York, 1977).
4. Foreign Ministry, *Shūsen shiroku*, pp. 633–635.
5. Kase to Tōgō, Aug. 8, 1945, JFMA.
6. JIS memo, Oct. 22, 1945, JIS 80/5/M, JCSD.

BIBLIOGRAPHY

Published materials

Acheson, Dean G. *Present at the Creation: My Years in the State Department.* New York, 1969.

Agawa Hiroyuki et al., eds. *Taiheiyō kaisen.* Tokyo, 1964.

Allen, Louis. *The End of the War in Asia.* London, 1976.

————. *Singapore, 1941–1945.* London, 1977.

Alperovitz, Gar. *Atomic Diplomacy: Hiroshima and Potsdam: The Use of the Atomic Bomb and the American Confrontation with Soviet Power.* New York, 1965.

Anderson, Irvine H. *The Standard-Vacuum Oil Company and United States East Asian Policy, 1933–1941.* Princeton, 1945.

Aoyama Kazuo. *Han-sen seiryaku.* Tokyo, 1972.

Arisue Seizō kaikoroku. Tokyo, 1974.

Asahi shimbun. Tokyo, 1941–1945.

Ashida Hitoshi. *Dainiji sekai taisen gaikō-shi.* Tokyo, 1959.

Ashizawa Noriyuki. *Aru sakusen sanbō no higeki.* Tokyo, 1974.

Beard, Charles A., and G. H. Smith. *The Open Door at Home.* New York, 1934.

Beitzell, Robert. *The Uneasy Alliance: America, Britain, and Russia, 1941–1943.* New York, 1972.

Bernstein, Barton J. "The Peril and Politics of Surrender: Ending the War with Japan and Avoiding the Third Atomic Bomb," *Pacific Historical Review,* 46.1 (Feb. 1977).

Blaker, Michael. *Japanese International Negotiating Style.* New York, 1977.

Blum, John Morton, ed. *From the Morgenthau Diaries: Years of War, 1941–1945.* Boston, 1967.

————, ed. *The Price of Vision: The Diary of Henry A. Wallace, 1942–1946.* Boston, 1973.

————. *Roosevelt and Morgenthau.* Boston, 1970.

————. *V Was for Victory: Politics and American Culture during World War II.* New York, 1976.

Bohlen, Charles E. *Witness to History, 1929–1969.* New York, 1973.

Borg, Dorothy. *The United States and the Far Eastern Crisis of 1933–1938: From the Manchurian Incident through the Initial Stage of the Undeclared Sino-Japanese War.* Cambridge, Mass., 1964.

————, and Shumpei Okamoto, eds. *Pearl Harbor as History: Japanese-American Relations, 1931–1941.* New York, 1973.

————, and Waldo Heinrichs, eds. *Uncertain Years: Chinese-American Relations, 1947–1950.* New York, 1980.

Boyle, John Hunter. *China and Japan at War, 1937–1945: Politics of Collaboration.* Stanford, 1972.

Buhite, Russell D. *Patrick J. Hurley and American Foreign Policy.* Ithaca, N.Y., 1973.

Burns, James MacGregor. *Roosevelt: The Soldier of Freedom.* New York, 1970.

Butow, Robert J. C. *Japan's Decision to Surrender.* Stanford, 1954.

———. *John Dow Associates: Backdoor Diplomacy for Peace.* Stanford, 1974.

———. *Tōjō and the Coming of the War.* Stanford, 1961.

Calvocoressi, Peter, and Guy Wint. *Total War.* London, 1972.

Campbell, Thomas M. *Masquerade Peace: America's UN Policy, 1944–1945.* Tallahassee, Fla., 1973.

Chern, Kenneth. *Dilemma in China: America's Policy Debate, 1945.* Hamden, Conn., 1980.

Chiang tsung-t'ung yen-lun hui-pien. Vol. 16. Taipei, 1956.

China, Kuo-fang-pu, ed. *Chung-Jih chan-cheng shih-lüeh.* Taipei, 1968.

Chūōkōron. Tokyo, 1941–1945.

Churchill, Winston S. *The Second World War.* 6 vols. London, 1948–1954.

Clemens, Diane Shaver. *Yalta.* New York, 1970.

Cohen, Warren I. *The Chinese Connection: Roger S. Greene, Thomas W. Lamont, George E. Sokolsky and American–East Asian Relations.* New York, 1978.

Cole, Wayne S. *Charles A. Lindbergh and the Battle against American Intervention in World War II.* New York, 1974.

The Collected Wartime Messages of Generalissimo Chiang Kai-shek, 1937–1945. Vol. 2. New York, 1945.

Crowley, James B. *Japan's Quest for Autonomy: National Security and Foreign Policy, 1930–1938.* Princeton, 1966.

———, ed. *Modern East Asia: Essays in Interpretation.* New York, 1970.

Dallek, Robert. *Franklin D. Roosevelt and American Foreign Policy, 1932–1945.* New York, 1979.

Darilek, Richard E. *A Loyal Opposition in the Time of War: The Republican Party and the Politics of Foreign Policy from Pearl Harbor to Yalta.* Westport, Conn., 1976.

Davies, John Paton, Jr. *Dragon by the Tail: American, British, Japanese, and Russian Encounters with China and One Another.* New York, 1972.

Davis, Lynn E. *The Cold War Begins.* Princeton, 1974.

Dilks, David, ed. *The Diaries of Sir Alexander Cadogan, 1938–1945.* New York, 1972.

Divine, Robert A. *Roosevelt and World War II.* Baltimore, 1969.

———. *Second Chance: The Triumph of Internationalism in America during World War II.* New York, 1967.

Dunn, F. S. *Peacemaking and the Settlement with Japan.* Princeton, 1963.

Eastman, Lloyd E. *The Abortive Revolution: China under Nationalist Rule, 1927–1937.* Cambridge, Mass., 1974.

Eckes, Alfred E., Jr. *A Search for Solvency: Bretton Woods and the International Monetary System, 1941–1971.* Austin, Tex., 1975.

Emmerson, John K. *The Japanese Thread: A Life in the U.S. Foreign Service.* New York, 1978.

Endicott, Stephen Lyon. *Diplomacy and Enterprise: British China Policy, 1933–1937.* Vancouver, 1975.

Etō Jun. *Mōhitotsu no sengo-shi.* Tokyo, 1978.

Feis, Herbert. *Between War and Peace: The Potsdam Conference.* Princeton, 1960.

———. *The China Tangle: The American Effort in China from Pearl Harbor to the Marshall Mission.* Princeton, 1953.

———. *Churchill, Roosevelt, and Stalin: The War They Waged and the Peace They Sought.* Princeton, 1957.

———. *Japan Subdued: The Atomic Bomb and the End of the War in the Pacific.* Princeton, 1961.

———. *The Road to Pearl Harbor: The Coming of the War between the United States and Japan.* Princeton, 1950.

Fifield, Russell H. *Americans in Southeast Asia.* New York, 1973.

Friend, Theodore. *Between Two Empires.* New Haven, 1965.

Fukai Eigo. *Sūmitsuin jūyō giji oboegaki.* Tokyo, 1953.

Gaddis, John Lewis. *The United States and the Origins of the Cold War, 1941–1947.* New York, 1972.

Gardner, Lloyd C. *Architects of Illusion: Men and Ideas in American Foreign Policy, 1941–1949.* Chicago, 1970.

Gardner, Richard N. *Sterling-Dollar Diplomacy.* Oxford, 1956.

Genda Mironu. *Kaigun kōkūtai shimatsuki.* Tokyo, 1962.

Guillain, Robert, *Le peuple japonais et la guerre.* Paris, 1947.

Harriman, W. Averell. *Special Envoy to Churchill and Stalin, 1941–1946.* New York, 1975.

Hata Ikuhiko. *Taiheiyō kokusai kankei-shi.* Tokyo, 1972.

Hattori Takushirō. *Daitōa sensō zenshi.* Tokyo, 1965.

Havens, Thomas. *Valley of Darkness: The Japanese People and World War Two.* New York, 1978.

Hayashi Saburō. *Kantōgun to Kyokutō Sorengun.* Tokyo, 1974.

Heinrichs, Waldo H. *American Ambassador: Joseph C. Grew and the Development of the United States Diplomatic Tradition.* Boston, 1966.

Herring, George C. "The Truman Administration and the Restoration of French Sovereignty in Indochina," *Diplomatic History* 1.2 (Spring, 1977).

———. *America's Longest War: The United States and Vietnam, 1950–1975.* New York, 1979.

Hess, Gary R. *America Encounters India, 1941–1947.* Baltimore, 1971.

Hildebrand, Klaus. *The Foreign Policy of the Third Reich.* Berkeley, 1973.

Hinton, William. *Fanshen: A Documentary of Revolution in a Chinese Village.* New York, 1966.

Hiroike Toshio. *Tai-Men tetsudō.* Tokyo, 1971.

Hoshina Zenshirō. *Daitōa sensō hishi.* Tokyo, 1975.

Hosoya Chihiro. "George Sansom to haisen Nihon," *Chūōkōron* (Sept. 1975).

———, and Saitō Makoto, eds. *Washington taisei to Nichi-Bei kankei.* Tokyo, 1978.

Hughes, H. Stuart. *The Sea Change: The Migration of Social Thought, 1930–1965.* New York, 1975.

Hull, Cordell. *The Memoirs of Cordell Hull.* 2 vols. New York, 1948.

Ickes, Harold Le Claire. *The Secret Diary of Harold L. Ickes.* 3 vols. New York, 1953.

Ienaga Saburō. *The Pacific War: World War II and the Japanese, 1931–1945.* New York, 1978.

Imai Seiichi, et al. *Taiheiyō senso-shi.* Vols. 4, 5. Tokyo, 1972, 1973.

Iriye, Akira. *Across the Pacific: An Inner History of American-East Asian Relations.* New York, 1967.

———. *After Imperialism: The Search for a New Order in the Far East, 1921–1931.* Cambridge, Mass., 1965.

———, ed. *The Chinese and the Japanese: Studies in Political and Cultural Interactions.* Princeton, 1980.

———. *The Cold War in Asia: A Historical Introduction.* Englewood Cliffs, N.J., 1974.

———. *Nichi-Bei senso.* Tokyo, 1978.

———. *Pacific Estrangement: Japanese and American Expansion, 1897–1911.* Cambridge, Mass., 1972.

Ishikawa Junkichi. *Kokka sōdōin-shi: Shiryō-hen.* Vols. 3 and 4. Tokyo, 1975, 1976.

James, D. Clayton. *The Years of MacArthur.* Vol. 2. Boston, 1975.

Japan. Defense Agency. *Daihonei kaigunbu.* Vol. 2. Tokyo, 1975.

———. *Daihonei rikugunbu.* Vols. 2 and 5. Tokyo, 1968, 1973.

———. *Hoku-Shi no chiansen.* Vol. 2. Tokyo, 1971.

Japan. Foreign Ministry. *Gaimushō no hyakunen.* Vol. 2. Tokyo, 1969.

———. *Kakukoku tsūshō no dōkō to Nihon.* Tokyo, 1938.

———, ed. *Nihon gaikō nenpyō narabi shuyō bunsho.* Vol. 2. Tokyo, 1955.

———, ed. *Shūsen shiroku.* Tokyo, 1952.

Japan. General Staff, ed. *Haisen no kiroku.* Tokyo, 1967.

Japan. Ministry of Education. *Daitōa shinchitsujo kensetsu no igi.* Tokyo, 1942.

Japan. Ministry of Finance, ed. *Shōwa zaisei-shi.* Vol. 3. Tokyo, 1976.

Japan Institute of International Affairs, ed. *Taiheiyō sensō e no michi*. 8 vols. Tokyo, 1962–1963.

Johnson, Chalmers. *An Instance of Treason: Ozaki Hotsumi and the Sorge Spy Ring*. Stanford, 1964.

Jones, F. C. *Japan's New Order in Eastern Asia*. New York, 1954.

——, Hugh Borton, and B. R. Pearn. *The Far East, 1942–1946*. London, 1955.

Kami Shōichirō. *Manmō kaitaku seishōnen giyūgun*. Tokyo, 1973.

Kamiyama Shumpei. *Daitōa sensō no isan*. Tokyo, 1972.

Kennan, George F. *Memoirs, 1925–1950*. Boston, 1967.

Kennedy, Malcolm D. *The Estrangement of Great Britain and Japan*. Manchester, 1969.

Kidd, Benjamin. *The Control of the Tropics*. London and New York, 1898.

Kido Kōichi nikki. Vol. 2. Tokyo, 1966.

Kimball, Warren. *The Most Unsordid Act*. Baltimore, 1969.

King, F. P. *The New Internationalism*. Devon, 1973.

Kiyosawa Kiyoshi. *Ankoku nikki*. Tokyo, 1971.

Kodama Yoshio. *Akusei, jūsei, ransei*. Tokyo, 1974.

Koiso Kuniaki. *Katsuzan kōsō*. Tokyo, 1963.

Kolko, Gabriel. *The Politics of War: The World and United States Foreign Policy, 1943–1945*. New York, 1968.

Kubek, Anthony. *How the Far East Was Lost: American Policy and the Creation of Communist China, 1941–1949*. Chicago, 1963.

Kuklick, Bruce. *American Policy and the Division of Germany: The Clash with Russia over Reparations*. Ithaca, N.Y., 1972.

LaFeber, Walter. "Roosevelt, Churchill, and Indochina, 1942–1945," *American Historical Review* 80.5 (Dec. 1975).

Leahy, William D. *I Was There*. New York, 1950.

Lee, Bradford A. *Britain and the Sino-Japanese War, 1937–1939*. Stanford, 1973.

Lensen, George Alexander. *The Strange Neutrality: Soviet-Japanese Relations during the Second World War, 1941–1945*. Tallahassee, Fla., 1972.

Liang, Chin-tung. *General Stilwell, 1942–44: The Full Story*. New York, 1976.

Lingeman, Richard. *Don't You Know There's a War On?* New York, 1970.

Lippmann, Walter. *United States War Aims*. New York, 1944.

Loewenheim, Francis L., et al., eds. *Roosevelt and Churchill: Their Secret Wartime Correspondence*. New York, 1975.

Louis, W. Roger. *British Strategy in the Far East, 1919–1939*. New York, 1971.

——. *Imperialism at Bay: The United States and the Decolonization of the British Empire, 1941–1945*. New York, 1978.

MacArthur, Douglas. *Reminiscences*. New York, 1964.

Manshikai, ed. *Manshū kaihatsu yonjūnen-shi*. Tokyo, 1964.

Matloff, Maurice, and E. M. Snell. *Strategic Planning for Coalition Warfare, 1941–1942*. Washington, 1953.

Matsumoto Shun-ichi and Andō Yoshirō, eds. *Nihon gaikō-shi*. Vol. 25. Tokyo, 1972.

Matsuoka Yōsuke: Sono hito to shōgai. Tokyo, 1974.

May, Ernest R. *"Lessons" of History: The Uses of History in American Foreign Policy*. New York, 1973.

Melosi, Martin V. *The Shadow of Pearl Harbor: Political Controversy over the Surprise Attack, 1941–1946*. College Station, Tex., 1977.

Miles, Milton E. *A Different Kind of War*. Garden City, N.Y., 1967.

Miyamoto Shizuo. *Java shūsen shoriki*. Tokyo, 1973.

Moran, Lord. *Winston Churchill: The Struggle for Survival, 1940–1965*. London, 1966.

Nagai Yōnosuke. *Reisen no kigen*. Tokyo, 1978.

———, and Akira Iriye, eds. *The Origins of the Cold War in Asia*. Tokyo and New York, 1977.

Nakajima Mineo. *Chū-So tairitsu to gendai*. Tokyo, 1978.

Nakamura Takafusa. "Japan's Economic Thrust into North China," in Akira Iriye, ed., *The Chinese and the Japanese: Studies in Political and Cultural Interactions*, Princeton, 1980.

Nashimoto Yūhei. *Chūgoku no naka no Nihonjin*. Tokyo, 1958.

Nihon keizai nenpō, 1942. Tokyo, 1942.

Offner, Arnold A. *American Appeasement: U.S. Foreign Policy and Germany, 1933–1938*. Cambridge, Mass., 1969.

———. "Appeasement Revisited: The United States, Great Britain, and Germany, 1933–1940," *Journal of American History* 64.2 (Sept. 1977).

Okagawa Eizō. *Manshū kaitaku nōson no settei keikaku*. Tokyo, 1944.

Okumura Kiwao. *Sonnō jōi no kessen*. Tokyo, 1943.

Ōno Katsumi. *Kasumigaseki gaikō*. Tokyo, 1978.

Ōsako Ichirō. *Hiroshima Shōwa nijūnen*. Tokyo, 1975.

Ostrower, Gary B. *Collective Insecurity: The United States and the League of Nations during the Early Thirties*. Lewisburg, Pa., 1979.

Ōta Jōtarō. *Biruma ni okeru Nihon gunsei-shi no kenkyū*. Tokyo, 1967.

Paterson, Thomas G. *Soviet-American Confrontation: Postwar Reconstruction and the Origins of the Cold War*. Baltimore, 1973.

Pelz, Stephen. *Race to Pearl Harbor*. Cambridge, Mass., 1974.

Piccigallo, Philip R. *The Japanese on Trial: Allied War Crimes Operations in the East, 1945–1951*. Austin Tex., 1979.

Pogue, Forrest C. *George C. Marshall: Organizer of Victory, 1943–1945*. New York, 1973.

Polenberg, Richard. *War and Society: The United States, 1941–1945*. Philadelphia, 1972.

Saitō Yoshie. *Tai-Shi keizai seisaku no aru kihon mondai*. Tokyo, 1938.

Satō Kenryō. *Daitōa sensō kaikoroku*. Tokyo, 1966.

Satō Seizaburō and Roger Dingman, eds. *Kindai Nihon no taigai taido*. Tokyo, 1974.

Schaller, Michael. *The U.S. Crusade in China, 1938–1945*. New York, 1979.

Selden, Mark. *The Yenan Way in Revolutionary China*. Cambridge, Mass., 1971.

Service, John S. *Lost Chance in China: The World War II Despatches of John S. Service*. New York, 1974.

Sharp, Tony. *The Wartime Alliance and the Zonal Division of Germany*. London, 1975.

Sherwin, Martin J. *A World Destroyed: The Atomic Bomb and the Grand Alliance*. New York, 1975.

Shewmaker, Kenneth E. *Americans and Chinese Communists, 1927–1945: A Persuading Encounter*. Ithaca, N.Y., 1971.

Shigemitsu Mamoru. *Shōwa no dōran*. Vol. 2. Tokyo, 1952.

Shimizu Shin. *Nihon kokumin undō no kihon mondai*. Tokyo, 1943.

Shimizu Takehisa. *Soren no tai-Nichi sensō to Yalta kyōtei*. Tokyo, 1976.

Shinmyō Takeo, ed. *Kaigun sensō kentō kaigi kiroku*. Tokyo, 1976.

Sih, Paul K., ed. *Nationalist China during the Sino-Japanese War, 1937–1945*. New York, 1977.

Smith, Robert Freeman. *The United States and Revolutionary Nationalism in Mexico, 1916–1932*. Chicago, 1972.

Sommer, Theo. *Deutschland und Japan zwischen den Machten 1935–1940*. Tubingen, 1962.

Stephan, John J. *The Kurile Islands*. Oxford, 1974.

Stimson, Henry L., and McGeorge Bundy. *On Active Service in Peace and War*. New York, 1947.

Stoler, Mark A. *The Politics of the Second Front: American Military Planning in Coalition Warfare, 1941–1943*. Westport, Conn., 1977.

Sugiyama memo. Vol. 2. Tokyo, 1967.

Suzuki Yasuzō. *Seiji bunka no shinrinen*. Tokyo, 1942.

Ta Kung Pao. Chungking, 1941–1943.

Takagi Sōkichi. *Yonai Mitsumasa oboegaki*. Tokyo, 1968.

Tamura Shinsaku. *Miao Pin kōsaku*. Tokyo, 1954.

Tanemura Sakō. *Daihonei kimitsu nisshi*. Tokyo, 1952.

Thorne, Christopher G. *Allies of a Kind: The United States, Britain, and the War against Japan, 1941–1945*. London and New York, 1978.

————. "The Indochina Issue between Britain and the United States, 1942–1945," *Pacific Historical Review*, 45.1 (Feb. 1976).

————. *The Limits of Foreign Policy: The West, the League and the Far Eastern Crisis of 1931–1933*. London, 1972.

Tōgō Shigenori. *Jidai no ichimen*. Tokyo, 1952.

Tsunoda Jun, ed. *Ishihara Kanji shiryō*. Tokyo, 1967.

Uda Hisashi. *Tai-Shi bunka kōsaku sōan*. Tokyo, 1939.

United States. Department of State. *Papers Relating to the Foreign Relations of the United States*. Vols. for 1942–1945. Washington, 1961–1969.

————. *Papers Relating to the Foreign Relations of the United States, 1944: The Conference at Quebec*. Washington, 1972.

————. *Postwar Foreign Policy Preparation, 1939–1945*. Washington, 1949.

United States. Senate Committee on the Judiciary. *Morgenthau Diary (China)*. 2 vols. Washington, 1965.

Usui Katsumi. *Manshū jihen*. Tokyo, 1974.

Utsumi Nobuo. *Java shinchū no omoide*. Tokyo, 1969.

Vagts, Alfred. *A History of Militarism*. New York, 1959.

Varg, Paul A. *The Closing of the Door: Sino-American Relations, 1936–1946*. East Lansing, Mich., 1973.

Villa, Brian L. "The U.S. Army, Unconditional Surrender, and the Potsdam Proclamation," *Journal of American History*, 63.1 (June 1976).

Waseda University, ed. *Indonesia ni okeru Nihon gunsei no kenkyū*. Tokyo, 1959.

Wedemeyer, Albert C. *Wedemeyer Reports!* New York, 1958.

White, Theodore H., ed. *The Stilwell Papers*. New York, 1948.

Wilson, Theodore A. *The First Summit: Roosevelt and Churchill at Placentia Bay, 1941*. Boston, 1969.

Wohlstetter, Roberta. *Pearl Harbor: Warning and Decisions*. Stanford, 1962.

Woodward, Llewelyn. *British Foreign Policy in the Second World War*. Vols. 1–5. London, 1970–1976.

Yabe Ryūsaku. *Ajia mondai kōza*. Vol. 1. Tokyo, 1939.

Yabe Teiji. *Konoe Fumimaro*. 2 vols. Tokyo, 1952.

Yabe Teiji nikki. Vol. 1. Tokyo, 1974.

Yamamoto Chikao. *Daihonei kaigunbu*. Tokyo, 1974.

Yano Tōru. *Nanshin no keifu*. Tokyo, 1975.

Yatsugi Kazuo. *Shōwa dōran shishi*. Tokyo, 1971.

Yergin, Daniel. *Shattered Peace: The Origins of the Cold War and the National Security State*. Boston, 1977.

Yomiuri Shinbun, ed. *Shōwa-shi no tennō*. Vol. 1. Tokyo, 1967.

Yoshida Hideo. *Kobubō kokudo-gaku*. Tokyo, 1942.

Unpublished Materials

Great Britain
Public Record Office
Foreign Office Documents
Prime Minister's Files

Japan
    Defense Agency Archives
        Military Documents
    Foreign Ministry Archives
        Foreign Ministry Documents

United States
    National Archives
        Harley Notter Papers
        Joint Chiefs of Staff Documents
        Manhattan Engineering District Documents
        Office of War Information Papers
        State Department Documents
        State-War-Navy Coordinating Committee Papers
    Columbia University
        Institute of Pacific Relations Papers
    Harvard University
        Joseph C. Grew Papers
    Roosevelt Library, Hyde Park, New York
        Franklin D. Roosevelt Papers
    Stanford University
        Stanley K. Hornbeck Papers

INDEX

Acheson, Dean, 255–256, 263
Advisory Committee on Postwar
  Foreign Policy, 59, 74, 93, 168
Aleutians, 97, 142
Algeria, 89
Anami Korechika, 240
Armstrong, Hamilton Fish, 168
Asia, anticolonial movements in, 2
Asia, Northeast, 25–26, 28, 82, 89,
  91, 138, 140, 184, 223, 233,
  247, 267
Asia, Southeast, 6–7, 13, 15, 21, 25,
  27–28, 63, 66–67, 71–74, 80, 82,
  97, 112, 145, 155, 177, 184, 192–
  193, 201, 228–229, 232–233, 247,
  260, 264
Asia Minor, 221
Atlantic Charter, 29–31, 37, 75–76,
  80, 127, 130, 164, 241, 266
Atlantic Conference, 29
Atlantic Ocean, 25
Atomic bomb, 264, 265
Attlee, Clement, 261
Austin, Warren, 61
Australia, 52, 78, 91–92, 133, 144–
  145, 188–189, 192
Austria, 214

B-29 bombers, 186
Bagge, Widor, 237
Balkans, 181, 193, 195, 214, 218, 221
Ballantine, Joseph, 124–126, 129,
  166, 168, 208, 253
Baltic region, 20, 193
Ba Maw, 113
Barrett, David, 198
Batavia, 14
Beard, Charles A., 16
Béck, Ludwig, 181
Bengal, 155
Bering Strait, 90
Berle, A. A., 139, 189, 215–217
Berlin, 25, 181, 230, 252
Bern, 259, 263
Bishop, Max, 192
Black Sea, 82
Blaisdell, D. C., 203
Blakeslee, George, 129, 149–151
Blum, John Morton, 95
Bohlen, Charles E., 137–138, 194
Bohr, Niels, 217
Bolshevik Revolution, 2
Bonin Islands, 116, 134, 186–187

Borton, Hugh: on emperor issue, 168,
  206–208; on Japanese occupation
  and reforms, 166, 203, 209; on
  postwar Japan, 149–153
Bowman, Isaiah, 61
Boxer protocol, 110
Boxer Protocol Army, 4
Bretton Woods Conference, 191
British Commonwealth, 20
Brussels Conference, 22
Bucharest, 26
Buck, Pearl S., 75–76
Bulgaria, 217
Burma, 52, 67, 92, 97, 102, 112, 162,
  228; Allied offensive in, 115–116;
  independence of, 113–114; Japa-
  nese prisoners in, 211
Bush, Vannevar, 217, 220
Byrd, Richard E., 129
Byrnes, James F., 255–256, 263

Cairo Conference, 153–157, 161–
  164, 166
Cairo declaration, 246, 250, 253, 261
Canada, 144
Cannon, Cavendish W., 128, 145
Canton, 173
Caroline Islands, 97, 116, 189
Casablanca, 121–122
Caucasus, 82
Celebes, 186
Ceylon, 52, 92, 192
Chamberlain, Neville, 18
Changsha, 173
Chase, Augustus S., 146
Ch'en Kung-po, 47, 224
Chennault, Claire, 29, 56, 142
Chiang Kai-shek, 9, 22–24, 41, 48–
  49, 54–56, 141–143, 146–147, 163,
  223–224, 228–229, 232; on Asia,
  159; and Burma operation, 155–
  156, 159; and Cairo Conference,
  154–155; and Indochina, 162, 184;
  and Miao Pin, 237; on national
  resistance, 107; policy toward
  Yenan, 109; request for American
  aid, 156–159; and Roosevelt, 155–
  156; and Stilwell affair, 197–201
Chiang Kai-shek, Madame, 141
China, 2, 9, 21, 31, 51, 72, 88, 90,
  124, 126, 134, 155, 169, 171–172,
  177, 192, 202–203, 221, 226, 235,

China—*Cont.*
249, 264; in Allied strategy, 53; in big-power collaboration, 135; and First World War, 46; and Great Britain, 42; and Indochina, 233; and Japanese peace overtures, 23–25, 107; and Korea, 92; National Military Council, 200; and postwar security, 93–94; and Southeast Asia, 145, 232–233; and Soviet Union, 24; and United States, 25, 42, (in American strategy) 21–22, 142, 184–185, 201, 228–230, (operations against Japan) 180, 185–186
China-Burma-India theater, 211, 228
China incident, 24, 26, 33–34
Chinese Communists, 24, 42, 48, 107, 146, 172–173, 197–200, 224, 229; and American aid, 55; growth of influence, 108; party, 9, 42, 108, 198; resistance against Japan, 109–110
Chinese Eastern Railway, 222
Chou En-lai, 146
Chou Fo-hai, 224
Churchill, Winston S., 29, 53, 82, 152, 163, 216–219, 225, 252; and Cairo Conference, 154–155; at Casablanca, 121; on China, 162; and Potsdam, 261; and Quebec Conference, 135–137; on Soviet expansion, 138; at Teheran, 155; in Washington, 77; at Yalta, 230, 232
Chu Shen, 104–105
Cohen, Benjamin, 60, 80
Cold War, 1, 264
Collins, V. Lansing, 78
Colombo, 192
Comintern, 2, 24, 84; dissolution of, 108–109
Conant, James B., 217, 220
Connally, Tom, 60
Coronet operation, 243, 252
Council on Foreign Relations, 74
Coville, Cabot, 124–125
Craig, H. A., 254–255
Czechoslovakia, 19, 214

Dairen, 160, 230
Dallek, Robert, 136
Davies, John Paton, 146–147, 157–158
Davis, Elmer, 167
Deane, John, 185–186
Dickover, E. R., 203, 206–209

Dooman, E. H., 203, 227, 244–245, 256, 263
Dulles, Allen, 259
Dumbarton Oaks Conference, 193, 196
Dutch East Indies, 21, 28, 77–79, 133, 162, 169, 192

East Asian Association, 104
East Asian Conference, second, 240–241; declaration, 248
Eaton, Charles A., 143, 145
Eden, Anthony, 135, 140, 143
Emmerson, John K., 58–59, 211–212
Emperor system: American views of, 37, 50, 59, 124–125, 151, 166, 168, 206–208; Japanese views of, 39–40, 182
Ethiopia, 17
Europe: Central, 17, 22, 258; Eastern, 193, 195, 201, 214–215, 232, 246, 258

Fearey, Robert, 126–127
Fiji, 91
Finland, 20
First World War, 46, 121, 154–155
Flying Tigers, 29
Foote, Walter A., 78
Formosa, *see* Taiwan
Forrestal, James V., 246
France, 20, 63, 155, 192, 264; Allied invasion of, 82, 214, 184; and Indochina, 162, 184; and postwar security, 137
Franco, Francisco, 20
Fujisawa Chikao, 9
Fukai Eigo, 69

Gauss, Clarence E., 50, 56, 156–157, 232
Germany, 17, 19, 63, 72, 125, 159, 169, 185, 214, 219, 222, 225, 227, 240, 264; and Great Britain, 14; and Japan, 20–21, 83, 163, 187, 223; occupation of, 203, 245; and Soviet Union, 25–27, 82–83, 85–88, 90, 118; surrender of, 238, 241, 243, 248, 263
Giles, Barney M., 231–232
Graves, Leslie R., 218, 245
Great Britain, 14, 19, 22, 31, 63, 72, 92–93, 139, 144, 169, 171, 173, 192, 202–203, 224, 226, 235, 264; and big-power collaboration, 77, 135; and China, 51, 100–101, 107,

Great Britain—*Cont.*
111, 141; and Germany, 3, 25, 53,
122; and occupation policy for
Japan, 262; power of, 196; in Southeast Asia, 201; and Soviet Union,
53, 137–138, 163, 196
Great East Asia Conference, 110,
118–119, 153–154; declaration
compared with Atlantic Charter,
119–121, 164, 266
Great East Asian war, 64, 112
Greece, 216–217
Grew, Joseph C., 208–209, 256, 263;
statement on Japanese surrender,
250, 252–253
Guadalcanal, 96–97, 177
Guam, 189

Hamilton, Maxwell, 61, 73, 76, 144
Hankow, 173
Harriman, Averell, 185, 194
Hata Shunroku, 45, 104, 177, 239
Hawaii, 37
Hengyang, 173
Hidaka Shinrokurō, 45–46
Hilldring, J. H., 202–203, 205, 210
Himalayas, 56
Hirano Yoshitarō, 9
Hiranuma Kiichirō, 10, 176–177, 239
Hirohito, Emperor, 32–33, 96, 98,
116, 179, 234, 243, 252, 255; and
Koiso-Yonai cabinet, 177–178;
and Soviet issue, 177, 180; and
Tōjō's replacement, 177
Hiroshima, 245, 264–265
Hirota Kōki, 176–177, 223, 239,
251–252
Hiss, Alger, 167
Hitler, Adolf, 11, 18, 25, 83, 181
Ho Chi Minh, 237
Hokkaido, 219, 222, 231, 253, 262
Hong Kong, 67, 154, 224
Honshu, 219–220, 253, 262
Hoover, Herbert, 17, 250, 252
Hopkins, Harry, 157, 251
Horn, Thomas S., 78
Hornbeck, Stanley E., 22, 56, 59–61,
81, 146, 149, 153, 158, 167–168;
on U.S.-Chinese relations, 144; on
pan-Asianism, 159; on postwar
Asia, 139–140, 152
Hosokawa Morisada, 176
House, E. M., 19
Ho Ying-ch'in, 200
Hsin-min Hui (People's Renovation

Society), 8–9, 42–43, 103–106,
237
Hull, Cordell, 19, 29, 31, 131, 150,
153, 190, 194, 210, 217; on big-
power collaboration, 139; and
Quebec Conference, 135–136
Hurley, Patrick J., 199–201, 228–
229, 232

Ichigō operation, 173, 197
India, 52, 85, 91, 113, 152, 211, 215,
228
Indian Ocean, 52, 85, 180
Indochina, 21, 27–28, 31, 63, 92,
133, 161–162, 184, 192, 203, 233,
237, 247
Indonesia, 116
Institute of Pacific Relations, 74
Iran, 85, 137–138, 221
Iraq, 215, 221
Ishihara Kanji, 48
Ishii Itarō, 32
Ishii Kikujirō, 69
Italy, 17, 26, 63, 72, 88
Iwo Jima, 230

Japan: "absolute defense perimeter,"
116, 174, 179; and Asia, (development of) 65–66, 71, (policy in)
7, 66–69, 97–98, 112, (postwar)
164–165; and Burma, 113–114;
and China, 4, 6–10, 13, 15, 26, 28,
31–32, 36, 38–52, 71, 90–97,
101–104, 173–174, 180, 249,
(policy toward Chungking) 109–
112, 154, 223–224, (rapprochement with) 223–224, 237,
(strategy in) 98–102, 105–106;
and Chinese Communists, 106,
172; and Cairo Conference, 155,
162–164; and Dutch East Indies,
276n51; East Asian Ministry, 69–
72, 102; and Europe, 6–7, 10; and
France, 51; and Germany, 12, 25–
27, 31–33, 41, 84–89, (alliance
with) 11, 13, (and separate peace
with Russia) 180–181, (views of
defeated) 259, 263; and Great
Britain, 2, 8, 27, 31–34, 41, 48–
50, 69, 98, 112–113, 182–183,
273n37; and Hiroshima bombing,
265–266; and Italy, 12, 31, 41, 83,
87; and Manchukuo, 4, 6–7; and
Manchuria, 3–4, 6, 17, 48; Ministry
of Colonial Affairs, 69; Ministry of
Munitions, 179; and Nanking gov-

Japan—*Cont.*
ernment, 98–99, 106; and north
China, 3–4, 6, 17, 103–106; and
Philippines, 115–116; Planning
Board, 4, 7, 66–69; and Southeast
Asia, 6–7, 13, 15; surrender of,
249, 265; and Soviet Union, 12,
25–28, 102, 173–174, 180, 221,
258, (anti-Comintern pact) 222,
(entry into war) 181–182, 234,
(neutrality pact) 13, 83–85, 160,
(possibility of war with) 8, 83–84,
89–90, 273n32, (rapprochement
with) 244, 248, 252, 258–259,
(separation from Allies) 84–87, 91,
140, 160, 172, 182–183, 220–223,
241; and Teheran Conference,
162–164; and United States,
(peace terms) 248–251, 254, 257–
259, (trade with) 6–7; and Yalta
Conference, 234–235
Java, 67, 78, 97, 116

Kabayama Aisuke, 165
Kamimura Shin'ichi, 33–34
Kanda Jōtarō, 258
Kanto plain, 243
Karafuto, *see* Sakhalin
Kase Shun'ichi, 119
Kase Toshikazu, 259, 263, 265–266
Kerr, George, 166–167, 170
Kidd, Benjamin, 15
Kido Kōichi, 70, 151, 165, 180, 235,
239; on postwar regional coopera-
tion, 169–171; on Sino-Japanese
ties, 172; on Soviet mediation for
peace, 170–172; and Tōjō's re-
moval, 174–175, 177
King, E. J., 186
Kirk, Grayson, L., 122–126, 128, 133,
145
Kiyosawa Kiyoshi, 106, 119–121,
164, 169, 175–176
Koiso Kuniaki, 177–181, 183, 220,
222, 237–239
Kokura arsenal, 245
Kokusaku Kenkyūkai (Society for the
Study of National Policy), 10
Konoe Fumimaro, 9, 12, 27, 32, 151,
165, 174–175, 177, 237–238, 249,
258; on relations with Allies, 235–
236; fear of revolution, 176
Korea, 38, 60, 126, 129, 134, 154,
177; discussed at Cairo, 161; trusteeship for, 92, 203, 205

Kuomintang, 9, 24, 55–56, 142, 146,
157, 159, 173, 198, 200
Kurile Islands, 60, 90, 92, 116, 134,
154, 160–161, 222, 230–231, 260
Kuybyshev, 85
Kwantung Army, 26, 84, 245
Kyoto, 48, 245
Kyushu, 186–187, 219–220, 243, 253,
262

Latin America, 17, 63
Laurel, José, 115
League of Nations, 2–3, 15, 17, 82,
114
Leahy, William, 196, 233
Leningrad, 82
Levant states, 215
Lincoln, George, 229
Lin Piao, 146
Lippmann, Walter, 75–76
Litvinov, Maxim M., 53, 55, 77
Low Countries, 214
Luzon, 186, 230

MacArthur, Douglas, 29, 186, 192,
242–243
McCloy, John J., 253
McCormick, Anne O'Hare, 60
MacLeish, Archibald, 255–256, 263
MacMurray, John V., 145
Makino Nobuaki, 166
Malaya, 92, 116
Malik, Yakov, 251–252
Manchukuo, 4, 7, 9, 26–27, 41, 169,
171–172
Manchuria, 3, 17, 25–26, 51, 71, 74,
126, 129, 134, 154, 157, 169, 171,
203, 220, 222–224, 230–232, 237,
249; and Soviet encroachment,
238, 246–247
Manchurian incident, 33, 36
Manhattan project, 217–218, 245
Manila, 115
Mao Tse-tung, 24, 109, 198
Mariana Islands, 116, 174, 186
Marshall, George C., 89, 142, 220,
228, 242, 245
Marshall Islands, 97, 174, 189
Marxism, 39
Masland, John, 145
Matsudaira Tsuneo, 151, 166
Matsuoka Yōsuke, 6–7, 11–13, 26,
48
Mediterranean, 82, 181, 215
Meiji Restoration, 1
Melanesia, 91

Melbourne, 78
Miao Pin, 9, 237–238
Micronesia, 91
Middle East, 32, 53, 82, 137–138, 196, 214, 267
Miki Kiyoshi, 9–10
Miles, Milton, 56
Mindanao, 186
Molotov, V. M., 53, 55, 77, 85, 223, 258
Mongolia, 224; Inner, 222–223; Outer, 90
Morgenthau, Henry, 22, 157
Morishima Gorō, 182, 225
Morocco, 89
Moscow, 82, 84; conference of foreign ministers, 150, 152–153, 156–157; declaration, 188
Mountbatten, Lord Louis, 155, 184, 192
Munich, 18
Mussolini, Benito, 18

Nagano Osami, 97
Nagayo Yoshio, 36
Nanking government, 107, 173; declaration of war on Allies, 45, 98–100
Nashimoto Yūhei, 44
National Security Council, 227
Naval Group China (NGC), 56
Nazi-Soviet nonaggression pact, 10, 19
Netherlands, 31, 92, 144, 192
New Caledonia, 91
New Guinea, 97, 186
New Zealand, 92, 133, 144–145, 188–189
Nimitz, Chester, 242–243
Nomonhan, battle of, 8, 11
Nomura Kichisaburō, 31
Normandy, 181
North China Area Army, 41
North China Development Company, 4
North China Hsin-min Youth Corps, 43
North China Political Affairs Council, 44, 103–105

Oder River, 230
Office of Strategic Services, 259
Office of War Information (OWI), 167, 257

Ogata Taketora, 259
Ogata Yūkichi, 69
Okada Keisuke, 165, 281n30
Okakura Tenshin, 6
Okamoto Suemasa, 225, 259
Okamura Neiji, 41, 109
Okinawa, 60, 240, 254
Okumura Kiwao, 39, 42, 65
Olive, John, 128
Olympic operation, 243, 252
Osaka, 245
Ōshima Hiroshi, 14, 25–26, 31–33, 87, 181
Ozaki Hotsumi, 9

Pacific and European wars compared, 187
Pacific Ocean, 49, 80, 89, 91, 130, 174, 187, 201, 233
Pacific War Council, 144
Pan-Asianism, 4–9, 23, 34–36, 45, 48, 64, 74, 111, 153, 170–171, 182, 224; American views of, 49, 51–52; and China, 144
Pearl Harbor, 34, 36–37, 41, 44, 47, 49, 51, 57, 66, 69, 83, 88, 97, 116, 168, 186; first anniversary of, 93, 96; inevitability of, 169
Peffer, Nathaniel, 57–58
Peking (Peiping), 8, 99, 110, 173
Pence, H. L., 123–125, 129, 202–203, 205, 210
People's Renovation Society, see Hsin-min Hui
Perry, Matthew C., 58
Persian Gulf, 215
Pescadores, 154
Philippines, 29, 92, 112, 114–115, 129, 144, 162, 178–179, 186, 189, 219, 230, 234, 264
Poland, 19–20
Port Arthur, 230
Portugal, 192
Potsdam Conference, 252–257, 261, 263, 265
Potsdam declaration, 261–266

Quebec Conference, (1943) 135–137, 152–153, 156, 190, (1944) 218–219

Rangoon, 113
Republican party, 53
Rhine River, 230
Ribbentrop, Joachim von, 181

Roosevelt, Franklin D., 16, 18–19, 22, 29–30, 37, 52–53, 74, 82, 91–92, 127, 131, 160, 163, 171, 216, 220, 225, 228, 238, 242; on atomic development, 136–137, 217–218; and big-power collaboration, 52–53, 77, 79–80, 92, 94, 130, 133, 193–194, 242; and Cairo Conference, 154–155; at Casablanca, 121; and Chiang Kai-shek, 142–143, 146–147, 152, 157, 197; and China, 53–55, 140–144, 185, 230–231; on Indochina, 161–162; and oil embargo policy, 273n36; and postwar security, 136–138; and Quebec Conference, 135–137; and Stilwell affair, 197–201, 231; at Teheran, 155; on U.S. in postwar Asia, 129–130, 187–188; at Yalta, 230, 232
Root, Elihu, 15
Rōyama Masamichi, 9–10
Rumania, 217
Russia, *see* Soviet Union
Russo-Japanese War (1904–1905), 73–74
Ryukyu Islands, 134, 154, 186–187, 219, 230
Ryū Shintarō, 259

Saipan, 174–175, 177, 186
Saitō Yoshie, 6–7
Sakai Kōji, 175
Sakhalin, 60, 90, 92, 154, 160, 222, 260; North, 85, 118, 160, 172; South, 126, 129, 134, 139, 161, 203–205, 222, 230
Sakomizu Hisatsune, 281n80
Sandifer, Durward V., 128
Sansom, George, 250
Satō Kenryō, 87
Satō Naotake, 220, 222–223, 258, 263; and conciliatory policy toward Russia, 85–86, 89, 225; and peace with U.S., 259
Service, John S., 198–199
Shanghai, 237
Shensi, 229
Shibayama Kaneshirō, 224
Shidehara Kijūrō, 65
Shigemitsu Mamoru, 46, 103, 111, 113–116, 120, 172, 180–183, 225, 239; efforts to end war, 165–166, 169–170; policy toward Russia, 118, 220–223, 237; and removal of

Tōjō, 174–175; on war aims, 117, 121
Shikoku, 253, 262
Shimada Shigetarō, 281n30
Siberia, 26, 83–84, 88, 90–92, 138–139, 185–186, 231
Singapore, 13, 50, 52, 75, 133
Sino-Japanese War (1894–95), 134
Sino-Japanese War (1937–1945), 4–6, 13, 21
Smetanin, Constantin, 84–85
Solomon Islands, 96–98
Sorge spy ring, 84
South Asia Development Corporation, 71
Southeast Asia Command (SEAC), 155, 184, 192
South Manchuria Railway, 3–4
Soviet Far East, 160
Soviet Union, 11, 20, 31, 72, 134, 165–167, 169, 172, 202, 226, 260, 264; in Asia, 82, 148, 249; and big-power collaboration, 135; and China, 26, 108, 158, 231; and Chinese Communists, 108, 146–147, 159; defense in Far East, 82; entry into Asian war, 157, 159–160, 185–186, 203–204, 219–220, 251, 264; in Europe, 82, 201, 214, 232; and Germany, 24, 53, 155; and Great Britain, 181–182; and Japan, (conflict in Northeast Asia) 138–139, (neutrality pact with) 25–26, 238, (war against) 155; and Korea, 92, 161; and postwar influence, 82, 89, 92, 137–138, 160–161; and postwar security, 93–94; and United States, 1, 181–182
Stalin, Joseph, 92, 135, 162–163, 185–186, 194, 216–219, 225, 251–252, 258; on entry into Asian war, 172; and Potsdam, 261; at Teheran, 155; at Yalta, 230, 232
Stalingrad, 82–83
State-War-Navy Coordinating Committee (SWNCC), 210, 227–228, 231, 233–234, 244, 246, 256
Stettinius, Edward, 190, 217
Stilwell, Joseph W., 54–57, 142, 155, 157, 197–201, 228
Stimson, Henry L. 29, 196, 218, 220, 245, 250, 253, 262
Stockholm, 225, 259
Strong, George V., 227
Sugiyama Gen, 27, 96–97, 116, 179, 240

Sumatra, 67, 97
Sun Yat-sen, 107–108
Suzuki Kantarō, 238–241, 245, 248, 263–264
Suzuki Yasuzō, 65, 71–72
Suzuki Yoshimichi, 42
Sweden, 234, 240, 248
Switzerland, 169, 234, 248, 258

Taft, William Howard, 15–16
Taiwan, 38, 60, 126, 129, 134, 154, 184, 186
Tajiri Aigi, 102
Takada Shinji, 275n47
Takamatsu, Prince, 175
Takigawa Seijirō, 5–6, 9
Tamura Shinsaku, 237
Tani Toshiyuki, 100
Teheran Conference, 155, 160–164, 166, 186
Terauchi Juichi, 177
Thailand, 31
Thomas, Elbert, 143
Tientsin, 110
Tientsin Army, 4
Tōa Kenkyūjo (East Asian Institute), 7, 66–67
Tōgō Shigenori, 84–85, 100, 169, 239, 263; efforts to end war, 165–166; on German-Soviet conciliation, 86–87, 89; opposition to East Asian Ministry, 69–70; and Tōjō's removal, 174; and second East Asian conference, 240–241; strategy toward Russia, 248–251, 258–259; on unconditional surrender, 257–258
Tōjō Hideki, 34, 40, 67, 83, 96, 98, 116, 177, 212, 239; Asian policy, 65, 69–71, 117; and Burma, 113; on Cairo and Teheran conferences, 163–164; China policy, 99–101, 111; efforts to remove, 165–166, 169–170, 281n30; fall of cabinet, 174–176; on Filipino independence, 115; in Nanking, 104; on relations with Russia, 172; on relations with U.S., 33
Tokuda Shūsei, 36
Tokyo, 245
Tokyo Imperial University, 95, 168
Toyoda Teijirō, 31
Train, Harold C., 227
Trans-Siberian Railway, 90
Truk, 174

Truman, Harry S., 238, 241, 245, 248, 250–251, 253–254; and emperor issue, 263; and Potsdam, 261; and relations with Russia, 241–242; and Soviet entry into Asian war, 252; and use of atomic bombs, 264
Tsugaru Strait, 222
Tsutsui Kiyoshi, 26
Turkey, 215

Uda Hisashi, 5
Ukraine, 87
Umezu Yoshijirō, 180
United Nations conference, 240
United States: and Asia, 53, 74, 129, 187–189, 201–202; and atomic weaponry, 220, 245, 247, 267; and China, 17, 27–29, 38, 49, 51, 53–56, 59–60, 63, 111, 197, 231–232, (abrogation of extraterritoriality) 107, 141, (collaboration) 77, 139–141, 144–147, 184–185, (policy toward) 56–57, 61–62, 100–101, (postwar) 149, (views of internal strife) 146, (views of wartime efforts) 141–142; and Chinese Communists, 147, 157–158; and colonial question, 72–73, 131–134, 184; economic interests in Southeast Asia, 17; and emperor issue, 202–203, 205–209, 211–212, 227, 234, 250–251, 254–257, 265; and Europe, 25, 53; and France, 76, 133, 233, 247; and Germany, 17, 22, 53; and Great Britain, 18–20, 22, 29–30, 33, 52–53, 62, 76, 133, 145, 196–197, 214, 247, (aid to Russia) 88, (atomic cooperation) 136–138, 218; and Japanese approaches to China, 98, 100–101, 147, 159–160; and Korea, 92; Pacific offensive, 174, 183, 186; and Philippines, 115; and postwar international relations, 134–135, 169, 190–193, 201, 203, 216; postwar policy toward Japan, 122–128, 202–210, 227, 234, 244–245, 256–257, 262; postwar security plans, 92–94; and Soviet Union, 53, 62, 85, 89–92, 185, (atomic weaponry) 218–219, (collaboration against Japan) 138, 184, 186, 230–231, (entry into Asian war) 242, 245–246, (in Europe) 220, 246, (postwar relations) 61–62, 139–140, 193–197,

United States—*Cont.*
  230, (power confrontation) 267–
  268, (recognition of) 17, 82, 93,
  (view of postwar) 149; surrender
  terms for Japan, 226, 244, 250–
  257, 259

Vagts, Alfred, 39–40
Vandenbosch, Amry, 145
Van Wickel, Jesse F., 78
Vatican, 234
Vichy regime: in Indochina, 233,
  237; of occupied France, 20–21
Vincent, John Carter, 199
Vladivostok, 185

Wakatsuki Reijirō, 151, 176–177
Wake Island, 142, 189
Wallace, Henry, 200
Wang Ching-wei, 9, 22–23, 44–47,
  99, 104–107, 154, 159, 173

Wang K'o-min, 9, 105
Washington Conference, 101; trea-
  ties, 2–3
Wedemeyer, Albert C., 228, 233
Welles, Sumner, 18–19, 60–61, 79–
  80, 130, 143
Williams, F. S., 153, 168
Wilson, Woodrow, 2, 16, 125
Wilsonianism, 15–19, 30–31, 33–34,
  80–81, 120, 125, 127, 132, 150,
  190, 241, 248, 266–268

Yabe Teiji, 168–169
Yalta Conference, 194, 230–233, 237;
  agreements, 238, 248, 260–261,
  264, 266–267
Yenan, 38, 106, 109, 173, 198, 224
Yokohama, 245
Yonai Mitsumasa, 176–179, 240
Yoshida Shigeru, 235
Yugoslavia, 216–217